PRAISE FOR
SHADOW MAGICK COMPENDIUM

"According to Jung, children become adults through a process called individuation. As the world of magick moves boldly into the twenty-first century, it is time that magick, too, individuates from its eighteenth- and nineteenth-century parents and its twentieth-century childhood. Part of this maturation is the realization that wherever there is light, there is also shadow...Jung pointed out that our most famous myths are variations of a universal "Hero's Journey." *Shadow Magick Compendium* doesn't merely share this mythic Journey, it gives you keys and guidance to follow it yourself."
—Donald Michael Kraig, author of *Modern Magick* and *Modern Tantra*

"An exceptional guide to exploring the shadow side for a fully integrated path of magickal and spiritual enlightenment."
—Rosemary Ellen Guiley, author of *The Encyclopedia of Witches, Witchcraft & Wicca*

"*Shadow Magick Compendium* opens the way for us to reconcile our visible self with our shadow self...Once a lamp is lifted into the darkness, there is nothing left to fear."
—Leilah Wendell, author of *The Necromantic Ritual Book* and *Our Name is Melancholy: The Complete Books of Azrael*

"Raven joins the writers and authors giving the world workable occult technologies—systems of understanding to prepare individuals for the dangerous journey to wisdom and fulfillment. *Shadow Magick Compendium* is a treasury of resources for just that."
—Robin Artisson, author of *The Witching Way of the Hollow Hill* and *Letters from the Devil's Forest: An Anthology of Writings on Traditional Witchcraft, Spiritual Ecology & Provenance Traditionalism*

"A guide to unearthing the darker aspects of our self as well as a guide to integrating them in both the beginning and advanced practitioner."
—David Allen Hulse, author of *The Western Mysteries* and *The Eastern Mysteries*

"To recognize the Shadow and embrace it is the first step in learning to harness its limitless potential. This book shows that the dark side of our inner nature can illuminate and liberate just as readily as it can curse."
—Donald Tyson, author of *The Power of the Word*

"By examining how magic works in various realms from the internal to the external and beyond, Raven shows how Shadow energy can be tapped as a positive force in bringing balance back into one's life…this book is a wellspring of information that competently transcends all religious and spiritual paths. Well done!"
—Ann Moura, author of the *Green Witchcraft* series

"Many mainstream spiritual texts limit themselves to working the 'light.' Raven's approach, however, is to embrace the shadow self so as to attain self-awareness and balance, rather than focusing on pure light or pure darkness. The meditations and rituals allow readers to experience Raven's approach in a very real, practical sense."
—Tony Mierzwicki, author of *Graeco-Egyptian Magick: Everyday Empowerment*

"Each of us responds to the darkness in our soul differently—some with fear, avoidance, and denial; others with courage, curiosity, and sorrow. For the courageous, this book provides strategies, ideas, and knowledge…Digitalis draws from the wisdom of older cultures and religions as well as from younger, radical cultures."
—Gail Wood, author of *Rituals of the Dark Moon* and *The Shamanic Witch*

"One of the most basic tenets of Witchcraft is also its most challenging: Know Thyself. Raven Digitalis, author of *Goth Craft*, gives us a new tool for this important task…a 'must have' for White Witches, Dark Witches, and everyone in between."
—Deborah Blake, author of *The Everyday Witch* series

"This important book belongs in the library of any serious student of magic, self-evolution, and spirituality…Amid a wealth of fascinating information and inspiring exercises, Raven not only covers the psychology of magic—perhaps its foundation stone—but also the history of modern magical practice, in terms of the Shadow…It's truly refreshing to find a book on magic that has new things to say, as well as including thoughtful interpretations of existing beliefs and practices."
—Storm Constantine, author of the *Wraeththu* novels

"Full of inventive rituals, meditations, exercises, and practices, this book can help guide readers into a fuller understanding of their own dark natures and provide them with grounding, balance, and healing."
—Timothy Roderick, author of *Wicca: A Year & A Day* and *Dark Moon Mysteries*

A Witch's Shadow Magick Compendium

ABOUT THE AUTHOR

Raven Digitalis (USA) is the author of numerous books on Llewellyn Worldwide. Originally trained in Georgian Witchcraft, Raven has been an earth-based practitioner since 1999, a Priest since 2003, a Freemason since 2012, and an empath all of his life. He holds a degree in cultural anthropology from the University of Montana, co-operated a nonprofit Pagan Temple for 16 years, and is also a professional Tarot reader, editor, card-carrying magician, and animal rights advocate.

www.ravendigitalis.com
www.facebook.com/ravendigitalis
www.instagram.com/ravendigitalis

A Witch's Shadow Magick Compendium

Raven Digitalis

Chicago, Illinois

A Witch's Shadow Magick Compendium © 2023 by Raven Digitalis. All rights reserved. No part of this book may be reproduced in any manner whatsoever without written permission from Crossed Crow Books, except in the case of brief quotations embodied in critical articles and reviews.

Second Edition.
Second Printing. 2023.

Paperback ISBN: 979-8-9856281-4-2
Library of Congress Control Number on file.

Cover design by Wycke Malliway.
Typesetting by Gianna Rini.
Edited by Becca Fleming.

Disclaimer: Crossed Crow Books, LLC does not participate in, endorse, or have any authority or responsibility concerning private business transactions between our authors and the public. Any internet references contained in this work were found to be valid during the time of publication, however, the publisher cannot guarantee that a specific reference will continue to be maintained. This book's material is not intended to diagnose, treat, cure, or prevent any disease, disorder, ailment, or any physical or psychological condition. The author, publisher, and its associates shall not be held liable for the reader's choices when approaching this book's material. The views and opinions expressed within this book are those of the author alone and do not necessarily reflect the views and opinions of the publisher.

Published by:
Crossed Crow Books, LLC
6934 N Glenwood Ave, Suite C
Chicago, IL 60626
www.crossedcrowbooks.com

Printed in the United States of America.

MORE BY RAVEN DIGITALIS:

The Empath's Oracle Deck (art by Konstantin Bax)

The Everyday Empath: Achieve Energetic Balance in Your Life

*Esoteric Empathy:
A Magickal & Metaphysical Guide to Emotional Sensitivity*

*Planetary Spells & Rituals:
Practicing Dark & Light Magick Aligned with the Cosmic Bodies*

Goth Craft: The Magickal Side of Dark Culture

DEDICATION

This tome is a Lunar offering; one whose alignments correspond to the sphere of Yesod in Qabalah's Tree of Life.

Common occult philosophy views these qualities as uniquely feminine.

I dedicate this tome to the countless loving, wise, brilliant, diverse, and inspirational women in my life: you know who you are.
You have deeply (in)formed my existence, my work, and my ethics.
Bless you beyond measure, forever and a day.

With violet hues, and days anew,
the Goddess is me,
the Goddess is you.

999

CALL TO THE DARK MOTHER

Behold! She who holds the mysteries I seek under shroud of night. Nocturnal Mistress, I fear thee not. I call thee forth with love and humility. Hail the Dark Mother; She who turns the Wheel, She who is the Shadow Tide, She whose mysteries are the blood; She who is the moon eclipsed. O Dark Mother, She who is known by many names: Hekate, Persephone, Cerridwen, Rhiannon, Ereshkigal, Lilith, Babalon, Hel, and Maa Kali. Descend upon me this dark eve, consume my fear and inhibitions. Be at my side as I dare to see the unseen. Let me know the ways of nocturnal grace. Surround my soul as I tread your infinite waters. Accompany my rites this eve, in balance and in wisdom. I call thee forth, my Mother, my Sister, my Matrix.

Hail and Welcome. So Mote It Be.

CALL TO THE DARK FATHER

Behold! He who holds the mysteries I seek under shroud of night. Nocturnal Master, I fear thee not. I call thee forth with love and humility. Hail the Dark Father; He who oversees the falling of all things great and small. He who is the shadow having come from sun's light; He who is the sun eclipsed. O Dark Father, He who is known by many names: Osiris, Anubis, Hades, Pluto, Pan, Dionysus, Baphomet, Cernnunos, and Shani Dev. Descend upon me this dark eve, devour my trepidations and fright. Be at my side as I dare to feel the unfelt. Let me know the ways of dark enchantment. Enter my world as I journey your endless terrain. Accompany my rites this eve, in truth and in steadfast devotion. I call thee forth, my Father, my Brother, my Patrix.

Hail and Welcome. So Mote It Be.

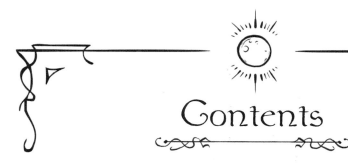

Contents

About the Author II
Foreword XVII

Chapter Zero
INTRODUCTION

DISCERNING THE SHADOW 1
   Shadow as the Holy Child 3
   Interpreting Shadow Magick 10

MAGICK & HOW WE USE IT 15
   Occulty Ethics 17
   The Nature of Darkness & the Color Black 20
   Will: The 93 Current 23
   Giving Thanks 26

CURSING, HEXING & CROSSING 27
   Injustice be Damned 28
   The Art of Binding 29
   Contemplating Karma 30
   The Place of Mindfulness 31
   Enlighten Up! 31

Chapter One
THE INTERNAL SHADOW

UNDERSTANDING NEGATIVE BEHAVIOR CYCLES . . 35
   Internal Shadow Magick: A Self-Evaluation 36
   Earth: Shadow Traits 39
   What Lies Behind Behavior? 42

Magick for Cyclical Change 45
Ritual Meditation: Purging Negative Shadow 46

MYSTICISM: THE PARADOX BEHIND THE VEIL 50
Jewish Mysticism & the Qabalah. 53
The Shadow of Da'ath 55
The Mystical Valleys of Sufism 58
Achieving the Mystical State. 61

DRUG USE IN SPIRITUAL PRACTICE. 62
Shamanic Drug Use. 63
Drugs & Witchcraft 68

UTILIZING EMOTIONAL ENERGY 74
Thoughts & Emotions in Witchcraft. 76
Emotional Awareness 77
Empathy. 78
Positive Thinking. 78
Follow Your Thoughts 79
Cognitive & Emotional Influences 80
Mental & Emotional Overload 82
Sadness & Grief 85
The Dark Night of the Soul. 87
Effigies & Emotional Channeling 89
Ritual Meditation: Cultivating Love & Compassion . . . 90

Chapter Two
THE EXTERNAL SHADOW

INVOCATION & GODFORM ASSUMPTION 96
Aspects of Aspecting. 100
Drawing Down 101

FASTING & SELF-SACRIFICE 102
Cross-Cultural Fasting 104
Planning Fasts. 107
Ritual Meditation: A Ceremony of Silence 123

MAGICKAL JEWELRY & METALS 127
    Bigghes. 128
    Chinese Mysticism, Taoism & Metal. 128
    Additional Pointers on Magickal Jewelry. 130
    Magickal Properties of Metals. 134

DIVINATION: READING THE SIGNS 145
    Obscure Methods of Divination 145

Chapter Three
THE ASTRAL SHADOW

ASTRAL TRAVEL & SOUL RETRIEVAL. 149
    Ritual Meditation: Shamanic Soul Retrieval 152

DARK ANIMAL GUIDES & ALLIES 157
    The Spirit Animal 158
    The Power Animal. 160
    The Totem Animal. 161
    The Familiar 162
    A Darkly Bestiary 163
    Ritual Meditation: Discovering Your Spirit Animal. . . 177

WHEN INVASIVE SPIRITS COME AROUND 182
    Trust Your Instincts. 183
    The Act of Discernment 184
    A Strange Encounter. 185
    Ritual Meditation: Understanding an Encounter. 187
    Spirit Cleansing 188

Chapter Four
THE SHADOW OF NATURE

ROMANCING THE MOON. 190
    Regenerative Introspection: The Dark Moon 191
    Celestial Shadows: Lunar & Solar Eclipses 192
    Connecting to the Eclipse: A Ritual Meditation 195

THE DARKNESS OF THE SOLAR YEAR............ 297
    Autumnal Glory 198
    Halloween: Honoring the Other Side 200
    The Day of the Dead 202

HERBCRAFT & WORTCUNNING:
A DARKLY HERBAL 204
    Some Cautions & Recommendations 207
    Ye Olde Flying Ointment 225
    The Weird Sisters of Macbeth 228

Chapter Five
THE SHADOW OF SOCIETY

A SAD & BEAUTIFUL WORLD 232
    Fantasy Magick: A Shadow
    Side of the Occult Scene 237

DECONSTRUCTING THE BURNING TIMES 240
    The European Witch Hunts 241
    The Etymology of Witchcraft 242
    Magick in the Middle Ages.................... 243
    The Hunt Begins............................ 244
    The Revival of Roman Law 245
    The Height of the Witch Hunts 246
    The Witches' Sabbath 246
    Thou Shalt Not Suffer a *What* to Live? 248
    The Malleus Maleficarum or
    The Hammer of Witches...................... 249
    Torture & Witch Testing...................... 250
    The Spanish Inquisition...................... 252
    The Burning Times 253
    The Accused: Midwives,
    Herbalists & Goddess-Worshippers?............. 254
    The Oppression of Women 256

Chapter Six
THE SHADOW OF DEATH

DEATH MAGICK 259
   The Requiem. 262
   The Afterworld 265

BLOOD MAGICK 269
   Risks in Bloodwork. 271

MEMENTO MORI: NECROMANCY 273
   Ancient Necromancy. 274
   Modern Necromancy. 277
   Ritual Meditation:
   Encountering the Angel of Death 280

Conclusion 286
Bibliography. 289

Foreword

As a young child, my father would take me to the public library every Saturday. I remember us walking out of the library with armloads of books each time. As I got older and more independent, I would ride my bike down to the neighborhood library several miles away from my house (this was the 70s, a very different time) and load up my backpack to bring home the precious books I'd found.

Needless to say, I've never lost my love of reading. The walls of my house are covered with bookcases whose shelves sag under the weight of books on every possible subject. If there's a free spot on a table, it likely has a stack of books on it.

Books have made me who I am. Every book I've read has left a mark on my life. Some books, though, have made a more significant impact than others. There are books that I've read that have completely changed the path that I walk.

The books of Raven Digitalis are examples of those life-changing books.

A Witch's Shadow Magick Compendium is essential reading in Dark Paganism. While there are different definitions of Dark Paganism, for me, Dark Paganism is a positive, life-affirming Pagan spirituality that honors and cultivates the self. It avoids the opposite extremes of selfishness and selflessness. Dark Paganism uses reason and magick to search for a healthy understanding of the self and its relation with others. Ultimately, Dark Pagans seek to cultivate the self to enhance one's humanity.

Dark Paganism was first introduced to the world in 2001 by John J. Coughlin in his book *Out of the Shadows*. Coughlin, a friend of Digitalis, explains that darkness isn't evil. Instead, "dark" is a metaphor for a spiritual path of introspection and knowledge of the self. Rather than looking for personal meaning as coming from the external, the Dark Pagan seeks existential truth internally through self-knowledge.

Self-knowledge is an ancient Pagan concept. The Greek aphorism "Know Thyself" was carved on the walls at the Oracle of Delphi. It was the Greek philosopher Aristotle who wrote that wisdom begins with self-knowledge (Stavopoulos, 2003). And it was Sun Tzu who wrote, "If ignorant both of your enemy and yourself, you are certain to be in peril" (Tipton & Nozaki, 2012). Dark Paganism continues this ancient Pagan practice of striving for self-knowledge.

A vital part of knowing oneself is to understand one's shadow. Carl Jung explained that "Everyone carries a shadow, and the less it is embodied in the individual's conscious life, the blacker and denser it is" (Jung, 2003). What is this mysterious-sounding shadow? James Hollis, PhD, executive director of the Jung Educational Center of Houston, explains that the shadow consists of "all those aspects of ourselves that tend to make us uncomfortable with ourselves" (Hollis 2008). While we may not like what we find in our shadow, knowing and accepting the shadow is essential for knowing and accepting oneself.

Because of its essential role in self-knowledge, incorporating the shadow into our lives plays an integral part in Dark Paganism. Coughlin writes about it in his book *Out of the Shadows*. I write about the shadow in my book, *The Philosophy of Dark Paganism*. And Kate Freuler writes about the shadow in her fantastic Dark Pagan book *Of Blood & Bones*.

A Witch's Shadow Magick Compendium is different from other Dark Pagan books because it's exclusively about the shadow. Raven Digitalis brings together a wide range of subjects to help readers understand and incorporate their shadow into their conscious lives. He shows us how the shadow impacts magick and how we can use it in our craft. Digitalis also shows us how the shadow impacts society as a whole and how we can recognize its influence.

If this is the first time you've read the work of Digitalis, I envy you; you're in for a real treat. I remember how impressed I was when I read his first edition of this book, *Shadow Magick Compendium*. If memory serves, I acquired it at a family-owned local occult shop that I frequent. I recall being amazed at the wealth of knowledge and the practical exercises in the book. I reread it regularly, and I learn something new every time.

For those who've read the first edition, you also have a lot to look forward to in the *A Witch's Shadow Magick Compendium*. This new edition has more than a new name and a new cover. It contains fresh and updated material to aid the reader in exploring their shadow.

I encourage the reader to take their time with this book. You'll benefit from pacing yourself. Read a chapter, meditate on what you've learned, and practice the rituals. Then, when ready, move on to the next chapter. This book isn't fast food magick. It's too important.

But most importantly, the reader should allow themselves to enjoy the book. Raven Digitalis's writing style is easy to read yet full of information. His writing makes learning fun. Yet, he doesn't dumb down the subject. *A Witch's Shadow Magick Compendium* strikes the perfect balance.

—Frater Tenebris
author of *The Philosophy of Dark Paganism*

Chapter Zero

Introduction

"Although many people equate Awakening with a spiritual epiphany, it's not always a matter of turning on a light in a dark room, and then you're Awakened. It's more like lighting a candle in a dark cave, only to discover that the light of this one candle reveals many more candles and a far more extensive cavern than you'd ever imagined."

—Michelle Belanger,
*Vampires in Their Own Words:
An Anthology of Vampire Voices*

DISCERNING THE SHADOW

Witches, much like the practice of magick itself, have long been viewed as mysterious…unique. We come in countless forms and from an incredible variety of backgrounds, but one thing remains true among us: we *are* mysterious; it is our nature. We are, whether by training or by natural inclination, tapped into hidden realms of mystery. We see things differently than most people do, and with good reason. Knowing that there is much more to life than it immediately seems, we walk gently, with one foot in the mundane world and one foot in the other.

The very essence of the concept of "shadow" is ambiguous. Throughout the ages and around the world, various cultures, religions, and individual philosophies have approached this idea in various ways, often discovering deep wells of meaning in the Divine polarity of "light" and "dark." A number of animistic religions, including those Indigenous to Asia, Europe, and the Americas, have long recognized the portion of the self-deemed "the shadow" for its role in human spiritual development and understanding. The view of shadow as a spiritual force has also been carried into a number of modern religions, philosophies, and lifestyles. It is from the shadowed aspects of the psyche that our magickal reality is brought into vision.

No single tradition, no single person or book—including this one—can fully capture the meaning of shadow, because its significance is so deeply personal. It is my hope that this book will inspire readers to explore and interpret esoteric darkness in their own ways, taking into consideration the suggested and proposed interpretations of shadow herein.

To begin this exploration, it's essential to make note of the Swiss psychiatrist Carl Gustav Jung. A student of Sigmund Freud, Jung recognized the shadow self as the often nonconscious aspect of the human psyche that contains repressed thoughts and impulses. It is the portion of our mind that usually goes unrecognized, harboring fear and other unpleasant emotions that we have consciously rejected for one reason or another.

In Jung's own words, "Everyone carries a shadow, and the less it is embodied in the individual's conscious life, the blacker and denser it is." That is, the more repressed one's shadow self is, the darker—and more intense—it becomes. Jung also notes, "The shadow is a moral problem that challenges the whole ego-personality, for no one can become conscious of the shadow without considerable moral effort. To become conscious of it involves recognizing the dark aspects of the personality as present and real. This act is the essential condition for any kind of self-knowledge." With this psychoanalytical concept of the shadow, Jung suggests that recognizing internal darkness leads to self-awareness. The more we ignore our darker aspects, the more burdened we actually become, even though it may seem quite the opposite in the immediate sense.

Modern industrialized humans have, generally speaking, come to fear the shadow, maligning and conflating it with concepts of evil. Jung's concept further recognizes that when the shadow self is ignored, people tend to project their own shadows onto others, shifting their own darker characteristics to anyone but themselves. It's no wonder that we in Western culture—a society that fears and maligns the internal shadow—are masters of the blame game.

Introduction

SHADOW AS THE HOLY CHILD

Both actually and metaphorically, the shadow is the essence from which all things come into manifestation. A few cross-cultural examples will show the shadow's profound significance in humankind's stories and mythologies through the ages. One fascinating example is E. Elias Merhige's 1991 silent dark art film *Begotten*. The film's opening scene depicts a robed, veiled figure killing itself with a blade. The figure is visually distressed as it welcomes a suicidal death out of what seems to be necessity. From the gruesome wreckage of the disemboweled figure—who is cited as "God Killing Himself" in the credits—a masked Venusian woman, Mother Earth, appears. Upon masturbating the fallen god, she impregnates herself with his seed.

The corpselike "child" the woman gives birth to appears as a quivering, helpless, and constantly convulsing humanoid, said to be the "Son of Earth: Flesh on Bone." A quote at the beginning of the film refers to this figure as representing humankind: "Like a flame burning away the darkness, life is flesh on bone convulsing above the ground."

The characters in *Begotten* portray a particular archetypal pattern seen in many of the world's ancient spiritual systems. The representation of the Divine Mother, Father, and Child is seen across the board, mythologically speaking. Also common in religious pantheons is the theme of death—or representational death—of the father figure. These archetypes are of particular importance to anyone living a spiritually progressive path, especially those who actively practice magick and Nature worship. In truth, all deities are but psychological imprints representing aspects of the human psyche or the psyche's perception of the natural world. The gods exist within us as representatives of our experience. They also exist outside of us as egregores, or independent, energetic embodiments in the mental and astral planes. This spiritual dichotomy—the Hermetic "As Above, So Below," the Principle of Correspondence—both creates and maintains our very own existence. Did the gods create us, or did we create the gods? At the end of the day, the answer is of little consequence; after all, are these questions *actually* mutually exclusive? I tend to think not.

The cycle of reproduction fuels all aspects of reality, from the microcosm of humans, animals, and plants to the macrocosm: the creative and destructive ebb and flow of the birth and death of planets and stars. Because this cycle reigns over all experience, it's of utmost importance to spiritual practitioners.

Just as a biological male and biological female can create a child, certain deities represent these forces in virtually all mythological systems. In this example, because motherhood, fatherhood, procreation, and birth occur on the physical plane, these forces are in turn mythologized and even anthropomorphized into recognizable forms. Whether the deities were actually humans who were later deified or whether they were created as thoughtforms, the archetypes live on.

Understandably, ancient pantheons deified natural forces in all their aspects. Across cultures, we see deital representations of the birth of plants, the birth of animals, and the birth of humans, as well as the corresponding equal-opposite representations of their deaths and appropriate harbingers of death. Virtually all aspects of reality have been deified in one theistic culture or another. For when a deity is said to represent or rule a force of Nature, this ethereal vibration can be tapped into, and the deity's specific alignments worked with magickally. This old truth is now rebirthing itself in the minds of spiritual seekers, much as a "begotten" child of the old ways appears in a new aeon.

The word "begotten" is a form of the verb "beget." To beget something means to bring it forth. More often than not, fatherly associations are drawn: this fathered that. In many mythological systems, and thus in many ancient and modern societies, the father or paternal deity passes his power, in whatever form it takes, on to his male offspring. The father or paternal figure's death, whether it comes before or after this transfer, serves to solidify this passing down of energy.

Many ancient and modern societies, both patriarchal and matriarchal, tend to view the Divine Feminine as a constant force that never truly dies; this idea is also seen in their mythos. Thus, although power is distributed from mother to daughter, the two remain aspects of one another. The male, however, dies and is regenerated.

Wicca and many forms of Neopaganism tend to accept this view of the Great Goddess and Great God. The Goddess is viewed in her many aspects through the solar year cycle. But her two consort gods, the Oak King and the Holly King, actually die; the Holy Father's energy is mutable and regenerating while the Goddess's energy fluxes but never ceases.

To mirror the seasonal shifts, the Oak King is killed by his Holly King brother at Midsummer, and vice versa at Midwinter. Each aspect of the Divine Masculine rules half the year. Starting on the Sabbat following his death, each brother again begins the process of being reborn by the Goddess, our Mother Earth, so he can again rise to metaphorically slay the opposing Doppelgänger. These brothers depict the balancing forces of Nature; the Oak King aligned to fertility, life, and the Upperworld, and the Holly King aligned to decay, death, and the Underworld. They are both simultaneously the Holy Father and Holy Child, one always equally opposing the other. The Holy Mother stands as a consort. The mythos of the Holly King and the Oak King entered traditional Wicca by way of Robert Graves's poetic work *The White Goddess*.

In another modern spiritual tradition, Jesus the Christ, a healer, shaman, and master of compassion, is deified as the "only begotten son of God." Like many deities, both God and Jesus in Christian mythology can represent many aspects of the human psyche, depending on the account in which the godform appears.

Archetypally, Jesus's mother Mary represents the virginal, untainted aspect of the Mother Goddess. Like other mythological Holy Mothers, she was blessed as the chosen individual to birth a highly spiritual being into the earth plane. Jesus, like his counterparts in many other myth traditions, was born as a pure beacon of merciful guiding light. He is also an avatar, a prophet in this case, much like Lord Krishna and other deities. The Christian God, like many other Divine Father figures, conceived Jesus in a nontraditional or occult (that is, a "hidden" or "shrouded") manner. Thus, the story of the Christ, including the tale of his resurrection, is nearly identical to the messianic tales of numerous ancient mythic traditions. It is simply one retelling of similar preexisting archetypal mythologies.

Arguably, the religion of ancient Egypt served as the framework for all Western religions. Looking at its pantheon, we see Isis and Osiris as an aspect of the Great Mother and Great Father. Isis, the goddess of love, is consort to Osiris, a king of the earthly realm.

According to the mythos, Osiris's brother Set (Seth) manipulated him with a malevolent joke that ended in Osiris's live entombment in a coffin cast to the Nile. After a period of searching and mourning, Isis recovered her dead lover's coffin. But before Isis could perform the customary funerary rites and take the coffin to a proper burial ground, Set and his men tracked down and destroyed Osiris's corpse, distributing his body parts across the land in a fit of rage. With the help of her sister Nephthys and nephew Anubis (in some accounts), Isis eventually recovered all of her husband's body parts except for his penis. In a solitary magick rite, Isis pieced together and mummified Osiris's body parts. She then thaumaturgically created a phallus, breathed life into the corpse, and made love to him in his momentary reanimation. (In some accounts of this myth, Isis made love to a reanimated Osiris directly after finding him dead in the Nile-cast coffin. After this sacred coitus, Set then scattered Osiris's body parts. After Isis gathered them together, she gave Osiris his eternal afterlife.)

The Holy Child conceived was the hawk-headed Horus (also called the baby Harpocrates or Hoor-pa-kraat), the ruler of the skies, whose eyes represent the sun and the moon. Some believe that Horus is the metaphorical reincarnation of Osiris and also carries multiple aspects of his mother Isis. Horus is now considered the Crowned and Conquering Child of the new aeon in many occult circles, including orders of Thelema. Therein he is often referred to as Ra-hoor-khuit, Horus's older and syncretized Ra-exalted aspect, or as Heru-ra-ha, his dualistic aspect (both the younger and older Horus). Ra-hoor-khuit is the child of the macrocosmic and infinitely expanded sky goddess Nuit, and the microcosmic and infinitely contracted Hadit; the Isis-Osiris myth plays out one phase of this Holy Trinity.

In fact, Thelemites believe that the present and newly unfolding Age of Horus was preceded by the Age of Osiris (overseeing patriarchal ideology and masculine worship), which was preceded by the Age of Isis (overseeing matriarchal ideology and feminine worship). It is believed that the present Aeon of Horus is that of the great balancer, that which will merge the positive principles of the two preceding ages.

Taking a look at Hinduism, we see Lord Krishna (Krsna) as an avatar, or human emanation, of Lord Vishnu the Preserver. Vishnu is an aspect of Hinduism's trimurti of three great gods, the others being Lord Brahma the Creator and Lord Shiva (Siva) the Destroyer/Regenerator. (The Great Goddess, of course, also takes innumerable forms—not least of whom is the amalgam Lady Durga—and the vast majority of Hindu deities are viewed as simultaneously male and female; there is no Shiva without Shakti, and there is no Krishna without Radha.)

Though he is mythologized as having been born a deity, Krishna was the eighth child of the human parents King Vasudev and Princess Devaki. In the myth, Devaki's brother King Kamsa planned to put Devaki's eighth child to death because a prophecy said that this child would grow up to kill him. But luckily, with Vishnu's intervention, the child Krishna was saved. Krishna grew up to become a holy warrior, prince, and charioteer for his friend Arjuna, the King of India… and he did indeed kill the evil King Kamsa. These stories and more are preserved in the *Bhagavad Gita*, a story of Krishna from the later Vedic epic poem called the *Mahabharata*.

In many ways, and certainly to Hindus who worship Krishna as the central deity, Krishna is seen as a Holy Child. A god in human form, he is seen as transcending the human predicament. His associations as a miracle worker and supreme godhead have earned him much adoration. (Much the same, beloved Lord Ganesha also embodies the Holy Child archetype.)

The epicenters of Eastern spiritual thought, Hinduism and Buddhism, are two of the world's largest religions. In Buddhism, the story of the Buddha's birth is a mythologized and fanciful tale, with imagery noticeably borrowed from the vibrant spiritual legends of Hinduism. According to the story, the child Siddhartha Gautama of the Shakya tribe was a god before birth; a god who chose to be born human. He descended from the Heaven of the Contented, a Divine realm, and entered his mother Mayadevi's womb, which created an immeasurable light in even the darkest realms of consciousness.

It is said that the Buddha was of a "pure birth." Purity, if course, is entirely subjective. The Buddha was born "from his mother's right side," according to early Pali-language Buddhist canonical texts; the non-vaginal birth implying that he was delivered either from his mother's actual side, below the ribs and above the hip, or from her armpit. In common Indian thought , the armpit is seen as an area similar to the pubic region but is rather less "impure."

Siddhartha was dry at birth, clean of any "contaminating" blood or amniotic fluid. After his birth, his mother passed away and is said to have been reborn in the Heaven of the Contented. Legend says that when the Buddha was born, a cool and warm stream of water poured from the heavens for Siddhartha and his mother to bathe in. The young Buddha then stood upright, took seven steps to the north, the land, and declared himself a king of the world. Some tell of lotuses growing from the child Buddha's footprints.

Though the story tells of sacred birth, most Buddhists understand it as mythical truth rather than historical truth, and as one portrayal of the birth of the Holy Child. However, because the Buddha is recognized as entirely human, simply enlightened, there is no direct representation of the Holy Father and Holy Mother (unless one counts Mayadevi as a Holy Mother figure), a factor that separates Buddhism from common theistic religions.

The spiritual tripartite of the Great Mother (life/nature), Great Father (death/destruction) and Holy Child (resurrection/redeemer) is expressed in many Western Mystery Traditions as the Greek Gnostic mantra of Iota-Alpha-Omega (IAΩ), each letter representing a phase in this infinite pattern. These letters also correspond to the three Hebrew Mother Letters of Shin, Mem, and Aleph. Many occultists attribute "I" to Isis, the Giver of Life; "A" to Apophis, the Destroyer; and "Ω" to Osiris, the Redeemer or the offspring of I and A. This is the sequential progression of light to darkness to the supremely transcendental balance of the two polarities. IAΩ is also another term for the Demiurge (the power of creation itself), or an archon thereof.

It may be worth noting that the Fool card of modern Tarot holds the position of zero in the deck. Being both the "highest" and the "lowest" card of the pack simultaneously, the Fool represents, amongst other things, naivety and carefree-ness, which are characteristics of children (and frequently of the inexperienced or uninitiated). The rediscovery of the truly pure and innocent Self is often viewed as the ultimate goal of magicians of many varieties. It can be said that reconnecting to humility, egolessness, and spiritual surrender are true keys to enlightenment—a truth reflected in both the Tarot and the Holy Child mythologies. It also correlates with the common Qabalistic saying that "Kether is in Malkuth and Malkuth is in Kether."

In esoteric Qabalah, the Holy Trinity of the Supernal Triad also has deep creational significance; these are the Sephiroth (spheres) above Da'ath on the Tree of Life. From Kether the Crown, Chokmah was born, followed by Binah. In terms of the Holy Mother-Father-Child association, the supernal Sephiroth on which these are aligned can be interpreted in various ways.

Introduction

In all cross-cultural depictions, the Holy Child is the outcome of the Holy Mother and Father, and it is this offspring who perpetuates the cycle. It is this Child who is the redeemer of sins, the peaceful balancer, the radiant light-bearer, and the bringer of the new age: *this* age! His vast incarnations remind us of a very important fact: images of the Holy Child represent humankind's potential.

Each and every one of us is a sacred being who was physically birthed from male and female biological systems. Likewise, the masculine and feminine currents rule the cycles of Nature and ourselves. In all aspects, the yin and yang, the Holy Mother and Holy Father—the God and Goddess, if you will—mirror our human experience. Our physical bodies and the balancing energies of the earth plane have arisen from these forces.

Every single thing we do is significant. Every thought, every action, every reaction and interaction is of absolute importance. Every step of the way, we co-create our lives. Magick permeates every person's being and, through our thoughts and actions, we are constantly casting magick—manipulating reality—throughout the day, whether we are aware of it or not. The whole of our Earth Experience manifests from our own consciousness: a fact that confers the utmost responsibility, and the goal of self-awareness, on all those who dedicate themselves to a spiritual path.

The myths and metaphors retold here can remind us of the importance of the self in this game we call "reality." Far too many people ignore the greatness, value, and mind-blowing mystery of life itself—many forget to realize that they're actually alive and conscious in the present moment, experiencing a paradigm like none other. In a modern world where it's all too easy to get trapped in the charade of everyday life and lose touch with the cycles that forge our evolution, it's equally easy to forget our own power—or what's worse, place our power entirely in temporary mundanity.

The healing, conquering, compassionate, and venerably enlightened aspects the Holy Child represents are mirrors of who exactly we can be and ought to strive to be; for we are indeed the children of the gods and our influence echoes through the planes. *We* are the Holy Children of this world, and we are the Divine Light birthed from the depths of shadow!

Interpreting Shadow Magick

This book examines different ways we can harness and understand the shadow, in its various forms, for spiritually transformative purposes.

I believe that shadow magick, particularly internal shadow magick, is about embracing the Holy Child. It's about reaching into the womblike darkness and depths of our minds and our experiences to uncover an internal diamond in the rough. It's about examining the extremes and rediscovering balance. This is the work of the shaman. The archetype of the Holy Child suggests that the offspring is more balanced than its progenitors—the Mother and Father—and thus brings a balanced light of blessing, discernment, and wholeness to the world.

To embrace "O" we must not only realize "I" but dance with "A." To know the self we must understand the Divine polarity in all its forms. We can't know the day unless we know the night; we can't perceive the glory of light until we examine the darkness; we can't go outside of ourselves until we go within.

Those who describe themselves as Dark Witches or Dark (Neo) Pagans tend to practice shadow magick in one form or another. The term "Dark Pagan" was coined by magician Cliff H. Low in the early 1990s, and is used by many Pagans who are attracted to darker energies, philosophies, and methods of working magick.

Many magickal-spiritual individuals who do not identify themselves as "dark" also practice shadow magick, finding that an emphasis on light alone proves incomplete. Because interpretations are so personal, what one person might deem magick aligned with "shadow," another might not. Some people might interpret shadow magick as magick that works with the Jungian-defined shadow self, others see it as magick dealing with external occult forces, and others may simply view it as Witchcraft or magickal spirituality practiced at night. It would be silly to think that any one person or group understands every aspect of shadow magick—all of us have a different view, a different angle to share on the topic.

A Witch's Shadow Magick Compendium is not a book about black magick, cursing, demonic conjuration, infernal working, nor abyssal magick, and it only somewhat dips its finger in Left Hand Path material as it walks gently on the Middle Path. This book does not emphasize the esoteric use of shadow for destructive or manipulative purposes. This is not a book of black Witchcraft, predatory sorcery, or self-aggrandizement. While self-service is necessary to an extent and should (in my belief) be balanced with honest altruism, the magick I proffer focuses more on knowing the mind and journeying the beautiful (yet sometimes dreadful) shadows than on dominating one's environment. Nor is this book simply glorified Wicca in a darker guise; the methods herein are all over the map in terms of Witchcraft and variations of shadow-work, regardless of one's own Crafty leanings.

This is not a basic beginners' book. Readers with some familiarity with basic principles of Witchcraft, spirituality, and the Magickal Arts will be best prepared for the more obscured elements of magick covered here. The material is wide-ranging: some is introductory, some advanced, some historical, some academic, some psychological, some goofy, and some practical. Some material is dark and heavy, and some is light and fun. It is a compendium, after all! As such, it is perhaps best called an intermediate-level book, considering its wide spectrum of material for a wide spectrum of readers!

I have also included various rituals and meditations throughout, but have chosen not to include specific spells or recipes for the sake of space. Meditation is the biggest focus because it is invaluable for any spiritual seeker. These exercises are best done sequentially, as the reader progresses experientially through the book. A variety of simpler exercises, chants, and spell suggestions are also included. All of these practices are designed to be done at night, ideally by candlelight or outside in a safe, natural environment. The ideal time of night is midnight, the "Witching hour," or around three a.m., which is the peak of stillness and astral quietude. The liminal time of dusk is also an excellent time to perform magick working with shadow.

All the possible topics and subtopics under the term "shadow magick" could fill encyclopedic volumes of text—an impossible prospect! Instead, I'll focus on the ones that I find most relevant and that have the most practical value. (Various books mentioned throughout this text are also ideal companions to this tome.) The material herein leans neither too far toward the Left Hand nor the Right: it stands solidly in the Middle. Its focus is neither entirely negative nor entirely positive. It focuses mainly on one's personal connection to the Divine darkness and the manner in which we dance hand in hand with life and death, light and darkness—the father and mother of us all. It would be naive to think that spirituality and magick have ever been entirely about love and light. Love and light are incredibly powerful, transcendent, and ultimately illuminating forces, but fully partaking of those currents isn't always easy. True light is often buried beneath chaos and turmoil that can take years or lifetimes to come to terms with. Contrary to popular belief—even in magickal circles—those who are drawn to and work predominantly with the "darkness" are not to be feared nor shunned. Sure, there are those occasional pervs or power-mongers who are drawn to every imaginable religious expression, but they certainly do not represent the whole range of shadow magicians. Indeed, those who *humbly* work with the shadow, in its multitude of forms, are not so very different from their other magickal kindred. The only real difference is the approach to magickal and spiritual evolution.

Those who practice shadow magick do not worship the darkness but seek to understand it and actualize it for positive ends. Embracing the darkness is part of Divine balance. While some would like to disregard the darker aspects of Deity and pretend they don't exist, that whole half of the spectrum is waiting to be understood. While it may be comfortable to believe that spirituality is pure blissful light, this is only half of the equation. Spirit is the paradox; it is both, it is neither. We would not have the light gods if it weren't for the dark ones, and vice versa. Nearly all occult paths, including Witchcraft, emphasize balance rather than pure light or pure darkness.

The Western world continues to see a stronger and steadier resurgence in ancient spirituality, occultism, and syncretized religious thought. Some would say that spirituality took an ascending path at the dawn of the commonly recognized Aeon of Horus (a Thelemic concept, as mentioned earlier) in 1904, and has risen at an unprecedented rate ever since. The Hermetic Order of the Golden Dawn had been founded in 1888, and Witchcraft was revived in the twentieth century, confirming the trend. From Helena Petrovna Blavatsky's takes on (mostly Hindu) ideas of reincarnation and Karma in her system of Theosophy, to the rising interest in Masonic and Hermetic occult systems, the New Age movement rapidly gained momentum. Later, it would be particularly embraced by the 1960s countercultural movements and psychedelic explorations. Meanwhile, orthodox and dogmatic forms of religion were losing their appeal, and their fear factor, on a mass scale.

Still, the force of darkness was never entirely negated. As Ms. Blavatsky noted in her 1888 book *The Secret Doctrine*, "According to the tenets of Eastern occultism, darkness is the one true actuality, the basis and the root of light, without which the latter could never manifest itself, nor even exist. Light is matter, and darkness pure Spirit. Darkness, in its radical, metaphysical basis, is subjective and absolute light; while the latter in all its seeming effulgence and glory, is merely a mass of shadows, as it can never be eternal, and is simply an illusion." It's unfortunate that such ideas about the positive attributes of darkness were never expounded upon as the New Age movement evolved.

Currently, "New Age" serves as an umbrella term for a number of spiritual paths, often loosely encompassing Paganism, Witchcraft, and occultism. Of course, many adherents to these paths abhor the association, but truth be told, we're all interconnected in terms of spiritual exploration. Unfortunately, some so-called New Agers wish not to focus on personal and global darkness, instead emphasizing "light" as a mechanism—sometimes the only mechanism—for spiritual progress. But if darkness is suppressed or ignored, a dangerous and imbalanced lifestyle results. Many who focus solely on the lighter side of spirituality are just as imbalanced as those who give thought only to its darker aspects. Self-awareness includes acknowledging both the shadow and the light—within ourselves as well as the world around us.

Beneath a candy coating of light often lies a rotten core. This fact demands to be addressed when one is engulfed in spiritual work and practice. No matter how much white light a person is surrounded with, if the darker portions are pushed back and not constructively released, no real balance can be had. Declaring pure love, light, and transcendental awareness without reclaiming inner and outer darkness can push a person to a delusional state of mind, forcing the darker currents to manifest in negative and often harmful ways. Perfectly natural feelings such as sorrow, discontent, lust, anger, and dissatisfaction can snowball if ignored, often resulting in nervous breakdowns and extreme depressions as a counterbalance.

Shamans (and those who may be termed shamans) across the globe have long understood the necessary balance of the light and dark, both within and without. From these shamanic ways, many of our own healing and magickal practices have been born, including aspects of Paganism and many occult rites of initiation, divination methods, and views of the ethereal planes . Balance is rare these days. Goddess knows only a handful of people have truly achieved it; the rest of us are still trying to find proper footing! Many forms of shadow magick, particularly those that emphasize the shadow self, are mechanisms for regaining balance. Certainly, one must practice both "light" and "dark" magicks to achieve this equilibrium.

A number of things that could be considered shadow magick fall in the negative realm. (In general, I use the term "negative" to refer to what is harmful, while noting that both positive and negative currents are necessary to sustain our existence. The term is shorthand.)

Qabalists and other magicians refer to harmful, destructive, or consuming energies as belonging to the Left Hand Path, or the Pillar of Severity on the Tree of Life. This pillar serves as a necessary balance for the Pillar of Mercy (the Right Hand Path), the two of which frame the Middle Pillar of Equilibrium. The Left Hand Path (LHP) encompasses religions like Satanism, Luciferianism, Setianism, Demonolatry, and others. Without question, many people who claim to follow "light" paths are instead treading in negative darkness: just look at the religious extremists! Immoral and amoral people of all kinds, religious or not, can be viewed as living a Left Hand lifestyle; this we can easily see in statistics of violence, assault, and murder as well as in the ever-more-obvious instances of political, religious, and corporate crime. Still, other cultures might classify a "Left Hand Pather" as anyone who goes heavily against the norm—even the ascetic saddhus of India who practice extreme self-mortification. Those who blatantly go against the grain can be perceived as threatening to the masses. To use the age-old saying, people fear what they don't understand. Undoubtedly, "freaks" of Western culture, such as us kooky magickal folk, are viewed by many as Left Hand Pathers, at least socially, even if that view may be inaccurate.

Shadow magick is not a "negative" practice. However, it does require coming to terms with the shadow self. Reaching into those crevices of the mind is sometimes perceived as a negative experience. Seeing reality and the self as objectively as possible is essential to the spiritual seeker and most definitely so to the Witch or magician. Within the vibration we call shadow lie energies both beneficial and maleficent. The focus of this book is spiritual evolution; thus, we must analyze both the "negative" and "positive" aspects of shadow. Often, these polarities are defined by interpretation alone. The aspects of shadow magick range widely. In many ways, those that deal with the internal darkness of the self can be considered positive in nature: practices such as magickal work on the emotional plane, mysticism, and types of deep meditation. Other Arts, such as divination, astral projection, automatic writing, and dreamwalking, are clearly not negative in nature (and are in fact shared by nearly all Witches). Still, some shadow magick can be deemed more negative in nature: demonic evocation, Qlippothic or Goetic work, uncontrolled psychic vampyrism, cursing, and some types of necromancy, for example. While I respect those who cautiously and compassionately practice Left Hand Arts, I do not delve too deeply into them here. I'll leave that to the professionals!

MAGICK & HOW WE USE IT

Magick is one of the most appealing and interesting aspects of Witchcraft. Some people find themselves researching the Craft solely because of its inclusion of magickal practice. Contrary to popular belief, the actual practice of ritual magick is only a small part of Witchcraft as a whole. The Craft is, first and foremost, a spiritual system. Magick is certainly a very important aspect of Witchcraft and other forms of Paganism, but it should not take precedence over spirituality. Rather, magick is aligned with spiritual principle, not a substitute for it.

The magick of the Dark Witch draws upon nocturnal or unseen energies to weave intention into manifestation. The darkness is an extremely powerful force that can be utilized for all types of spiritual workings. The darkness is everybody's own experience—energies of the darkness are subjective in nature. When dark energy is drawn upon, the results can be miraculous, serene, and intense. Nearly anything can be accomplished so long as fear doesn't interfere. I encourage the reader to safely and knowledgably experiment on their own. I offer this information on tools, protection methods, circle casting, and so forth, as assistance in the magickal journey. At the same time, it's only brushing the surface of the magickal world.

Magick works. Life itself is a grand magickal operation. I don't intend to defend my belief in the validity of magick because I imagine that most of the readers have experience in the Arts and are well past the point of uncertainty in this field. If you are relatively inexperienced in magick and/or have uncertainty about magick and its validity, I commend you. All too many people approach ideas and belief systems without questioning, researching, and experimenting. Blind belief is a downfall of any religion or way of life because all sound paths must be built on a foundation of experience. Otherwise, they're only daydreams.

Like most practitioners, I find myself performing minor magick every day. When running late to an appointment, I envision my path to be clear so that I may arrive on due time. If an ambulance passes nearby, I'm sure to project a good amount of healing light at the vehicle so that it may surround the person whom the paramedics are speeding to help. When washing dishes or taking out the trash (how mundane can you get?!), I make it a process of releasing old energy in order to embrace the new. Practical, minor instant-magicks can be performed at the drop of a hat. Projecting intention into reality doesn't take a million crystals and pounds of incense. Every one of us is weaving magick constantly, whether we know it or not! Every thought we have is an act of creation.

The actual process of spellcasting is one form of magick that is considered by Witches to be "amplified prayer." That's it. Though the formulas may be complex and the energy raised extreme, spellcraft is just like prayer work. Likewise, common prayers are spells themselves. The only difference is how much energy is put into each projection of energy. Spells generally contain more oomph than short prayers, but not in all cases.

When I was exploring Christianity in my early teenage years, a friend of mine at the time took me to a fundamentalist Evangelical church. After sitting through a series of seemingly endless and judgmental lectures, the youth pastor instructed everyone to take pieces of paper and write down the names of friends and family who needed to find Jesus in order to be "saved." Everyone did this but me (go figure!) and the pastor gathered the papers and put them in a shoebox. He instructed everyone to gather around the shoebox, hold their hands outstretched to it, and pray vocally simultaneously. I took note of how much energy was being projected into the box as a result of everyone's combined intent. They were, in fact, performing Witchcraft without even realizing it. This was an act of projecting energy to the people at hand, comparable to burning a written petition in a Pagan ritual. This, in addition to entering trancelike states, exorcising "demons," and speaking in tongues, confirmed for me that energy is energy and magick is magick, regardless of the religious skin it wears or the deity it serves.

Occult Ethics

All religions have their own systems of ethics. The word ethics is inherently subjective and a never-ending topic in philosophical discussion. What is ethical for one person or group of people may not be for another, and vice versa. Ethics are culturally relevant. Moral codes differ in every culture, society, and belief system. There is no universal code of right and wrong.

Magickal lifestyles rarely consist of direct codes of ethics and morality. In most forms of Witchcraft and occultism, accountability is placed directly on the back of the practitioner. This is an enormous weight of responsibility, but also one that should never be forgotten as we go about our lives. The Pagan path is a very personal one, especially in that each practitioner decides for themselves what is ethical and what is not. There are no commandments in the Craft. Ethical principles are not the same for every Pagan, but are personally determined instead. This is a lot of personal responsibility and is actually off-putting to those who feel more comfortable following another person's written code of ethics instead of their own. At the same time, some Witches feel more comfortable following guidelines like the Wiccan Rede or a similar moral code. Unlike most religions' moral codes, the Wiccan Rede is but a general guideline emphasizing "harm none," a profound yet simple code designed to influence the ways in which practitioners conduct their lives.

I personally believe that we inherently know the difference between right and wrong. Instead of expounding on this, I will say that each of us has absolute responsibility for our actions and reactions. If little mind is given to the way we conduct our lives—including how we treat other people, which industries we support, what food we eat, where we shop, which ideologies we proclaim, and how we conduct our magick—we are not properly living the magickal/spiritual lifestyle. The cultivation of personal spiritual awareness must encompass humanitarian ethics and conscious behavior. When the cycles we create are given sufficient attention, we become more self-aware and our lives are lived in greater metaphysical consciousness.

"Dark" Witches are not afraid to perform hexing and cursing if there is no other option. (However, I have discovered a new, successful, and even ethical approach to cursing, which will be discussed shortly. Still, tried-and-true specific curses *do* have their place if it's legitimately for the greater good.) For a true Witch to perform a cursing, the situation must be extreme and there must be no other option. Where many Witches and magickal practitioners are more comfortable sending healing light to any given situation, Dark Witches understand that this isn't always the most beneficial plan of action. Witches do not take enjoyment in cursing another person; very, very few cases actually call for such magickal work. Though it isn't true for 99 percent of cases, sometimes a cursing can cause the greatest degree of positive change. While most people only need to see and embrace healing to enter its realm, for others it takes a cosmic bitch-slap to wake them up to that reality. For example, if a serial rapist was the target of magickal work, the last thing I'd want to do is send them love and light in hopes that they will come to see it. The reason for this is that an emergency situation requires emergency action, whether on the physical plane or etheric planes. The perpetrator must be stopped in their tracks, even if it takes a "Karma booster" to make that happen. Of course, this type of dark spellcraft must be well thought out before being executed. Magick is not nearly as effective (actually and karmically) without spiritual grounding and rational thought behind it. Casting unjustified spells only creates chaos upon chaos, which ends up being ultimately consuming, rendering the caster jaded and drained of power. Witchcraft is about flowing with Nature, not going against it. Witches harness and help move the constant ebb and flow of the Universe; at times this is healing and at times destroying; it simply depends on which is best for the greater balance.

Personally, I rarely perform cursing and have only done so a couple times in the past—both of which had positive outcomes after the magick was brought into fruition. If I ever need to perform a cursing or a crossing, an element of light is always added with the intention of "if cursing is not the best possible way to bring this person to a more enlightened state, may they come to that state with no ill effects." Both light and dark elements are required for successful magick, and the order of the Universe mustn't be forgotten for the sake of personal agenda. Shortly, I will discuss a new approach to cursing that is more effective in the majority of cases.

I maintain the idea that people studying spiritual philosophies and the Magickal Arts for purely harmful reasons, like cursing, end up ditching the material as fast as they picked it up, having grown tired of "inapplicable" ideas and failed attempts at selfish magick. Not to mention, they never really "get it." If spiritual principles do not become interwoven into one's life, no satisfaction comes about beyond temporary egotism, and disinterest is soon to follow.

When it comes to the topic of people perusing magick just for a sense of power, an esoteric Qabalist would call these delusions of grandeur the Illusion of Tiphareth. In Qabalistic terms, the sephira Tiphareth is a lower emanation of the highest sphere, Kether. Like a reflection of the sun on a lake, Tiphareth reminds the magician of their own potential for reaching enlightenment. If this acknowledgment isn't heeded, the magician may mistake this emanation for actual enlightenment. Rather than seeing an affirmation of their gifts as a confirmation, they believe themselves to have metaphorically reached Kether, existing at the top of the metaphysical food chain. Behaviors accompanying the Illusion of Tiphareth are purely ego-based, pompous, and foolish. Must this display of delusion be perpetuated in the Craft? Who's got time for *that*?

The Nature of Darkness & the Color Black

The shadow is darkness, and the darkest color of all is black. Simply said, the color black plays a role in shadow magick because of its embodiment of dark energies. It is primordial. Its very essence is ancient and mysterious, containing the entirety of the past and future, retaining memories in its cosmic space.

Neither light nor darkness is inherently "evil." I don't believe anyone or anything is completely good or evil, completely this or that. Reality works through varying degrees: not in black or white, but instead in shades of gray (and there are *way* more than fifty shades). Nothing fully embodies one end of the spectrum or the other. Similarly, the light would not exist without the dark, and vice versa.

Black forms a polarity with light. But this should not be confused with the polarity of good and evil: they are two separate things entirely. Polarities exist to depend on one another. Hot and cold, active and passive, sweet and bitter, male and female: one is a positive pole, the other a negative. Obviously, this doesn't mean that one is inherently evil or equatable with any other polarity. Each has its own individual essence. The Taoist yin-yang symbol exemplifies the philosophy that nothing can exist without its equal but opposite balance; each extreme is dependent on the other, including light and dark in all its forms. The examples are limitless and are directly reflected in Nature. Pagans of all types celebrate Deity in a variety of forms, and this is reflected in the Wheel of the Year. Each major Sabbat is equally important. As the Wheel turns to its darker tide, the death and rebirth of the season is respected and celebrated. If death did not happen, there would be no life. If life did not happen, there would be no death. The light and the dark are not separate entities but are very much one whole, holding the equal balance that is necessary to sustain it.

Those who work with the shadow understand the need for destruction but don't glorify it. At the same time, lightness is understood but we choose not to be blinded by it. An abundance of light is just as consuming as an abundance of darkness; a balance between the two truly is the Middle Path. An important way to express the lightness is through our healing work and everyday optimism. An important way to express the darkness is through art and introspection. Both forces must operate to cultivate balance.

Introduction

Most creation myths begin with darkness. Even the biblical "Let there be light" implies that, yes, darkness was prior…*gasp*! From the darkness, the light of spirituality—the light of life itself—springs forth. Black is the color of the cosmos whence we came and whither we go again upon death. The sun and other stars act as beacons in a vast expanse of black nothingness. In occultism, black is most often associated with two things in addition to creation: energetic protection and the destruction of negativity. When banishing harmful influences, Witches burn black candles to vanquish the energy, and magicians of all types use black as a general protective shield. Black is the combination of all colors *and* is the lack of color. The same is true for white. Black is white, and white is black.

When black is worn on the body, it surrounds the person with a rampart of protection, a cloak shielding them from surrounding energies. Just as light is drawn to dark colors, black also absorbs such energies. Instead of letting them pass further (such as into the wearer's sphere), it banishes them into its own darkness. Nowadays, the color black is most often associated with death and dying, and in many cultures, it is the color of preference worn at wakes and funeral services. It is certainly a color of mourning, as it draws upon energies shrouded and obscured. Black can represent the unfathomable and unknowable, the Great Beyond, the infinite dreamscape entered when dreaming and upon death. It can also be associated with "blacking out" or the loss of consciousness. After the death of a close friend or relative, some people are naturally inclined to wear black clothing for therapeutic reasons, as to cope with the reality of death. Expressing one's mourning in blackness can provide a deep-seated comfort. Plus black goes with, like, literally *everything*.

People who are depressed are often subconsciously drawn to the color because it can contain their energy, whereas extending energy outward could open them to potential harm. In magick, items intended to keep a very specific energy pattern are covered in black cloth and stored in the dark. This cloaks the item, not allowing adverse vibrations to penetrate.

Black represents no thing: nothingness…the Abyss or the void into which anything unwanted can be cast (or drawn from). Black stones, candles, and fabric are best used in spells of banishment and releasing. Black is said to help remove hexes and also aid in binding or cursing when need be. Black is associated with the womb of the earth in some cultures; it may be used for grounding and reconnecting with humankind's roots by way of ancestral communication and past-life regression. Just like white, black is an all-purpose color. It is associated with the night, rebirth, divination, and the eternal journey of awakening to spiritual truth.

Black has different associations for every culture. For some, like most Western cultures, it's a color of mourning, sorrow, and despair. For others, it's the color of rebirth and coming back to the center of the soul. It is a symbol of both release and cultivation, and may be seen as a neutral color. Black not only represents nothing, but also paradoxically represents everything—all colors and energies—and is ideal when used for boosting the conduction of energy in a sacred circle. Most Witches I know weave their magick under the cloak of night because of its calm and mysterious implications . Certainly, daylight has its own distinct vibration that should also be utilized as needed.

We have a good idea about how Westerners commonly view the color black. What about others? Many spiritual folk associate black with the darkness of the dreamscape, as well as the starry, infinite night sky (Nuit). One very interesting association is seen in the traditional Egyptian viewpoint: *Khem* means black in Coptic and refers to the fertile soil on the banks of the Nile River. Khem is also the root word for alchemy. Egypt and its surrounding areas are often called Kemet, or "the black land." Because of this fertile soil's wide-ranging yield of crops, black gained sacred associations with sustenance and abundance.

While the general New Age community commonly links the color white with purity and transcendence, other cultures associate it directly with death. White is the color of bones and the paleness of a body before decomposition. White is a color of purity and the release of mundane ties at the moment of death.

Many of these associations are widely held in many parts of Asia in particular. Some Asian cultures, such as Chinese and Indian, see death itself as tainting or polluting. Thus, the color white is worn in mourning to purge the individual of these associative impurities, creating a rampart of reflective protection around the individual so that death energy cannot enter their space. Because the color white is not bound by any color on the light spectrum, it can esoterically disallow perceived "impure" energies from entering the spirit of the individual in mourning. It may, along similar lines, prevent the soul of the departed from entering into another's physical vehicle as well.

Another example of white as a death color: male members of the Masai peoples of Kenya and Tanzania cover themselves in white chalk at the point in their lives when they transition between warrior and eligible husband status. In this Rite of Passage, white represents their status as "socially dead," in the liminal space between boy and man, being members of neither rank. In ritual, the men engage in ecstatic dance, heavy chanting, trance, and spirit possession (invocation). Obviously, the group of men can still be seen by others, but they are individually unidentifiable due to their ghostly appearances during the ceremony.

In this case, white represents the realm between the death of old social status and the rebirth of a new role. White also physically represents the semen of males and the maternal milk of females, and has associations with fertility across many cultures . So, cross-culturally, both black and white are associated with death and birth! This is only appropriate because death is a form of life, as an entrance into the Otherworld, and life is a form of death, as we are all in a constant process of physically dying while incarnate. The processes of birth and death are really not as separate from one another as they may seem, and neither are the colors black and white.

WILL: THE 93 CURRENT

In his book *Magick in Theory and Practice*, Aleister Crowley defines magick as "The Science and Art of causing Change to occur in conformity with Will." This may sound like a very simple and straightforward definition, which it is, but the magician must really dissect what these words mean in order to come to a fuller grasp of the process. I have found Mr. Crowley's definition to be not too far off from many other occultists' personal viewpoints, regardless of their level of respect for the guy. To analyze this statement, we must first understand what Crowley meant by "will." To draw a correlation with modern Witchcraft, the final stanza of the fifty-two-line Wiccan Rede is this:

Eight words the Wiccan Rede fulfill: An' it harm none, do what ye will.

This is a modification of Crowley's spiritual principle "Do what thou Wilt shall be the whole of the Law." This is one of the primary phrases of Thelemic philosophy, alongside "Love is the Law"; both phrases are said to have been delivered by spiritual means to Crowley and his wife while in Cairo on their honeymoon.

After his wife Rose began experiencing a number of occurrences in which she channeled arcane spiritual messages, Crowley administered a sequence of tests that showed that Rose possessed information impossible to know without massive amounts of prior research, apparently delivered to her from legitimate external sources. Crowley later identified these sources as the Secret Chiefs (Masters) of the Great White Brotherhood (or Lodge), who are seen as a number of Ascended Masters who uphold evolutionary consciousness on earth.

The height of the Cairo working was the instruction for Crowley to sit in a temple at noon for an hour on three successive days to receive a channeling from an external source. It was then that Crowley received a transmission that became known as *Liber AL vel Legis* (*Liber CCXX*): *The Book of the Law*. The book was later researched and declared genuine by a number of occultists. The being that delivered the information identified itself as Aiwass, who became recognized as Crowley's personal Holy Guardian Angel.

The cryptic Egypt-centered philosophies delivered in *The Book of the Law* became the primary teachings of the path of Thelema, the magick of which works to push the practitioner to individually find the way to connect with the higher, cosmic self or God-self, thus uncovering one's True Will (cosmic destiny) in order to achieve the Great Work: that which we are destined to achieve during our incarnation, similar to the Vedic view of *dharma*. Another message delivered in the channelings of Aiwass was "Thou hast no right but to do thy Will," stating that all things done in life in accordance with one's True Will are correct and spiritual, while anything done out of line and against one's will is incorrect and thus sinful.

Like Uncle Al's channeled philosophies, the final line of the Wiccan Rede does not mean "go ahead and do whatever the eff you want." If the Thelemic definition of will is taken into account, it portrays the fact that all acts of magick are part of one's life plan and that magickal practitioners help uphold the world in which we exist. This includes 100 percent personal responsibility for any action one takes. It does not mean pursuing all temptations and pleasures of the flesh, nor does it mean to invite ego or chaos above morality. At the same time, it doesn't mean to disregard them. It means uncover your destiny and follow it accordingly through conscious thought. One's destiny is one's life path; that which is meant to be accomplished. This includes both one's *greater destiny*, or life's work, as well as *every moment* of life—that which constructs the bigger picture. Thelemic magicians call the accurate following of one's True Will the "Great Work."

Gerald Gardner and Mr. Crowley were in contact whilst developing their own magickal systems: Crowley, the Thelemic magick of the OTO under his leadership, and Gardner, modern Wicca. They exchanged an unknown amount of material to help one another form their magickal systems. They also interacted with other magicians and Witches of the time, who exchanged multiple ideas and traditions between themselves. We *do* know that Gardner was initiated in Crowley's OTO. While Gardner and Crowley's relationship remains more or less ambiguous to this day, it's speculated that the final lines of the Rede, which are seen in a similar form in Gardner's Old Laws (Gardner did not write the Rede we are now familiar with), are modifications of Crowley's input. It has even been speculated that Crowley actually wrote most of Gardner's original Book of Shadows upon receiving payment to do so! Still others believe that Gerald Gardner modified Doreen Valiente's writing The Witches' Creed to form portions of his Old Laws, or that he created lines now integrated in the Rede as a combination of the Creed and the Thelemic Law. Other theorists who believe Gardner had a strong influence in the creation of the Rede believe that he simply borrowed lines from Crowley's material in the process of creating Wicca. For example, a couple of lines from Crowley's Gnostic Mass are used word-for-word in the invocation of Drawing Down the Moon. The Drawing Down is accredited to Doreen Valiente, the first Priestess of Gardnerian Wicca.

In the Ostara 1975 issue of *The Green Egg* periodical, Lady Gwen (Gwynne) Thompson published *The Rede of the Wiccae* (which is the Wiccan Rede), attributing the material to her deceased paternal grandmother Adriana Porter, who was said to have gotten it from earlier sources. Is this the origin of the Rede, and if so, how did Ms. Porter compile her material? We do know that Lady Gwen's version was circulated among members of the New England Covens of Traditionalist Witches (NECTW). Regardless of the text's origins, which are as of now unknown, the idea of will in both systems remains very much aligned. They are very similar and carry the same message: do the life's work that you are meant to do.

Giving Thanks

Giving thanks to Spirit is one of the most beneficial and profound things that one can do. I've had a surprising number of people ask me lately, "How do I give thanks and show my appreciation in ritual?" The answer is actually quite simple: do what you feel is right! Do what's appropriate for the situation, and honor the Divine as you see fit, so long as it's in honesty and humility. If working with a particular deity, offerings should be left for them that previous cultures have deemed appropriate. For example, Hekate prefers apples, honey, keys, candles, and myrrh. I've found that Baphomet prefers eggs, tobacco, wine, and a few drops of the magician's own blood. Find out what offerings your patron deity or deities favor and leave them outdoors or at the base of the god's effigy for them to take of the item's essence. Many Witches leave offerings of blended herbs to the deities. Though not nearly as personalized, this is a great way to show thanks and ask for blessings. I like to carry a blend to the cemetery and offer it to restless spirits, power centers, and astral guardians of the land.

In her book *The Circle Within: Creating A Wiccan Spiritual Tradition* (Llewellyn, 2003), Dianne Sylvan suggests cornmeal in addition to other herbs for a "general offering" blend. I've found that some versatile additional herbs are mugwort, yarrow, tobacco, mullein, and lavender. Blends such as these are also ideal for offerings in general magickal workings in which elementals are summoned but no actual deities are invoked. Offerings can be left after magick or simply as homage to the Universe for providing you with abundance—it's never the wrong time to give thanks.

The most important part of giving thanks is the intention. As the offerings are given, contemplate the essence of the one being offered to, really thinking about what they mean and how their energy applies to your own. Allow the energy of true gratitude to rise within you, letting it manifest before you in the form of a material offering. Your internal voice is heard; this is the essence of giving thanks and is a vital part of living the magickal life.

CURSING, HEXING & CROSSING

Because of this book's title, the "black magick" stone will undoubtedly be cast by a handful of people. Whether the commentary is "This is a book of black magick!" or "Why is there no black magick in here!?" I should at least clarify my stance on this subject! Unnecessarily harmful magick is a pathetic display of powerlessness. "Black" magick, as some would term it, can be defined as magick that seeks to control another person's free will, gain dominance over them, or inflict unnecessary harm for personal fulfillment.

As discussed earlier, "black" magick can be seen as manipulation for personal gain. Such practices are almost always used for boosting the ego for the sake of personal validation. Intimidating and dominating other individuals is no more advanced than the behavior of the schoolyard bully.

Anything that violates another person's free will can be called black magick, though most Witches and magicians prefer to simply call it "harmful" or "baneful" magick. This places less emphasis on color, and more on intention.

Deep-seated torment underlies harmfully sadistic behavior, be it in the invisible realm or the physical realm. This harmful conduct, whether it's that of the playground bully or the adult using manipulative magick, is a form of psychological projection: the person inflicting such harm is themselves hurting dreadfully within, and feels a type of comfort in making others suffer. This is, in other words, an external projection of an aspect of a person's internal shadow. Harming others can momentarily relieve loneliness, giving the attacker a sense of justification for the internal pain they so desperately wish to avoid. What's more unfortunate is that this behavioral mistreatment can perpetuate through generations of children, never really healing until someone chooses consciously and decisively to break the vicious cycle.

It is said that a Witch who doesn't know how to curse doesn't know how to heal. True enough! I'm certainly not one to say that cursing and the like never have their time and place. They do. I, like most Witches, have used manipulative and necessarily harmful magick—but never without objective and intelligent reason, and certainly never nonchalantly. The purpose of cursing should, at least in my eyes, always be progressive—for the spiritual benefit of all involved. Not for revenge, not for a display of power, but with the intention of helping another person see the light and discover healing.

It seems to hold true that, for example, an abusive and apathetically self-serving individual will respond better to a Karmic magickal jolt of chaos rather than a visualization of healing white light. Again, the need for performing harmful magick is exceedingly rare, and it should only be practiced after deep consideration and down-to-earth logical contemplation. I once heard that, after the decision has been made to cast *any* spell, a person should wait twenty-four or forty-eight hours to perform the magick. This ensures that the mind is in a balanced and objective state. Any Witch or magician worth their salt knows that the misuse of magickal powers is a spiritual death wish. I'm not necessarily talking about Wicca's (commonly misunderstood and superstitious) "rule of three" here; I'm talking about universal Karma. What goes around comes around, and our behavior, magickal and otherwise, directly influences every day of our lives.

Injustice be Damned

There are times when we will hear news about horrific abuses toward innocent people and animals. The sad reality is that these horrors exist in the world and deserve to be exposed on platforms of public media. It's not enough to shut off and shut out the news. We have to be a part of the change, even if it's merely energetic. For empathic and highly sensitive spiritual souls, merely thinking about involving oneself in these energies can be cause for anxiety and stress—but we must power through. We have taken this spiritual path for a reason. Perhaps the most significant aspect of our spiritual paths is to serve others and uplift the world however we are able.

When learning about issues of abuse and exploitation in the news, one's first magickal instinct may be to unleash a curse, a hex, a spell of revenge. But injustices happen every day, and it would be exhausting and unwise to spend our daily energy trying to inflict the harm of retribution. We must be wise with how we expend our energy. I mean, a financial donation and/or volunteer work with an organization that strives to end suffering can be miles more effective than casting a spell for twenty minutes. Hey, why not do both?!

Sometimes cursing, hexing, crossing, and binding seem far more justified, such as in the case of witnessing or firsthand experiencing abuse and exploitation. In these instances, one should seek legal help and physical protection alongside magickal work. In cases such as these, laying curses and "black magick" are understandable responses.

THE ART OF BINDING

As you're likely aware, there is a fantastic scene in 1996's groundbreaking film *The Craft* where protagonist Sarah binds Coven-sister-gone-Goth-wackadoodle Nancy "from doing harm; harm against other people and harm against yourself." You can bet dollars to donuts that thousands of teenagers performed binding spells as a result of this scene back in the 90s—myself included!

Most Witches, Pagans, and magicians agree that binding rituals can be very positive magickal acts that influence *restriction* on the violator and *protection* for the violated. Typical binding magick is different from cursing or hexing because it affirms safety for the violator and the violated, although it still directly influences a person's freewill. Like anything, binding can take numerous forms and is a spectrum of ethics just as nuanced as cursing itself.

Cursing, hexing, and binding are all complicated subjects too vast to thoroughly explore in these pages. For readers curious about diving deeply into the ethics of these topics, I recommend looking up the article *The Hex Appeal of Activism* on patheos.com, wherein journalist and author Mat Auryn interviews twenty-eight public Witches and magicians (including myself), exploring the intricacies of hexing, cursing, and binding in modern practice. I wholeheartedly recommend this article for all readers, as its wisdom is indispensable for magickal practitioners of every variety.

Contemplating Karma

Wicca is one of the most influential Western magickal paths in modern times. Since its creation in the late 1940s, the "law of threefold return" has been interpreted under various meanings, the most common of which assumes that a person will "get back" what they "send out," times three. However, many modern practitioners see this belief as more of a superstition than a natural law. This is because Nature is balanced; everything is an equal give-and-take. Anything beyond a "law of equal return" simply does not make sense because reality itself is a balancing act of equilibrium, not amplification.

In numerous Eastern mystical traditions, *samskaras* are understood as "Karmic formations," or vibrational imprints that are created through certain actions or inactions in a person's life. (The Sanskrit word Karma itself translates to "action.") Taking out the trash, for example, does not affect Karma and does not create a samskara; it's just part of our duty. However, intentionally throwing recyclables in the trash because it feels "amusing" would be something that creates a samskara or reinforces a preexisting Karmic pattern. On the flipside, organizing an earth-based sustainability rally to spread education about reducing waste may also create a samskara. In other words, it's not always a bad thing. If we choose to make positive, progressive, and compassionate lifestyle choices toward ourselves and others (including our thoughts!), those energies become peacefully affixed to our spheres, encouraging more positivity day by day.

Karma is neither good nor bad. Like gravity or oxygen, Karma ("action") is a natural force that upholds existence, although its effects may not be immediately observed and can't be simply tested in a laboratory. I should also mention here that recognizing, understanding, and resolving deep-seated Karmic patterns takes lifetimes. When we humbly dedicate ourselves to a path of spiritual growth, whether Witchcraft, Yoga, or something else, we become more aligned with spiritual currents that encourage the learning and settling of old Karmic patterns. Seemingly "negative" Karmas can be resolved through self-awareness, humility, and *seva*: selfless service.

Introduction

The Place of Mindfulness

I'm a big fan of Buddhist perspectives on mindfulness. Now a common phrase, mindfulness implies a certain conscientiousness and self-awareness when it comes to responding to life's ups and downs. Moreover, mindfulness can be likened more to an experience of *observing* life rather than instinctively *reacting*.

Self-awareness is greatly borne of mindfulness, and both terms imply an ability to emotionally step back before responding to the human drama around us. Wisdom takes numerous forms and is valued in virtually all cultures and traditions. If we can more objectively look at our minds and the way we think and respond to our experiences, we can more wisely choose where and how to expend our energies and efforts. This most certainly applies to our intentional practices.

Enlighten Up!

Humans, and all things in reality, are fractions of the Great Whole. The singular forms in which we perceive ourselves (bodies) and to which we affix an ego (identification) are but a grand illusion. No thing is apart from you, me, or our surroundings—however, we need this vision of separateness in order to function. Because all things are undeniably connected, if a person consciously harms a point on the fabric of reality, they in fact are harming themselves.

Everyone deserves self-awareness. Many of the world's problems arise from traumatic imprints latent in the spirits and psyches of individuals who, having been violated themselves, *become* violators. Psychological and sociological sciences of interpersonal violence, control, and cruelty are vastly nuanced subjects. When it comes to the magick of the "enlighten up" variety, the reasons, whys, and wherefores of the violator(s) take a backseat to the desperate need for increased self-awareness.

I am pleased to offer this perspective: my personal take on an alternative to cursing. The best part of "enlighten up" magick is the fact that it *will not* harm a person if they are in fact innocent in a situation. If performed with kindness rather than maliciousness or spite, this sort of magick will assist the other on their path of knowledge. If the person or people *are* guilty of causing intentional harm, however, a blast of enlightened energy may *appear* to them as a curse because of the intensity of the *"enlighten up by any means necessary"* intention. It is not always easy to learn deep-seated life lessons and to get on the right track. Sometimes it takes a lot of discomfort for the most necessary lessons to be learned.

This form of magick is concerned with helping a person or people become more enlightened and self-aware so that they can stop causing harm. After all, who doesn't want more awareness? Who doesn't need more loving-kindness in their life? We all need it and we all deserve it, even the most wicked of souls.

As an ethical alternative to cursing—one that is often far more powerful—I encourage attempting the following or a variation thereof. This should only be performed alongside magickal and "real world" action toward safety, protection, and criminal justice if the case is severe. (If laws have been broken and if you or someone else is in danger, contact your local emergency department and legal authorities immediately.)

Throughout this working, make a concerted effort not to cast any maliciousness toward this person or group; send only peace and compassion to the best of your ability. This is often much more easily said than done. If this simply feels impossible, do not direct magick toward this person.

Keep in mind that you will, to some extent, be *forcing* the energy of self-awareness onto another person or people. In many ways, this can be likened to a "binding of light," and may even be viewed as "black" magick in a "light" skin. If this does not sit right or feels unethical, please do not perform this sort of magick. Everything in life is situational, and every circumstance is different, so the practitioner must be entirely confident that this magick is the proper and most ethical course of action.

1. Get comfortable in sacred space. Perform cleansing activities such as burning pure incense or sage, and asperging with saltwater. Light white candles. Perform the Lesser Banishing Ritual of the Pentagram (LBRP) or cast a circle if it is your practice. Call upon gods, guides, and guardians with whom you are familiar and who you feel represent the concept of

"enlightenment." This type of ritual is best performed at dawn or sometime before the sun reaches its daily pinnacle. Although not required, this working is most potent on a *Sun*day. (These are merely suggestions rather than necessities, and the practitioner should personally tailor all magickal workings to some extent.)

2. Facing the east (sitting or standing) with your eyes closed, envision the violator(s) in your mind's eye. See their face and recall the incidents that have led you to influence their reality in this manner. If anger, sadness, or difficult emotions arise, allow them to exist without becoming attached to the sensations. Try your best to become the "observer" of these emotions rather than the "experiencer."

3. Now it's time to get to work. If you are weaving a spell alongside this visualization (such as using a photo, candle, letter, or anything else), set out your crafting components and perform your additional work. (Note: certain herbs, incenses, and stones can also be utilized for this sort of metaphysical work, including jasmine, sandalwood, frankincense, benzoin, selenite, and lapis lazuli.)

4. When you feel as though you have accurately tapped into the emotional energy of the situation—and the energetic signature of the violator in question—visualize yourself looking straight into their eyes.

5. Doing your best to cultivate acceptance in your heart (which is not the same as forgiveness), speak directly to the violator. Rather than cursing them with your words, tell them the reason why you are taking a higher road in the situation. Feel free to scold them for their actions and speak to them as you would a child. Explain to their spirit why they deserve self-awareness, healing, and enlightenment just as much as anyone else.

6. Invoke *light*. Lift up your hands and spend some time visualizing your body growing in size, extending out into cosmic space. See yourself invoking the light of consciousness, life,

and the projective force of evolution. Contain these energies in a blinding-white astral ball between your hands. Visualize yourself coming back down to earth with this sphere in hand.

7. Forcefully project this sphere toward the violator in your mind's eye and/or the spell in front of you. See the person physically respond to the blast of light while you declare, *"Enlighten up—by any means necessary—NOW! NOW! NOW!"* Visualize this light entering every facet of their body. Come to terms with the fact that you are helping to quicken their soul's evolution.

8. Visualize the powerful light simultaneously opening their heart chakra (*Anahata*) and their third eye chakra (*Ajna*), as well as both of their hands. See these two chakra points and the hands all connected by this astral light, symbolizing a connection between awareness, compassion, and action. To seal these energies, envision the person's face growing in astonishment. Visualize them being able to accurately perceive and realize their violations. Visualize the light creating a state of "shaken awareness" for the individual who is now realizing the wrong they have done.

9. Finally, see the individual in your mind's eye humbly accept this light into themselves. Place your hands in the *Anjali* mudra (Namaste or prayer position) and bow to them. Communicate any final wishes aimed at their enlightenment, and genuinely wish them well on their journey. If Wicca is your practice, you may now wish to repeat a mantra such as the line "An' it harm none" from the Wiccan Rede. Follow your intuition in closing the spell.

10. Thank the gods and spirits at hand, as well as the other person's invisible guides, and be sure to ground down your energy however you see fit. Rest assured that you have performed work that is beneficial toward everyone in the situation, and be sure to follow up any castings with "real world" action concerned with safety and social justice.

Chapter One

The Internal Shadow

"Witches do not claim their power from darkness, as the dominant culture tells us. Witches claim their power through darkness. The word is an active one, and it implies that Witches actively pursue their power— it is not a manifestation of some external source. They honor their power from within."

— Timothy Roderick
from *Dark Moon Mysteries: Wisdom, Power & Magic of the Shadow World*

UNDERSTANDING NEGATIVE BEHAVIOR CYCLES

People attracted to both dark energies and the spiritual-Magickal Arts must, in some manner, work with the personal shadow on an everyday basis. Constantly monitoring the self and the mind is essential for magickal and spiritual progress. Shadow Spirituality requires looking at behaviors, actions, and reactions both regularly and as objectively as possible. One of the best ways to do this is by frequently practicing the self-evaluation exercise below. It appears here, in the first chapter, because this awareness must be honed before we move to other forms of shadow-work.

Our perceptions, actions, and reactions form our reality. It's easy to get so swept up in the drama of life that we lose focus of the vital role we play in building our experience. Objectively examining our own behavioral patterns is, in my view, the most important aspect of shadow magick. From there, it's just a matter of "How deep do you want to go?" We can only change the external world by transforming the internal; both simultaneously co-create each other. Every single one of us has behavioral and perceptual patterns that somehow hinder our full spiritual development—or else we wouldn't be here! Everything in existence is linked by an etheric web. This is not fancy New Age ideology, but a strict observation of the true nature of reality. Mystical paths have always recognized that no one thing is separate from the next; even modern science seamlessly backs this ancient notion. When one point on the multidimensional web of life changes, it naturally influences the rest of it, even ever so slightly. As we examine and positively change ourselves, we change our own reality cycles and influence all others' paradigms to shift.

If we let ourselves see the nature of our own psyche, we permit ourselves to heal on deep levels. If we actively recognize and change harmful patterning (even if it's an incredibly painful task), progress occurs both on the level of the earth's general energetic vibration and on the level of our own personal connections and daily experiences. It's a good idea to analyze your actions and reactions regularly—constantly, even. If you find it difficult to step "into the moment" and observe your mind, try meditating in the evening, rewinding and reviewing your day, piece by piece. The most significant points of energy exchange in the day will enter your consciousness first, letting you immediately analyze your own behavior and that of others. Were there moments when you overreacted to something? Were there instances of stress and frustration? What happened in your day that made you upset, sad, confused, or resentful? How could these emotional imbalances have been avoided through your own behavioral responses?

Internal Shadow Magick: A Self-Evaluation

I would like to propose a simple psychological self-evaluation. This exercise helps expose our most ingrained and deep-rooted patterns, opening us to accepting and healing them. Please grab a piece of paper and a pen, or get to your computer or what have you. No, seriously, do this right now. C'mon! *Pretty please, avec sucre?* This exercise is powerful, and the resulting material will be worthy of everyday reflection and expansion, if you wish. Over time, more observations will naturally come to you, especially if you do this self-reflection regularly. Then you can perform the magick you deem necessary to regain balance, even if it requires searching the deepest, most repressed portions of your mind.

Start by dimming your environment. Get some candles and natural incense going, turn off the phone, unplug the television…whatever you have to do to reach a comfortable and serene state of being that is at least somewhat different from everyday waking consciousness. Slow your mind. If it means getting some tea, turning on some music, and wrapping up in a warm blanket on your bed, go for it. If you put on music, make it peaceful and instrumental (nonvocal). If you feel that this exercise would best be performed in a properly cast circle, have at it. The deeper you go within, and the more time and effort you devote to this exercise, the more meaningful the results.

ELEMENTAL ALIGNMENTS

Even if you are already familiar with the common Neopagan and Hermetic concepts of elemental associations, first review them here, taking a few moments to center each element's qualities in your mind.

> EARTH concerns structure: Stability, security, sustenance, materials, and physical reality (plant, animal, and mineral).
>
> AIR concerns the mind: Perception, ideas, intellectuality, study, science, communication, society, and information.
>
> FIRE concerns activity: Motivation, invigoration, lust, sexuality, sensuality, passion, confidence, and transformation.
>
> WATER concerns intuition: Emotions, love, empathy, compassion, healing, psychic ability, astral travel, sleep, and dreaming.

Each of these lists could continue forever. Literally all aspects of reality are contained within these four elementals; this aspect of occultism is recognized across many traditions. One can attribute cardinal directions, planets, astrological signs, senses, seasons, emotions, colors, Tarot suits, deities, archangels, and countless other things to these four primaries—and I won't even touch on the Qabalistic associations!

Now consider what harmful cycles in the human psyche are suggested by these divisions, resulting from either an overabundance or a lack of the associated qualities. A person with hard-to-control anger issues could be seen as having too much Fire energy, whereas a person who has difficulty remembering things might be lacking in Earth energy. (These elemental assessments may or may not be related to your zodiacal birth chart; this is up to you to decide.)

The following four elemental lists show some such possibilities in the form of statements. Note that I have divided these examples by elements; I have found this the easiest way to put "name to form" for those of us who are naturally inclined to working with elemental powers. Browse these lists now, keeping yourself in mind, and read each item with an honest, analytical eye. On your paper, write the headings Earth, Air, Fire, and Water, and copy any statement that you feel applies to you. If you think of others not listed here, trust your intuition and write them down under the element that seems most appropriate. Take it slow, breathe deeply, and allow yourself to detach from your ego as you contemplate. If you're like most people, you'll probably have a sizable list of harmful behavioral cycles—many of which may be rooted in only a handful of life experiences; this is a process of narrowing down where our imprints originated, and many of them *do* tend to spring from the same place or small handful of experiences.

Is it wise to consider what other people have said about you? Sure, but only to some extent. Remember that insults and critiques are always subjective, and therefore may or may not be accurate assessments of our characters. At the same time, our own self-perceptions are subjective, too, and it often takes another person's perspective for us to finally illuminate our patterns and modes of being. Contemplate not only what others have said about you, but also behaviors that you often beat yourself up about. You may be surprised by the list you create as you go deeper within. Also, there's no shame in patting yourself on the back if you discover things about your character that you hadn't recognized before, or had chosen to ignore in the past! The further you immerse yourself in the shadow of your mind, uncovering that which is repressed or ignored, the deeper you allow self-awareness and healing to enter.

Earth: Shadow Traits

- I am often unmotivated in life.
- I often forget the borderline between fantasy and reality.
- I often turn to certain vices, and I may be an escapist.
- I tend to be neglectful of other people's needs.
- I tend to give too much, being neglectful of my own needs.
- I feel that everyone always hurts me in the end.
- I may be addicted to role-playing games.
- I stress about the order and structure of things.
- I disallow anyone from getting too close to me for fear of hurting or getting hurt.
- I could say that I live a double life.
- I only feel secure if I'm in a romantic relationship.
- I am very resentful toward my family and friends when I feel wronged by them.
- I sometimes think that people of a certain ethnicity, religion, orientation, age, class, gender, social identity, body type, culture, disability, and so on are inherently flawed.
- Money is usually the first thing on my mind.
- I often imagine myself having supernatural powers.
- I rarely follow through with plans I make.
- I frequently hold grudges.
- I stress about my obligations and requirements more than I should.
- It's often difficult for me to see other people's viewpoints.
- I only feel secure when surrounded by material abundance.
- I depend on others to carry me through life.
- I tend to consider people's social labels more than their character.
- I overwork myself to the point of exhaustion.
- I sometimes starve myself or purge what I've just eaten.
- I'm never really satisfied with anything.
- I am often apathetic and disinterested.

- I am often quite fearful and have many phobias.
- I rarely leave my home.
- I become fanatical and extremist about new ideas.
- I usually feel responsible for other people.

Air: Shadow Traits

- I have the habit of lying, exaggerating, and creating tall tales.
- I have a bad memory and am usually forgetful.
- I am often spacey, flighty, and ungrounded.
- I always need to have the last word.
- It's difficult for me to embrace new beginnings.
- I am obsessed with my image and public presentation.
- I almost always see people's negative qualities first.
- I feel unattractive without makeup or when naked.
- I feel I'm more aware and knowledgeable than almost everyone I know.
- I believe I never know enough and feel shame when others know more than I.
- I present myself as having more knowledge than I really may.
- I look down on others when I feel more intelligent.
- My attitude changes at the drop of a hat.
- I tend to manipulate other people.
- I often perceive myself as being nonhuman.
- I often get lost in my thoughts.
- I always doubt myself or my ideas.
- It's frequently difficult for me to communicate or to comprehend certain things.
- I try to appear differently to other people.
- I approach things from an extremely academic standpoint.
- I tend to eavesdrop on conversations.
- I usually believe everything that people say.
- I have a tendency to overanalyze.
- I am easily distracted.
- I place personal worth in what others say about me.
- I believe that others should be like me.
- I believe that I should be like others.

Fire: Shadow Traits

- I am usually nervous and anxious.
- I often regret being liberal with my sexual behavior.
- I have insecurities about sex and sexuality.
- I often violate other people's boundaries.
- I tend to lack self-confidence.
- I am fascinated by death and destruction.
- I feel the need to dominate conversations and draw attention to myself.
- I tend to cut myself or otherwise harm my body.
- I often have uncontrollable outbursts of anger.
- I have been known to destroy people's social identities.
- I have an erratic and spontaneous personality.
- I often steal things instead of paying for them.
- My personality is frequently bitter and critical.
- I often force people to see things my way.
- I sometimes have traumatic panic attacks.
- I get pleasure in seeing others suffer.
- I have an addictive personality.
- I often put others down to make myself feel better.
- I constantly seek attention from others.
- It would be very difficult for me to detach from technology.
- I am almost always overexcited and extroverted.
- I get overwhelmed and frustrated at even the smallest things.
- I am extremely rebellious.

Water: Shadow Traits

- I often don't want to wake up in the morning.
- I have difficulty escaping from certain memories.
- I find myself being unable to stop crying at times.
- I find myself unable to cry.
- I tend to overuse mind-altering substances.
- I am almost always introverted.
- I feel that I do not deserve to experience true love, joy, and happiness.

- I usually just "go with the flow" and am passive in life.
- I have a shy personality because I'm overly sensitive.
- I always go with my feelings instead of logic.
- I often make big deals over small occurrences.
- I can usually sense other people's emotional states to an uncomfortable degree.
- It's difficult for me to tell other people's emotions from my own.
- I often misread others' emotions.
- I always take insults to heart.
- I have a hard time being alone.
- I have difficulty "letting go."
- I often feel sorry for myself.
- The past never really seems to heal.
- I find myself reverting to childhood behavior frequently.
- I may be emotionally codependent in my relationships.
- I feel empty without others' sympathy.
- I often feel a rush to change.

What Lies Behind Behavior?

This is where things can get tricky. It's not sufficient to simply list our observations and consider the process complete. Nearly all of these negative cycles, whether directly from this list or from personal variations thereof, have underlying influences. Like layers of an onion, imbalances have the tendency to be shrouded by other imbalances: psychological imprints, emotional trauma, and social conditioning have a way of insidiously sitting in our unconscious mind, influencing our actions and behaviors in daily life.

The real shift from shadow to light happens when we consciously recognize what is psychologically occurring under the surface. For example, a person may recognize a pattern of manipulating other people, a trait linked with Air because it concerns the mental plane. This recognition is the first step in a progressive and positive shift of consciousness…but it is still just the springboard.

The next question is, why does this person manipulate others? It might be for the sake of fitting in and being accepted (Air: socialization), or to get some sort of attention (Fire: activity), or to gain material security (Earth: stability), or to receive a sympathetic emotional response from others (Water: emotion). Further, the underlying motivation itself can be traced to other influences more deeply embedded in the unconscious mind, usually having come about from triggers in childhood or adolescence. For each of us, behavioral cycles come from different sources; everyone reacts differently because we each have a unique life experience.

I've gotta be honest here: it takes *real, true, genuine humility* to accept and modify behaviors and ways of thinking that no longer serve ourselves or others. At times, *shame* is a bedfellow of spiritual humility—most notably in Christian-based religions. But we are Pagans. We are Witches. We are fill-in-the-blanks. With a healthy amount of humble confidence (but *not* ego-based pridefulness), we can gracefully accept our shortcomings, short-sightedness, and life lessons with a warm heart and gentle smile.

To use myself as an example, it wasn't until my midtwenties that I realized having issues accepting the validity of my *own* opinions and perspectives, and tended to keep quiet rather than speaking up. This seems to relate to the element Air because it has to do with ideas and perception. Just beneath that layer, however, was a lack of self-confidence, which relates to the element Fire because it has to do with the strength of assurance. Upon deeper introspection and meditation, I remembered two incidents in my past that had undermined my self-confidence more significantly than I had realized. The more recent incident was during freshman year in high school. After years of acting with a local theater, I tried out for the first school play of the semester. Unbeknownst to me, it was a musical production (they hadn't done musicals in years). When it was my turn to audition at the tryouts, I said to the teacher, "Umm, I can't really sing…" whereupon she held up my application form and, in front of a crowd of fellow would-be actors, ripped the paper in two and threw the pieces in the air, saying, "Then you will *not* be considered!" Because this incident involved a feeling of social rejection, it can be classified as an Air occurrence.

After digging deeper, I discovered an earlier imprint affecting my lack of self-esteem. Around the age of thirteen, I was involved in speech and debate. At this time, I was heavily interested in stage-performance illusory magic—go figure! After one presentation where the other kids gave their speeches and I did my tricks, I walked offstage in a silly way, showing off and being goofy the way kids do. Later, someone I knew (who was also my neighbor) asked me, "Why were you walking like that? You looked stupid."

Looking back, I see that this simple childhood comment damaged my self-esteem more than I realized at the time. Elementally, I would call it an Earth occurrence because of my immediate feeling that I did not fit into a certain structure. It had more to do with social roles and norms (Earth) than social acceptance (Air), especially because the person was a neighbor and thus part of my life off-campus. This initial Earth imbalance affected other elements, leading to a lack of self-confidence. Had I not caught this early in my adulthood, some seriously detrimental issues could have developed out of these *minor* incidents. There are additional areas of damage within my psyche that I've had the pleasure of reviewing and understanding with the help of a therapist; without a doubt, we all *deserve* counseling, therapy, coaching, and assistance with mental health...even my own therapist has a therapist!

Nothing heals instantly, but if a wound is dressed and cared for regularly, it will recover in due time. Similarly, if the wound is ignored, it grows, festers, and overtakes other areas: a perfect analogy for our psychospiritual ailments.

Because the subject of emotional triggers and psychospiritual deconstruction is so large, I'll leave the "root causes" description at what I've offered in these pages. I encourage readers to more deeply examine their own overarching behavioral patterns, underlying motivations, and embedded occurrences of psychospiritual and emotional damage, big or small. Even though many behavioral cycles can be easily deconstructed psychologically, each person's case is different. We must tread across the hidden darkness of our minds and journey through the psychic depths where these cycles originate. We must do this at our own pace, and often with the assistance of family, friends, and licensed professionals. In order to harness the limitless potential of shadow magick, we must begin with ourselves.

Magick for Cyclical Change

I strongly recommend meditating at length on each item on the list you've made. This will allow you to deconstruct and analyze all possible triggers for various thoughts, beliefs, and behaviors. When personal issues arise and beg to be conquered, spirituality and magick are our tools of transformation. We *can* all change our harmful patterns; we are *not* victims of circumstance. When dark personal cycles are brought into awareness, we can choose to change our everyday behaviors. Magick, meditation, and prayer most definitely assist in the process of transforming harmful patterns. When we send our intention for personal change into reality, and if we can catch ourselves "in the process," the mind shifts its own mechanisms to allow for a transformation to occur. With time, the damage remains where it should be: in the past.

There are endless ways to work with harmful behavioral cycles through magick. Because we worked with elemental classifications in the previous exercise, the most obvious way to balance oneself is to work directly with the imbalanced element. That means we consider our list of negative patterns, and regularly research, align with, and get to know the most imbalanced element or elements on it. There are countless ways to use spellcraft, meditation, and prayer to *respectfully* banish an overabundance of a certain element and cultivate an equal-opposite amount of another. The most powerful spells are those we create ourselves.

If you regularly work with Greek deities and are comfortable with them, I recommend calling forth Mnemosyne, the goddess of memory and mother of the nine Muses. If you'd like to create an entire ritual wherein her aid is invoked, go for it. Or perhaps, for this sort of work, you'd fancy working with a more primordial god or goddess, such as Ishtar or Saturn.

I would like to briefly suggest a meditative exercise that is a sort of regression into the past. Deeper forms of regression are not to be approached nonchalantly. I suggest having someone you know and trust assist you in these deeper levels; someone with whom you can be vulnerable and not face judgment. If you have a trusted spiritual friend, partner, or family member, ask for their help; perhaps you could aid one another in your voyages of mind, trading roles as you wish.

To summarize, another person (if possible) guides the other through a life timeline, listening and asking brief questions to help elicit stories. The person who is the "subject" enters meditation (lying down is okay), and recalls various significant life occurrences and describes them aloud for the other person to make note of. They may seem trivial at the time, but speaking freely is essential; it will reveal what may have been previously hidden. As the subject speaks, the other person quickly writes down those occurrences. And, of course, if the person revisits any seriously injurious moments in this meditation, the partner can help with calming the mind and grounding the other back in the present moment. If you don't have a magickal assistant, personal regressions can be done alone as long as you feel secure enough to endure potentially difficult moments on your own.

So, that's all there is to the exercise: strive uncover the deepest and darkest portions of the mind so you can influence personal healing accordingly. To do this, you must think back, and back, and back. Replay your history, record your results, and do it all over again. Cultivate fearlessness, brutal honesty, and steadfast empowerment. Even if it hurts to revisit painful experiences, you must, to some extent, live a piece of the trauma all over again to really know it—to really come to terms with it, to heal it. This is particularly important in cases of abuse, neglect, and social humiliation. "Heavier" cases may require assistance from a compassionate licensed therapist or other third party: there is absolutely no shame in this. To recognize and actively work with the deepest and most imbalanced aspects of our consciousness is to constructively dance with the shadow. It is brave and courageous, and allows us truly act on the ancient edict of "Know Thyself."

Ritual Meditation: Purging Negative Shadow

This meditation, which is separate from the meditation suggested above, can easily be incorporated with the preceding section or stand on its own as a separate exercise. Much of the material within the following exercise intertwines with information within this book as a whole, and its aim is to purge and banish harmful aspects of the self that you *consciously recognize*. It is best to perform this exercise at or just before the New Moon, ideally at dusk or midnight. If possible, abstain from food for at least three hours beforehand (nonalcoholic liquids are okay) or plan a fast for that day. I suggest a rice or juice fast (or both), and breaking the fast after the ritual. These are but suggestions; please follow your own instincts, intuition, and health needs.

In many forms of shadow magick, the aim is to rid oneself of unwanted negative cycles and to use the dark aspects of one's life as tools of empowerment. For example, if a person has experienced traumatic abuse in the past, the idea would be to acknowledge and work with the experience rather than to suppress or ignore it. Shadow magick is all about navigating darkness, both internal and cosmic, assimilating its strengths, and transforming it into something positive—something to grow from. Therefore, much of the apparent "negativity" in our lives may be used as fuel for advancement.

For this ritual, use a candle that is black throughout (rather than a white one with a black shell). First, "magnetize" the candle by stroking it from the center both upward and downward, alternating strokes, whilst thinking of the emotional, spiritual, and physical habits you wish to shed. Imbue the candle with thoughts of the changes you wish to make.

You might like to use some birch oil for this: it's incredibly evocative and smells like autumn in a bottle. This thick, black unguent is ideal for imbuing your candle with the essence of creative decay and transformation. A good substitute is real patchouli oil. For an incense that also helps set the atmosphere, try a blend of rue and dragon's blood resin, which will bring focus and protection to your work. As you burn this incense, carve into your anointed candle a symbol or symbols of what you would like to shed or transform in your life.

As with all meditations in this book, the following may be read in a monotone style by a friend, or it may be prerecorded. It may also be memorized and put to application, or you can jot down short notes to glance at throughout if this doesn't hinder the meditation.

If prerecorded, allow plenty of time between steps, as there is no telling what events will take place moment to moment. Not to mention that the passage of time often seems to "change" during ritual. As with all rituals and meditations, read through it first before undertaking.

Nearly all of the meditations in this book begin with the same first step, for the sake of consistency. Some initial steps include additional special instructions, so be careful not to gloss over it every time, even if you already have a procedure for entering an altered state of ritual consciousness.

1. Construct sacred space around you by casting a circle and calling the quarters as you normally would. Sit comfortably to start the journey. Begin by clearing your mind. Take three deep breaths in through the nose, then let them out through the mouth. Let the thoughts of the day drift away like moving clouds. This is not the time to focus on what happened today or what you need to do tomorrow…let the common world dissipate as you enter the sacred terrain of the mind. For several minutes, sense the oxygen entering your nostrils and exiting your lips. Bring absolute focus to your breath.

2. Close your eyes and imagine yourself sitting in a black egg, the egg of your own nativity. Envision blackness all around you; you can sense the egg's shell containing you fully. Push away all daily concerns and thoughts of yourself; let your mind float in the nurturing darkness, losing all sense of your small life—as you would when looking up at a starry night sky. Sense this egg and solidify it around your body. Around you is nothing, just darkness—the same above and the same below.

3. Your consciousness is germinal; your thoughts move in images now rather than words. Focus on this, allowing your mind to become more and more abstract. Visualize yourself freed of the negative cycles you no longer wish to participate in. Review these patterns in your mind, sending them out of your body and into the womblike atmosphere surrounding you. Eventually, as your anointed candle burns down and your senses are soothed by the incense and the candle's subtle smell of autumnal decay, the egg begins to slowly turn from black to dark purple, then to indigo.

4. Recite your own dark affirmation, or say these words:

    "By the Power of Night, by the Power of the Abyss, by the Power of Duality to create its equal and opposite reaction, I hereby shed my unwanted negative traits and replace them with wisdom and kindness."

5. At this point, you might like to paint, write, chant, or sing something that affirms the termination of these patterns, but try to sense this transformation rather than being overly intellectual about it. If you do decide to create art of any kind, have any needed supplies at hand so you can remain in a trancelike state. Following that, slip back into the meditation and see the indigo-colored egg surrounding you.

6. Now visualize the Grim Reaper, as seen in your favorite Tarot deck or painting, riding toward you on horseback, scythe in hand. Sense their presence from far in the distance as they get closer and closer to you. Hear the rhythmic percussion of the horse's trotting hooves, nearing you even more. Feel fear if that's what the image naturally evokes. Some may even feel a sense of comfort or relief.

7. The Reaper reaches you and swings their scythe in your direction: this shatters the eggshell that surrounds you. The Reaper gallops away from the scene. An eerie illumination floods in from above, highlighting the shards. Look at these images in your mind and remember anything that occurs to you. Perhaps pieces of the broken shell look like a symbol, a person, or an animal. Just gaze at it in your mind's eye and record what you see.

8. When you have gathered the information you were supposed to receive, emerge from your shattered past refreshed and reborn. Once the flame has burned past the symbols you have carved into the candle, burn a bit of your own hair in the flame to signify the transformation. Afterward, blow it out with a resounding *"And so it is"* or *"So mote it be."*

9. When finished, wave smoke around yourself using sage, frankincense, or a purifying incense blend. Alternatively, or additionally, take a shower to refresh yourself and wash away excess energy. Deconstruct the circle and dismiss the quarters as you normally would. Relax, unwind, and take it easy for the rest of the evening.

MYSTICISM:
THE PARADOX BEHIND THE VEIL

Mysticism is an invaluable part of the spiritual journey. I would go so far as to say that it lies at the core of legitimate spiritual practice. The Dark Witch does *not* involve themselves with the Magickal Arts merely to "do stuff" externally: instead, our journey has its footing in our *internal* landscape. It would be incredibly progressive, I believe, if all spiritual traditions either retained or developed mystical practices, but that's not the reality of things. For modern spiritual seekers, particularly the magicians and Witches of our time, mysticism in any form can serve as the mechanism for driving the spiritual journey home, solidifying our philosophies through personal experience.

I've heard a great number of Witches, occultists, and other spiritual folk of various paths say that "something is missing" from their practice. From my viewpoint, the missing element is the mystic experience; the transcendental connection—the Oneness or Gnosis—with All Things. It's one thing to think and speak about Oneness, another to actually experience it.

Spiritual paths require that our worldview shift to a more expanded state of operation. The mystical experience accomplishes this, giving the practitioner (regardless of tradition) a connection to both the self and the surrounding world that cannot be captured in words. I consider mystical experience an aspect of shadow magick because the practitioner emerges—internally, perceptually—into the subtle planes, the dimensions of reality that ordinarily remain hidden to waking consciousness.

Mysticism can be defined as the quest to attain union with the Divine. The best-known and best-documented mystic traditions are Jewish Kabbalism and Muslim Sufism, both of which I will review here. A variety of Christian mystics through the ages have also had their experiences and philosophies well-preserved. Mysticism has always occurred within Indigenous, animistic, and Pagan cultures. Ancient and modern shamans can easily be called mystics because their practices reach into the Otherworlds for purposes of healing, divination, journeying, and esoteric work.

Mystical thought often plays a key role in modern magickal practice, though many practitioners might not call it that. Unfortunately, a number of people drawn to the esoteric, occult, and magickal realms seek to alter the external world to their fancy rather than focus on the internal mechanisms that actually shape it.

In classical times, those who subscribed to Gnostic thought emphasized one's own transcendence into mystical states of awareness as a means of escaping the material world. Gnosticism is a classical religious movement and philosophy that holds that we, as humans, must escape our current mundane situation and return to a union with Spirit. Gnosis, meaning "saving wisdom," implies the reunification of man with God, so that we may understand our true nature and awaken from the dream that is common reality. Modern-day Gnostics also emphasize this ideology, as do some neo-mystical approaches such as chaos magick and ceremonial orders. By the same token, many adherents of Eastern religions speak of experiences of Oneness, enlightenment, and transcendence—though more often than not, these terms describe a perpetual state of being rather than an ephemeral one.

Judaism, Islam, and Christianity have long held strict religious standards. Thus, unsurprisingly, the pursuit of mystical experience hasn't always been viewed with empathetic kindness. Still, traditional doctrinaire religions have taken a variety of views regarding the place of the mystic. In Catholicism, mysticism is generally an honored practice (albeit, and in my opinion unfortunately, only pursued by the few), but one set clearly apart from everyday Catholicism; many of its mystics are actually regarded as saints and venerable figures.

Of the branches in the Christian movement, Eastern Orthodoxy tends to have the most respect for mystical traditions, whereas the Protestant Reformation of the sixteenth century did much to suppress mystical thought by maligning it in the public eye. Again, every tradition's stance on mystical practice is different.

During a mystical experience, a person perceives an intimate unity with the Divine. This is experiencing Spirit. For older, more animistic traditions, the Divine is perceived as Nature, or forces thereof. Monotheistic societies have perceived mystical union as being with God, while polytheistic societies have perceived it as being with either a number of gods or an individual deity depending on a person's spiritual alignments, such as with cults or tribes devoted to serving a specific godhead. Pantheistic and animistic societies seem to experience a unity with All Reality; a state of Oneness with the All That Is, due to their view of Spirit as permeating everything in existence.

A number of the features of the mystical experience have been distinguished by religious scholars, such as the twentieth-century professor of mysticism W. T. Stace. For our purposes, I include these points to further compare our own theurgic practices with those already documented. Many of the points made here have been influenced by the teachings of University of Montana professor Paul A. Dietrich.

A number of characteristics can define mysticism and accounts of mystical experiences:

INEFFABILITY: The sense that the experience is beyond the realm of words and impossible to accurately convey—it is purely experiential.

TRANSCENDENCE: The feeling that one has transcended space and time.

UNITY: The feeling of absolute Oneness with Divinity.

EQUANIMITY: Feelings of absolute peace, bliss, joy, and well-being.

PASSIVITY: The feeling that one is being acted upon rather than being an actor.

PARADOXICAL EXPERIENCE: Feeling the governing forces of reality and understanding the polarity of existence, often realizing that "everything exists, yet simultaneously nothing all at exists."

PERSISTING CHANGES: The life-changing events provoked by the mystical experience that stand the test of time; in many cases, this is conversion to a particular mystic tradition.

Jewish Mysticism & the Qabalah

Allow me to quickly review some aspects of traditional Judaism and how they intertwine with mystic branches of the religion, including the *traditional* form of Kabbalah. This summary is focused on written tradition and, unlike many religions, relies heavily on ancient commentary and rabbinic interpretations of canonical texts. The Hebrew Bible, also called the *Tanakh*, includes the *Torah*, also known as the Law of Moses or the Five Books of Moses. Those names refer to the books of Genesis, Exodus, Leviticus, Numbers, and Deuteronomy. The Old Testament includes these Hebrew-based scriptures, though the order in which they appear varies between the Hebrew Bible and the Old Testament.

Judaism emphasizes the practice of orthodoxy (called orthopraxy), and traditional Jews focus their lives on *mitzvoth*: pious deeds done with spiritually correct intention. In many ways, the Jewish tradition relies on doing the right thing over simply believing a certain way. Mitzvoth is said to have cosmic significance and is the act of aligning oneself with Holy Law.

Within Judaism, the first documented major mystical branch is called the *Ma'aseh Merkabah* ("Work of the Chariot"). This mystical system relies on the notion that a pious Jew may be carried through the heavenly spheres on a Holy Throne or Chariot (the Merkabah). This Chariot is mentioned in the book of Ezekiel in the Hebrew Bible and was viewed by Jewish mystics as an analogy for God's eminence and his influence on the realm of humankind. The tradition examines this Holy Throne in detail, including its seven heavens and angelic inhabitants. Merkabah mystics focused on experiencing Heaven while still in the earthly realm—why wait?

A book called the *Sepher ha-Zohar* is particularly significant to Jewish mystics and of utmost importance to modern Kabbalah (discussed in a minute). Also called the *Zohar*, the Book of Splendor, the Book of Radiance, the Book of Lights, and the Book of Enlightenment, the Zohar is an exegetic and hermeneutic midrash, meaning that it is both a mystical interpretation of and commentary about a sacred text: in this case, the Torah. The Zohar's written style is esoteric, meditational, and novelistic. It is meant to comment on the Torah, but also contains a wide array of additional material, including stories, narratives, and Kabbalistic treatises.

The Zohar was long accredited to a second-century Jew called Rabbi Shim'on (Shimon bar Yohai), who is said to have copied it from an even more ancient sacred book. According to Moses de León of Guadalajara, the Zohar was passed from teacher to student over many generations, eventually making its way to Moses de León in Spain in the late thirteenth century. However, the more recent discoveries of scholar Gershom Scholem (who passed away in 1982) suggest that the Zohar was almost undoubtedly written by Moses de León himself, a theory with which nineteenth-century Jewish historian Heinrich Graetz concurred. Regardless of authorship, the Zohar is considered a holy text of Jewish mysticism by traditional Kabbalists. It was from a little-known branch of Jewish mysticism called the *Ma'aseh Bereshit* ("Work of Creation") that one of the documents most influential in the development of the Kabbalah emerged.

In his book *Major Trends in Jewish Mysticism*, Gershom Scholem writes, "The existence of speculative Gnostic tendencies in the immediate neighborhood of Merkabah mysticism has its parallel in the writings grouped together under the name of Ma'aseh Bereshit. These include a document [the *Sepher Yetzirah*]...which represents a theoretical approach to the problems of cosmology and cosmogony." The Sepher Yetzirah chronicles the development of reality and is the oldest known document to mention the Tree of Life. Compact yet informative, the text was heavily influenced by Greek and Hellenistic thought, and it is connected with early Jewish mysticism because of its emphasis on theurgic magickal practice. The book is often attributed to Rabbi Akiba Ben Joseph (Rebbi Akiva) around the year 100 CE. This authorship is possible, as modern scholars estimate its origins between 100 BCE and 900 CE.

Earlier traditional sources attribute it to the prophet Abraham himself, though it is almost certainly *pseudepigraphic*, that is, a book falsely attributed to another author in order to establish its validity: either a single "ghostwriter" or a collection of individuals, as in most cases. Most, if not all, books of both the Hebrew and Christian Bibles are pseudepigraphic, as is the Zohar of early Kabbalism. (The Greek *Odyssey* and *Iliad*, accredited to Homer—and I don't mean Simpson—may also be pseudepigraphic literature.)

It is from the Sepher Yetzirah that we receive the concepts of the Kabbalistic Tree of Life, including descriptions of the Sephiroth (the spheres on the tree, also called the "fruits," "emanations," and "lights") and the paths that link them together. The twenty-two letters of the Hebrew alphabet correspond to these paths, and planetary associations are aligned with the Sephiroth. A virtually endless number of correspondences to these Sephiroth and paths, including Tarot cards, colors, scents, herbs, deities, stones, incenses, elements, materials, symbols, emotions, areas of the body, and many more, are currently recognized within the Qabalah of the Western Mystery Tradition, and much of this information was drawn from the Book of Formation.

Modern esoteric (Hermetic) Qabalah—spelled with a Q—is the most significant branch to modern esotericists, and is often spelled as such to distinguish it from traditional Jewish Kabbalism (or Cabalism) or any of its subsequent Christian interpretations. This esoteric, magickal Qabalah was greatly developed by Éliphas Lévi in the nineteenth century, building upon his studies of the traditional Kabbalah and his application of Hermeticism and comparative mythology. It was later significantly expounded upon by the Hermetic Order of the Golden Dawn, and it is from their teachings that many of our current views, practices, and metaphysical associations of the Tree of Life entered modern esoteric circles.

The Shadow of Da'ath

Within the Western Mystery Tradition, the sephira Da'ath (Da'at) on the Tree of Life (particularly in esoteric Qabalah) can be seen as resonating with the essence of shadow magick. Da'ath is called the eleventh, or hidden, sephira. This Hebrew word means "knowledge" and sounds surprisingly like the word "death" in English.

Though sometimes called "the non-sephira," this sphere, whose obscure origins are still debated, can be viewed as a shadowlike integration of the energies of the tree's upper fruits (the Supernal Triad), which is Kether, Binah, and Chokmah. Da'ath is situated on the Tree of Life just beneath this area, and is often called the Abyss. The Abyss is the space between the Supernal Triad and the others; the area where the ego, or sense of self, is released when journeying the Tree. Some believe that Da'ath acts as a seed for the upper spheres or as an invisible emanation of their excess energy. Unlike the Tree's other spheres, the energy of Da'ath is so enigmatic in nature that many practitioners do not feel a need to recognize it in their practices—this is especially the case for Judaism-based Kabbalists, who are themselves still considered fringe by orthodox Judaism. Because Da'ath is not definitive, it is often depicted with a dotted line on the Tree of Life, if at all.

Though some amount of darkness exists in each sephira, some occultists believe Da'ath to be the area in which the soul travels during the sorrowful Dark Night of the Soul, while others equate that experience to Binah. Like a black hole, the energy of Da'ath confronts us with the truth of impermanence, reminding us that nothing is fixed. It can be seen as the Underworld sephira, representing not only the depths of personal internal darkness, but also religious myths such as the Pagan Descent of the Goddess (particularly in the Greek pantheon) and the scriptural fall from Eden. Of course, associations such as these depend entirely on the view of the Qabalist or Kabbalist, or of their specific school of thought.

Da'ath embodies all that is mysterious and urges us to face both sides of our human nature. Author Rachel Pollack, in her book *The Kabbalah Tree: A Journey of Balance & Growth*, gives Da'ath psychosexual associations, assuming it to be the place of balance between the sexes (and any two polarities), wherein males metaphorically become females and females, males. This reinforces the idea of Da'ath as a place of paradoxical polarity, of both nothing and everything...the ultimate spiritual dichotomy.

Da'ath is situated between two polarities, and its accessibility is most favorable around Samhain or the New Moon. As a further correspondence, Da'ath can be seen as the gateway between two worlds: that of the living and that of the dead. Perhaps this is the point on the map in which souls depart from the physical world and enter the light of the Afterworld. In accordance with the Judeo-Christian worldview, it may be seen as the invisible realm where God enters and exits from the earthly plane to the others, and can be seen as the seat of life or consciousness. Qabalists often believe that Da'ath is the Tree's dark portal, leading to Hell-like realms of demons on the dark side of the Tree, which is often called the Qlippothic realm, as accessed via the "Tunnels of Set(h)," which are the dark underbellies of the Tree's paths.

Da'ath is situated in the Middle Pillar of the Tree and is said to align with the throat chakra on the human body. Because Da'ath exists on the Middle Pillar, it would be foolish to think that it's all bad. Qabalists have reported mistaking Da'ath for Kether in their magickal and meditative work, proclaiming it to be dangerous territory. Others believe that Da'ath is actually a lesser emanation of Kether (absolute enlightenment), similar to Tiphareth. As you can see, there are many views of what Da'ath truly is. For this reason, it is excluded from most depictions of the Tree, though it remains a part of it in essence nonetheless. In truth, everyone's experiences with the Sephiroth are quite different, and each sphere holds a somewhat subjective meaning for every magician.

Each Qabalistic sephira embodies a different vibration or energy pattern that can be seen in immediate reality. Taking this idea further, each person vibrates with a particular sephira over another. For example, a highly intellectual person would vibrate with the sphere Hod, while a daydreamer might vibrate with Hod's equal-opposite, Netzach. Da'ath is relevant to shadow magick because it embodies the mysterious and the unknowable. This does not mean that our attunement to a certain sephira is fixed. In fact, it's highly mutable. However, many people stay anchored to a particular vibratory state and branch out, always coming back to the base. Even though someone is almost always loving and compassionate (characteristic of Chesed), that doesn't mean that person cannot feel impassioned aggression (characteristic of Geburah). For people who often contemplate the darkness (in whatever form) or are introspective in a highly emotional way, Da'ath can be seen as that metaphorical base.

When it comes to Qabalistic pathworking, a certain entity or amalgam of energy is believed to sit at Da'ath, separating the lower sephira and the Supernal Triad. Called the Watcher on the Threshold or the Dweller on the Threshold, this spirit represents the sum of the magician's delusions, fears, accumulated negative Karma, misunderstandings, limiting beliefs, and anything else that can possibly interfere with the magician's path to enlightenment and spiritual attainment. The "Dweller in the Abyss," another title for this energy, is the ultimate embodiment of antispiritual ego. The entity Choronzon was originally recognized as a demonic figure by Edward Kelley and John Dee (Enochian magick), and later expounded on by Aleister Crowley. The entity is said to be the last thing the magician faces in their path toward enlightenment, and is quite often recognized as being an aspect of the magician's own mind, much like our internal mental "critic," rather than being an entirely external force. As Above, so Below; as Within, so Without.

If you feel trapped within barriers of over-introspection and unhealthy depression, I would recommend researching the Qabalah as part of your magickal path. Both Qabalism and balanced Witchcraft identify and work with darkness as a tool for spiritual expansion. If you end up working with Da'ath ritualistically or meditatively, I recommend you not try to comprehend the sphere in its entirety; to do so would be like attempting to figure out the full of the cosmos. Simply know that it exists and that you may tend to gravitate toward its energy. Trying to fully understand Da'ath is like trying to fully understand the reality of death: it is impossible without actually experiencing death itself. Da'ath is seen by many as a black hole of trickery that can suck people in deeper and deeper as they feel their knowledge of it expanding. It's also for this reason that *when* we emerge from a place of absolute sadness and darkness, having refused to be consumed by our own misery, we come out stronger and more aware of the shadow—our own Da'ath—as a result.

THE MYSTICAL VALLEYS OF SUFISM

The Sufi tradition of Islamic mysticism, also called *Tasawwuf*, originated as a response to traditional Arabian ideologies. Sufis place ultimate confidence in the *Shahadah* (one of the five Pillars of Din), or the profession of faith that "there is no god but God." Similarly, they believe that "all things are God (Allah)." This animistic view is an aspect of *tawhid*, an Arabic term for the Unity of Being. Sufis also view the term *jihad* as referencing the spiritual seeker's challenge to align with God, and the struggles of acquiring virtues in place of vices, though the term is frequently used in the West to refer to a narrow, extremist view of a "holy war on behalf of God." The word Islam means "surrendering to God's will." The word Sufi most likely comes from the Arabic word *suf*, referring to the coarse woolen garments that early Islamic mystics wore both to renounce materialism and to criticize the opulence throughout the Middle East.

Sufis interpret the *Qur'an* (*Koran*) in the manner that Kabbalists interpret the Zohar. Mohammad, the prophet of Islam, died in 632 CE. The Qur'an was edited around 650, and Sufism is commonly accepted as having begun in the ninth century. Similar to the birth of mystical commentaries from the Kabbalistic movement, a vast collection of poetry and literature arose from Sufism. The most well-known Sufi poet is Rumi, an esoteric writer and the founder of the *Mevlevi*, the order of Whirling Dervishes.

An earlier Islamic mystic writer was Farid ud-Din Attar, who influenced many of Rumi's viewpoints and writings. One of Attar's most renowned works is *The Conference of the Birds*, an allegorical story featuring a variety of birds for characters. This metaphorical writing style has been used throughout history as a way to convey viewpoints. In this case, each bird represents a particular human vice, or sin, as some would have it. Birds are a cross-culturally religious symbol of the soul, and their flight can represent a person's spiritual freedom and journey to higher consciousness. Here, Attar maps this journey in seven precise stages called "valleys." These stages encompass common mystical ideas found both within and outside of Sufism. These mystical valleys are said to be augmentative, in that the first leads to the second, which leads to the third, and so forth. Because of the strong identification that many mystics feel with these stages, let us review them here.

1. THE VALLEY OF THE QUEST

The first valley refers to the altruistic zeal or desire to embark on the path leading to the unification of Self with Spirit. Though hardships are a constant, a person's unquenchable desire to align with the Divine serves as fuel to the fire of endurance and progression. When this solid motivation is embraced, the succeeding stages become available.

ii. The Valley of Love

This valley refers to the state of absolute love for God and the spiritual journey. Affective rather than effective, this journey is more intimately connected to the emotional body than to the intellectual mind. Even if nothing else seems to remain, the limitless energy of transcendental love allows the spirit to hold on. This love is described as a consuming allegorical fire, within which all beings on the spiritual path must burn in the ecstasy of Spirit.

iii. The Valley of Knowledge

This stage points to actual insight into the reality of mystical states of consciousness. Transformative rather than informative, this knowledge offers but a glimpse into the constant state of being available to spiritual seekers if they continue on the journey. There are various outlets of expression for this insight, an endless variety of individual perceptions from which this knowledge can arise.

iv. The Valley of Detachment

A number of spiritual traditions also endorse this idea. A person must let go of not only "worldly" constraints, but also the very idea of enlightenment itself (this idea is also promoted in Buddhist schools of thought). Further, the seeker must detach from the ego—the entire identity of "self"—to deconstruct the internal blockages that naturally hinder the journey. This concept affirms a person's extraordinary yet minute place in the cosmos.

v. The Valley of Unity

Whereas the Valley of Knowledge is a reflection of the whole, the Valley of Unity is an unchanging integration of the Self and Spirit as One. This is the mystic's desired state of consciousness; a sustained experience of the interrelatedness of all things. From this platform, the greater picture comes into focus.

vi. The Valley of Bewilderment

The path of the mystic doesn't simply stop at the stage of Unity. "Bewilderment" refers to a person's reintroduction into the world after having experienced full metaphysical awareness. This can be called a reintegration or rehumanization, in that the mystical state of consciousness must blend with the terrestrial. This is the valley of lamentation, of absolute sorrow and void. Here, one does not know whether one *is* or *is not*. The experience of the paradox of all things leads to this experience of spiritual shock: a state of being in absolute awe toward the *miracle* of life itself.

vii. The Valley of Poverty

A curious final step, the Valley of Poverty is a declaration of nothingness. This is "obscure oblivion," a final rejection of the self and its vices. Here, the notion of self is said to be permanently forgotten. It is the ultimate annihilation of the hallucinatory view of the life-charade. This perception is beyond rational comprehension and relies on experience alone. Here, self-consciousness is nonexistent, and anything believed to be separate is realized, in fact, as One.

Achieving the Mystical State

Twentieth-century philosopher Abraham Maslow pointed out that mystical *"peak experiences"* could occur at various times: during prayer, whilst walking on the beach, when exercising, whilst making love, and so on. Even if it's unexpected, one can have a true mystical experience that defies description in words. Certainly, the idea of peak experiences could be expanded to encompass other experiences directly aimed at unification with the Divine, including deep meditation, ritual, dancing, Yoga, playing music, sweatlodge practices, entheogenic drug use, ascetic practices, and so on—all of which have spiritually transcendental potential.

Maslow also determined that people with nonhostile, self-actualized states of being, particularly *those with humility and respect, those who are personable, and those who have a sense of humor* (all of which are spiritual qualities in my eyes), were more likely to experience and report occurrences of mystical awareness. Mystical experiences by way of mind-altering substances, if I may expand on this particular method, are common in modern times, and were generally more common before widespread colonialism. Many would argue that drugs—particularly natural drugs such as cannabis, psychedelic mushrooms, peyote, *Salvia divinorum*, and so on—are holy gifts for us to attain unification with spiritual realities. I agree wholeheartedly, provided these experiences are approached with proper planning, research, and mindfulness of the substance consumed. It's all about *set and setting*. Uses of certain drugs under certain circumstances can, does, and historically has induced intense mystical experiences and deep awareness of the interconnectedness of all things. Still, with a "substance shortcut," some users associate the experience with the influence of the drug itself rather than the influence of the Limitless Divine. (It doesn't help that the vast majority of people who use drugs don't take them with the purpose of attaining mystical union with God or Nature.) One's approach and one's environment, both externally and internally, greatly construct the phenomena experienced.

DRUG USE IN SPIRITUAL PRACTICE

In modern society, the issue of drug use is considered taboo, usually filled with stereotypes and misconceptions. Many people avoid drugs altogether, even the most natural of substances. Others misuse intoxicating substances, having only self-centered intent, ignoring any possible spiritual implications that the substance may have to offer. While these instances are extremes, they're very much a part of modern culture, which is quite divorced from original concepts of mind-altering substances. For many ancients, the Middle Path was walked between these two extremes, emphasizing intelligent *use* instead of abuse, misuse, or overuse. This section will examine some aspects of ancient and modern drug use, and its significance to the magickal path and alternative spiritual lifestyle.

Physically, drugs affect the body by either mimicking a neurotransmitter such as dopamine or serotonin, or by increasing the rate in which certain neurotransmitters are released in the brain. Some inhibit a neuron by blocking certain receptors in the brain, disallowing the regular flow of chemicals, in turn causing a high. In other words, drugs change chemical levels in the body, which in turn causes sensations of altered consciousness. The same is true for many prescription drugs. Used in excess, drugs of any type can cause permanent damage to the brain and organs of our sacred Body Temple.

Mother Earth has gifted us with tools to be utilized for specific purposes. This view is accepted by most spiritually-minded individuals, namely practitioners of earth-based paths, both Indigenous and modern. Additionally, many followers of Eastern religions tend to accept some naturally high-inducing substances as normative and not inherently polluting, unlike the general view of many Judeo-Christian monotheistic traditions. Though some of these cultures may advocate the intelligent use of certain *natural* drugs, we find that chemical substances and designer drugs are generally looked down upon. When looking at "shamanic" and tribal traditions, spanning from times past to the present day, the influence of mind-altering substances mustn't be overlooked. Entheogenic plants are venerated because of the part they have played in shaping Native belief systems. Substance-induced visions can be spiritual experiences and, because of their profound effects on the user, are often viewed as real and valid happenings, allowing the user to see alternate layers of reality that would likely otherwise remain hidden. These perceived levels are recognized and included in the cosmology of the particular Indigenous belief system. It is for this reason that certain drugs are viewed as a spiritual sacrament. Again, this concerns the religious and ceremonial use of mind-altering substances, not casual or recreational use.

Shamanic Drug Use

The word *shamanism* actually originates from the Tungus people of Siberia. Anthropologically, the word was further applied to other cultures with similar tribal associations. Shamanism has now become a broad term, unrestricted to any one tribe or group of Indigenous people. A modern term popularized by the highly influential author Michael Harner is "core shamanism."

Shamanism has been practiced since the beginning of human culture in varying yet similar forms, and can be traced back to the

Paleolithic era. In pre-religious times, people relied on shamans for insight and healing. They were the Medicine People who utilized elements of the natural world for healing and spiritual discovery. They were the religious experts of old who helped a community maintain its spiritual roots. While the rest of the community had their specific duties to maintain the culture's survivalistic necessities like food and shelter, the shamans were (*and still are*, in many cultures) individuals who existed on the fringes of the greater society, and who had the distinct role of maintaining the society's connection to the ancestors, spirits, and deities—this would often occur by way of personal healing sessions for individuals, families, or the society at large.

Shamanic cultures, and those that may be termed "shamanic" in nature, have since their beginnings utilized hallucinogenic and mind-altering substances in ritual settings for esoteric purposes, including communing with the gods, embarking on astral journeys, contacting ancestors, breaking curses, performing deep healing, gaining past-life vision, utilizing divination, and learning secrets of existence too grand to put into words.

Generally speaking, when members of society would fall sick, shamans view(ed) them as having lost a portion of their souls. Shamanic healers, past and present, work with patients to draw back their spirits from the Otherworld in the case of illness—an act of spirit retrieval. Natural drugs assist in this process, opening up the shaman's perceptive ability and helping them to see an illness, locate a spirit, gain visions, and execute healing processes.

A number of modern psychotherapeutic methods even make use of "soul retrieval" in a psychological manner, such as IFS, or Internal Family Systems, in which the client is given an opportunity to gently communicate with past or fractured aspects of their own consciousness in order to regain holistic balance. This particular system does not include the use of drugs, nor does it term itself shamanic; however, I can personally vouch for the effectiveness of IFS.

Hallucinogens are classified as alkaloids, which are characterized by their bitter taste. This represents their toxic properties, which may be utilized by medicinal healers, or as poisons in overly large quantities. They have a molecular structure that includes two carbons and one nitrogen, and have long been used in methods of shamanic work across the globe.

AYAHUASCA

Ayahuasca is a Quechua Indian word that means "vine of the dead." This vine is used in Amazonian shamanic medicine to expand consciousness and increase spiritual communion through visionary experience. Ayahuasca refers to a combination of plants, not one singular compound. The plants are native to the Amazon River Basin. Each mixture is unique to its maker, as each shaman uses a different combination of plants for their medicine and uses a variable amount of each substance. The presence of two alkaloids seems to be common in all forms of ayahuasca—these are beta-carboline and tryptamine. Beta-carboline is typically extracted from the bark of the *Banisteriopsis caapi* vine, and tryptamine is typically extracted from the leaves of the *Psychotria viridis* bush, though different alkaloidic plants with similar genetic structures are also used.

The topic of modern-day ayahuasca use could fill volumes of text, so the focus here is on the traditional. Ayahuasca is rarely administered by smoking, but rather is made into a drinkable brew or powdered into a snuff. Traditionally, when ingested by the Amazonian shaman, the shaman begins to perceive the cause of a patient's illness. Once that has been determined, the shaman proceeds with ritual cleansing and healing to target the root of the ailment that the ayahuasca mixture's vision presented to them. The shaman doesn't treat every person who comes to them for help; but of those they do, ayahuasca is only administered for specific cases, especially those rooted in psychological ailments. Historically speaking, most of these ailments were deemed a result of negative magick ("Witchery") or bad medicine. The healer will only prescribe ayahuasca for certain cases, and during the actual healing ceremony will "suck" the bad medicine from an area of the patient's body and blow the smoke of specific plants on the wounded area in a metaphysical process of purification. Ayahuasca enables intense visions in the practitioner, which is helpful to both the practitioner and the greater society.

PEYOTE

The peyote cactus (*Lophophora williamsii*) has long been used by native cultures of the Americas. It grows no more than an inch above the ground (with much larger roots). The "buttons" contain mescaline, which acts as a strong hallucinogen. Peyote was first used by Mexican Indians, and its name is derived from the Aztec word *peyotl*. It was introduced to upper North American tribes around 1870, before European colonizers forged contact (or should I say *forced* contact!). A number of First Nations began to use peyote at this time, including the Comanche, Pawnee, Arapaho, and Kiowa Apache. Still, others felt that peyote was unnecessary in their practices, such as the Omaha, the Oklahoma Cheyenne, and the Menominee.

Peyote has a number of uses. Some peyotists (those who make use of peyote's medicine in accordance with tribal tradition) carry a button on them at all times as a magickal amulet against evil. Medicine healers administer the drug to patients and themselves to target and heal the cause of an illness or imbalance. It is particularly useful as a sedative and painkiller, and peyotists believe it is able to help heal any ailment. It can be administered by eating the buttons directly (dried or fresh), or as a tea, powder, or poultice.

Some nations continue to legally partake in large peyote ceremonies where all present are under the influence of the drug and gain vision as part of spiritual communion. If a peyotist does not gain a vision, they will experience telepathic connectedness with other participants or feel a transcendental bond with all of life. The peyotist ends up not focusing on extraneous thoughts that arise, instead keeping focused on the meaningful messages that are being delivered, due to a combination of the substance and the shaman's spiritual work. The intensity of the experience depends both on the amount taken and the tolerance of the user.

Similarly to administrators of ayahuasca, peyotists say that there is no ending point in learning what the drug has to teach, because something new is learned every time. Because the effects vary for each person, there is no telling what experience any given person will have. It must be assumed that it teaches each peyotist the lessons needed at the time. Because of its healing properties, a great number of Native Americans feel strongly about preserving its ceremonial use.

Members of the Native American Church of North America practice what they call the Peyote Way, incorporating it into many of their religious ceremonies. The Church was originally established in 1918 as an organization to preserve the Peyote Way as a sacred and legal practice. Still, the legal system has created a rollercoaster of ups and downs for peyotists, and the legality of the cactus fluctuates with the passing of every new law. Currently, every state has a different law associated with the use of peyote by which Native people are permitted exemption from some of the restrictions surrounding the controlled substance.

PSILOCYBIN MUSHROOMS

The Mazatec Indians of southern Mexico make use of the psilocybin mushroom. Entire families will eat mushrooms together and gain experiences of connectedness and kinship. Mazatecs use mushrooms for specific reasons like resolutions of problems, the curing of ailments, and for vision quests. Its use is most frequent among the tribe's shamans, who are respected as being attuned to both the healing energy of the mushroom consciousness and the journey to spiritual planes it takes the user on. Traditionally, they only make use of it during the nighttime, citing that one can go mad if mushrooms are eaten in the light. Because darkness represents the unknown, mysteries of life are more accessible to the user when they are under the influence at night. Personally speaking, I've had a few breathtaking visionary experiences observing the starry night sky (and faerie realms) with the help of psilocybin medicine. In fact, I am not afraid to say that the mindful ceremonial use of magick mushrooms has helped form my reality.

The Mazatec creation myth speaks of mushrooms as having grown from where the blood of the Aztec god Quetzalcoatl spilled upon the earth, becoming the food of life and wisdom. Until recently, the Mazatec had no form of medicine other than the mushroom. They are rarely eaten by the tribe except in the case of illness, where the healing medicine is said to target any and every form of physical and psychological imbalance, which is a similar viewpoint to the one held by peyotists about their own sacred substance. Mazatec shamans use mushrooms to open themselves to see hidden layers of reality both in the macrocosm (the surrounding world itself) and the microcosm (the layers of the human body and mind).

TOBACCO

Native Americans historically smoked and chewed 100 perfect natural, organic, cured tobacco leaf, and have maintained awareness of the herb and its effects on the user. In Native traditions, high respect is given to tobacco's medicine, and its use is quite often moderated under special ritualistic circumstances. The Jivaro Indians of the Ecuadorian Amazon drink the juice of green tobacco leaves on a regular basis to maintain awareness of possible attacks from rival groups. Tobacco has been used to maintain awareness in meditation, and to induce ecstatic trance when smoked in large amounts.

There is little to no evidence that Indigenous elders had lung cancer or other diseases as a result of tobacco use; chemicals were not introduced as additives until the early twentieth century. Whether chemicals or prolonged addictions to the plant are the reason for disease, the plant is still a toxin. Tobacco contains poisonous alkaloids and is a member of the nightshade family, related to mandrake, belladonna, tomato, potato, and eggplant. It grows between two and nine feet high with large, fleshy, oval-shaped leaves, thick stems, and funnel-shaped flowers. There are nine species of tobacco in North America. Wild tobacco (*Nicotiana rustica* or "Indian tobacco") is considered the most spiritually potent and is used specifically for ceremony, though all types are considered sacred when used respectfully. The herb opens doors to other realities and the psychological results, including addiction, can be devastating if the user does not treat the herb with utmost reverence.

DRUGS & WITCHCRAFT

Truth be told, drugs use has a long history in Witchcraft and magickal societies. (Note: we will explore the alleged Witch's flying ointment toward the end of chapter IV.) The consensus among Pagans is that minimal drug use can be acceptable if carried out in moderation and with personal awareness. Most believe that drug use only becomes problematic if the line between use and abuse is crossed.

Unfortunately, many people in the world choose to recklessly intoxicate, unaware of the spiritual gifts a substance has the capability of offering when approached correctly. This is most apparent in bar/club scenes, wherein mass amounts of alcohol and other substances are consumed purely for social reasons and often to excess. More deaths and injuries occur as a result of alcohol intoxication than any other substance. However, illegal or highly controlled substances are generally viewed as being much more dangerous than liquor. Much of this view is attributed to the government's portrayal of all illegal substances as untouchable evils. This is not to say that drugs are not harmful, but to emphasize the fact that there are many types of drugs and varying degrees of effects—physical, mental, and spiritual.

Goddess knows Pagans love mead! Okay, not all of us, but many of us. Also called honey wine, mead is created through a process of fermenting honey, usually with the addition of herbs, to create a sweet, intoxicating beverage. Many Pagans use mead or another wine as part of "cakes and ale" in ritual; those that have a family history of or predisposition to alcoholism—as well as those who simply do not enjoy drinking—prefer nonalcoholic mead, sparkling cider, or all-natural juices like pomegranate, apple, or berry. Traditionally, high rituals are ended with a feasting of cakes and a beverage for the sake of grounding and communion. The cakes are charged as the flesh of the gods and the drink as the blood (sound familiar?). Consuming the products represents the alignment of the self with the Mighty Ones.

Alcohol and other natural drugs aren't just here to help us get faded, though. Everything is designed with a purpose, and each substance can serve as a conduit to channel spiritual energies and open gateways of perception in the user. Additionally, many natural drugs have physical and metaphysical healing properties—although many have toxic properties as well. This is one reason why utmost care must be employed when using natural drugs (as well as synthetic, of course), for purposes spiritual or otherwise. If you have heard that the way to a profound spiritual experience is through drugs, I ask you to really give it some thought. If you have personally experienced or experimented with certain drugs, you likely have an idea as to what affects you and in what way. If you have little or no experience with drugs, you likely have little idea of what doors any given substance may open in you personally.

Drugs influence everybody differently. One person may try a substance once and quickly get hooked. Another person may experiment with that same substance at various points in their life and never get addicted. There is no way of telling how a drug will interact with a particular person unless they experiment and come to realize their own particular limits and boundaries. However, it is likely better to avoid substances altogether if there is no spiritual or medical need to experience their effects, or if there is any potential for harmful interactions with brain chemistry or prescription medications.

Some people become dependent on a given substance because the euphoria induced by the drug acts as a substitute for spiritual experience. For many people, the effects of certain drugs mimic what would be a spiritual high. When a user believes that their only outlet for expanding consciousness is by way of a substance, they will continue to use it to induce a similar effect. On a nonconscious level, the mind, body, and spirit are seeking freedom from the constraints of the everyday grind. This, for many people, is gained by way of a drug that seems to fill a void. For the magickally inclined, ritual and ecstatic trance induce similar highs, but with a greater purpose.

Those who become addicted to drugs seek union with the Divine—at least, on some level—but go about it improperly, knowing no other means of achieving bliss but through continual use. This sad reality is a product of our culture. The thing is, once a substance has been experienced and spiritual doors have been opened, they never really fully close: we can access these realms with or without the substance; it just takes dedicated focus and meditative discipline. Instead of realizing this and finding the proper ways to open these doors without drugs, many become dependent, unable to achieve the bliss of expanded consciousness without a certain substance.

Habits are difficult to break and must be caught early on before they consume the user and become full-blown addictions or dependencies. Many people use hard drugs habitually for an extended period of time before finally discovering that sobriety—life itself—is the grandest high. It may sound cliché but it's true. No substance in the world can take the place of the natural high of experiencing life itself. We mustn't constantly experience our life in a diluted and ultimately false manner by way of perpetual drug use. (Pharmaceutical or herbal prescriptions by licensed professionals are different, however, and can be greatly beneficial in helping an individual achieve mental and emotional balance.) *In general*, believe it healthy to mindfully experiment with relatively harmless drugs as long as the user does not become attached to the feeling and is able to come back to sobriety with no trouble whatsoever.

Most occultists agree that the best revelations come when sober, although they may use drugs sparingly as recreational or medicinal vehicles rather than strictly spiritual tools. Few magicians, especially Pagans, venture into the realms of synthetic drugs unless they are part of a physician's prescription plan. Synthetic or designer drugs are chemically manufactured by human hands and often mimic chemical compounds found in Nature. Instead of retaining the pure essence of a natural plant, the active compounds in the synthetic drug become nearly completely divided from their original biochemical context compounds—everything else inside the plant. Witches recognize that each plant has its own spirit, its own vibration. The same can be said for chemically produced substances.

"Drugs are bad, mmmkay? You shouldn't do drugs, mmmkay?" No, not really—all substances are ultimately neutral but *can* be bad, or good, depending on the substance, the person, and their unique physiology. Like magick, it's what we do or don't do with them that determines their goodness or badness. We spiritual folk must keep in mind that extended overuse of unnatural drugs creates a sort of astral "slime." This unhealthy sludge is difficult to shake and remains with the user on an etheric level that is even more potent during magickal work. Also, low-vibe, drug-induced energy attracts a wide variety of "astral nasties" like leeches, hungry ghosts, and unfriendly hangers-on. This is nothing to mess with. I have sadly witnessed substance dependencies consume the psyches of a handful of *incredibly* talented and metaphysically proficient individuals, even to the point of death. Furthermore, this energetic imbalance filters into levels of the physical body, where it can manifest as disorders, diseases, and neurosis. Please be careful, be mindful, and value yourself. Life is a miracle not worth tainting.

Utilizing specific drugs in a ritual setting is entirely different than using them at a party or in a mundane social setting. The environment is completely different, and thus the drug's effects are variable. Some practitioners of magick use drugs in exclusively ritual settings. Many Witches I know smoke cannabis in personal ritual, during meditation, or while creating art. Because of the minimal number of negative effects and profundity of positive effects if used wisely, cannabis is one of the most commonly used mind-altering substances in the world. Even the deities Bast/Bastet (Egyptian) and Shiva/Siva (Hinduism) are directly associated with marijuana, and many of their devotees will offer the herb to the deities and consume it for purposes of Divine communion. Smoking weed ritualistically, with the intention of gaining insight into the nature of reality, is on the opposite side of the spectrum from toking it up and playing video games.

Though I rarely smoke these days, I recognize the role cannabis played in my spiritual development. My very first experiences of multidimensional awareness were induced simply by smoking. I fully believe that marijuana medicine was the "push" I needed to *deeply* contemplate reality and our place in it. Though people can open their spiritual senses through different means, the rewarding effects that the intelligent use of drugs can have on human consciousness cannot be ignored. I'm extremely grateful to have had unspeakably profound spiritual experiences with cannabis, magick mushrooms, *Salvia divinorum*, and the like. And I in turn recommend that any spiritual seeker to consider the healing and medicinal properties of natural drugs before casting socially skewed judgment on certain substances—that is, *if* the use of any given substance agrees with one's biology and mental constitution. As amplifiers, drugs have potential to be life-changing—either rewarding or destructive, depending on the user's approach.

Certain Covens, training systems, and occult orders strictly forbid the use of mind-altering substances altogether, both inside the magickal circle and out. Though most circles are not severely straight-edged, the ones that choose to be approach such a decision with the philosophy that mind-altering substances only work against the spiritual seeker.

Some groups forbid drug use only within the magickal circle. This is understandable, as each person's energy not only alters the entirety of the energy being raised and focused within a group ritual, but also may invite unwanted vibrations into the confines of sacred space. All participants in group circles must be completely honest about their current states of being with the other members involved, including their mental, emotional, and physical health at the time of ceremony. This respectful transparency includes being honest about being under the influence of a substance, even if the magickal procedure at hand is only celebratory in nature. Withholding information that may be significant to other members involved is just as good as lying. If a participant consciously neglects informing other members of their insobriety, that person is breaking one of the most important ethics of circle: Perfect Love and Perfect Trust. If everyone in the circle is tight-knit, a person's shifted energy should be immediately detectable. Either way, everyone involved should be aware of one another on multiple levels so as to know what sort of energy is being raised throughout the working. In some Sabbatical celebrations, particularly Beltane, the ritual ends in music, dance, and merrymaking. Liquor and other drugs are definitely not required to have a good time, but if one decides to partake, utmost self-awareness must be exercised nonetheless.

Some groups of Witches and metaphysical folks actually gather to use certain drugs for specific spiritual purposes. Reasons include vision seeking, astral traveling, energetic healing, and divination, to name a few. In these circles, the drug use is entirely controlled and supervised. In the case of using something stronger than cannabis, a sober individual is usually present to "babysit" the users, monitoring the situation and helping anyone whose perceptions may become overwhelmed. Taking precautions is always the best option for keeping things from getting out of control if a substance is being used in the circle—especially a synthetic substance like ecstasy or LSD. Certainly, if a ceremony is centered on the use of a particular drug for spiritual purposes, all participants must be aware of the other members' states of being—including their limits before using and their state of being during the high.

If you are in a situation wherein you feel using drugs would be a good thing, you must look at the situation from all angles to better gauge it. If any possibility is left unaddressed, it could become a factor contributing to a bad high. Negative triggers can be overlooked if the situation is not fully examined. Who will you be surrounded with in an altered state…are they people who have earned your trust? What activities are planned for the day…could your high inhibit these things or enhance them? What is the purpose of using the substance…is it for social acceptance or an escape from your worries, or is there direct spiritual reasoning behind it? How much will you use and how might the substance affect you physically and mentally—and thus spiritually?

Every experience we have shapes us in some way; it may be grand or may be subtle, but nonetheless, our life experiences shape us holistically. When experience is amplified by a substance, it affects us to an even greater degree, and this is not something to be taken lightly on the magickal path.

UTILIZING EMOTIONAL ENERGY

So…what do emotions have to do with spirituality and magick? Everything! Change is triggered by magick, magick is triggered by intention, intention is triggered by thought, and thought is so often triggered by emotion. I thoroughly explore the conjunction of magickal spirituality and emotion in my book for Witchy and occult-minded empaths. If you consider yourself an empath, as many of us shadow-workers tend to, I urge you to purchase my primary book on the subject, *Esoteric Empathy*—not because I want more money, but because it really *will* help you in life! If you are a fan of Oracle cards, I would additionally suggest checking out my *Empath's Oracle* deck.

Spellcasting itself requires some level of emotional investment. The caster must project mental intention and emotional vibration in order for a working to be successful—this is because spells are not just empty "recipes," but are instead *activated* directly by the practitioner. Without emotions, a spell is just as mundane and insignificant as any other activity, and very little power is focused into the working. Emotions are our guide. Emotions connect us to unseen realms. They direct our lives, make our experiences real. They keep us interested in the world and give us a sense of fullness in the human experience. We have the unique gift of experiencing emotions and thus have the opportunity to embrace them as internal spiritual vehicles.

Ancient teachings, most notably those of Buddhism and other Eastern paths, advise us not to become attached to our emotions when we feel them. This means monitoring ourselves and our reactions, and how they relate to what's happening at any given time. This includes becoming aware of ourselves as souls embodying a temporary human frame and recognizing that our senses are interacting with stimuli in our surrounding environments.

If one is not emotionally or psychologically stable at a given time, studying the more intense aspects of occult science is like jumping down a rabbit hole while gripping a lit firecracker. This is also the case when studying or practicing shadow magick. When researching or practicing deep or complex spiritual subjects, it is essential to be in a state of psychological and emotional balance. The energies being worked with can be overwhelming and even scary if one's feet are not planted on stable ground first. Once this ground is reached though self-reflection, therapy, and basic methods of magick (such as Nature-based and elemental), a greater understanding of the mind can be reached, and certain esoteric information and practices become more attainable and feasible to immerse oneself in.

It is not easy to perceive multiple realities when the most important one is little understood. To understand emotions, one must be constantly aware of their emotional state. "What are the reasons I feel this way right now?" is a key question someone should ask themselves throughout the day. Emotions surface as reactions to stimuli. Follow this question up by asking, "Do I like feeling this way or not, and what can I do to change my current state?" Constantly becoming aware of and working on the emotional body will help the spiritual seeker understand their motivations and personality, gradually leading to the deconstruction of negative mental states. I have no qualms in saying that emotional work is the foundation of spiritual and magickal progression.

Everything we do influences the next moment. Every little thing. We all create a ripple, an echo. This spiritual fact of life is easily recognizable when looking at emotional spirals: if an individual is overtaken by emotion, be it happiness, depression, nervousness, or anything else in the sphere of experience, the aftershocks can be felt for quite some time. Emotionally sensitive people, including many Witches and magicians, naturally tend to internalize personal experience, dwelling on it for quite some time. These feelings must be worked with for metaphysical awareness to grow.

Emotions affect one's internal reality, thus weaving into external reality. If we feel sad, we will instinctively view life through a "sad filter." Likewise, if we are feeling optimistic, positivity seems to exist in abundance in our environment. I call this emotional filtration. This simple but very real psychological occurrence is in accordance with the Law of Attraction—you know, "like attracts like." If the aura is emanating a particular vibratory signature, similar energies are drawn toward it, creating an enhanced experience.

Chinese traditional medicine states that there are seven emotions in the human experience: joy, concentration, grief, anger, fear, anxiety, and fright. Buddhist philosophy often states that there are six basic emotions that are easy to become attached to: attachment (desire), anger, arrogance (pride), lack of awareness (ignorance, indecision, doubt), and opinionatedness (afflicted view). Many of these emotions are similar in nature and are derived from one another. A healthy balance of positive and negative emotions is necessary for the fully functioning spiritual person.

Thoughts & Emotions in Witchcraft

Our thoughts and emotions make us who we are. I'm happy to say that the majority of Witches and magickal practitioners I've met are deep-thinking, emotionally sensitive individuals. That's a fact I'm very grateful for because we all have such uniquely important roles to play in the world. Regardless of how we discovered the Craft, we find our hearts beating to the rhythm of Nature. We also find that the natural world is reflected within us, through the cycles and stages of development of our bodies and minds. Like our plant and animal comrades, we are extensions of the natural world. Yet unlike plants and other animals, our thoughts and emotions tend to be particularly complex. Nonhuman animals exhibit emotions, of course, but what sets us humans apart is our level of attachment to our experiences. We emotionally and cognitively process things somewhat differently than other animals—there's no denying it! While we do indeed function like other animals on base levels, including biological instincts and basic emotions, we humans are a distinctly complex species of overthinkers and overfeelers.

I think it's safe for me to assume that you, dear reader, have a decent understanding of what thoughts and emotions "are." Because thoughts and emotions are experiential, rattling off descriptions here and now would not do the subjects justice. In fact, numerous philosophers and theorists have cataloged the spectrums of human emotion and cognition in a multitude of ways—sometimes vastly different ways! However we choose to define them, our thoughts and emotions require recognition, responsibility, and awareness. If we own our thoughts and our emotions, we own our magickal lives.

Spellcasting, meditation, and prayer operate on both interior and exterior levels. Intentional focus in these scenarios, and indeed in life itself, resonate both cosmically (esoterically) and psychologically (mentally). The famed Hermetic axiom, "As Above, so Below" may also be applied to the saying, "As Within, so Without." Because of this connection between the micro (self) and macro (Universe), the ways in which we conduct our thoughts and our emotional responses have effects on both on our daily perspectives and the global spiritual landscape. Thoughts, we find, are often directly linked to our emotional responses. For this reason, a magickal practitioner has a unique responsibility to exercise emotional awareness and mental precision, whether it's in daily life or during our formal ritualistic endeavors.

Emotional Awareness

We humans, Witchy or otherwise, are creatures of feeling. Emotions enrich our experience of life, deeply influencing our daily modes of thought and, for us, our regular esoteric work. Aside from individuals who may suffer a medical condition that directly relates to affective functioning, the great majority of individuals have access to the full, beautiful spectrum of emotion. It's simply a matter of what we are tapped into at any given moment.

Everyone is psychologically wired differently, from birth and from experience (and undoubtedly from previous lifetimes), which is why no emotional issue ever has a single solution or remedy. Everyone connects with emotions in a different manner. Emotions and emotional responses are a personal thing. Everyone has different emotional strengths and hindrances.

Emotions are fragile, it's true, but we are powerful beings. As dedicated magickal folk, we must strive to be honest with ourselves as much as we possibly can. This includes emotional honesty. No one can be expected to function at 100 percent self-awareness every minute of the day, but if we can regularly keep our emotional tides in check, we will soon find that life's ups, downs, twists, and turns don't have to overtake us every single time.

Witches regularly practice "seeing through the veil," which also ideally applies to our personal veils! Sometimes the mind plays tricks; we can't believe everything that we think. Emotions can feel all-pervasive if we don't take a step back and become an observer…this is why Eastern spiritual paths are always talking about mindfulness and present-moment awareness. They've got a point!

Empathy

Empathy is a term that has gained great popularity in spiritual and psychological fields in recent years. In short, empathy is both biological and metaphysical, and involves the "stepping into" another person's emotional reality—or that of an animal, an environment, a story, and so on. The empathic experience involves not only emotional absorption, but also the response of compassion. Some individuals experience empathy on a regular basis, which can be overwhelming if not properly channeled, and these individuals can be called empaths.

Those who demonstrate strong and consistent empathic capacity have a number of things in common with each other. The similarities between empaths are plentiful, yet there are no hard-and-fast commonalities shared between all empaths or highly sensitive people, seeing as everyone experiences and reacts to life a bit differently.

As I mentioned earlier, I was fortunate enough to have the pleasure of researching the subject of empathy for many years in conjunction with my book *Esoteric Empathy*. There, I examine what it means to be an empath, how to work with extreme amounts of emotional sensitivity, and how an individual can apply these abilities to their magickal work. If you feel that you are an empath who needs to better understand your unique abilities, I encourage you to pick up a copy and let me know what you think!

Positive Thinking

While it might be easier said than done sometimes, positive thinking really is a key to our survival—not to mention our magickal success. If we can train our minds to default to optimism rather than pessimism, we find that the world is a beautiful place despite its dreadful challenges.

Choosing to think positively doesn't imply that we should put on happy masks or pretend that we're fine even when we're not. We can acknowledge our troubles and simultaneously choose to shift our mental focus to lighter and less somber states of perception.

Mindful redirection requires humility: one of the most valuable spiritual assets in the world. By remaining humble, we can easily learn from our mistakes and exercise forgiveness for ourselves and others. Through humility, we can gracefully step back from our mental and emotional bodies so that we can redirect ourselves in a more spiritually and magically conscious mindset—and we can encourage others to do the same!

It takes practice to invoke positive thinking into our daily routines. We need to exercise consistent self-awareness so that we can make the spiritual choice to reroute our minds' reactions as necessary. Keeping good humor and lightheartedness even at the worst of times can go a long way toward helping ourselves and helping others in our lives.

Just like pessimism, optimism is contagious. As Witches, it's our duty to be constantly aware of our effect on the world and the people with whom we interact. The more we work on our own thoughts and modes of communication, the more we can help turn the world in a positive direction, bit by bit, day by day, moment by moment—and that's some very powerful magickal work.

Follow Your Thoughts

When a great many people first find themselves attracted to Witchcraft and magickal spirituality, they are allured by the sense of power that can be gained from the "practical" applications of the Arts. I know I sure was! With time and experience, this perspective tends to shift into a focus on *empowerment* rather than power or control. And for good reason: self-control and self-awareness are a million times more spiritually relevant than "doing magick" to get something. But still, sitting down and performing a spell to alter our reality has its time and place.

In a sense, spellcasting occurs every day. Everyone actively co-creates reality, whether they realize it or not. Spells, prayers, and intentional magick are not limited to occult ritual. Ritualistic procedures can be fulfilling, potent, and transformational, but I strongly argue that the most important ritual we perform is our day-to-day experience. For this reason, we must follow our thoughts.

Because thought is linked with intention, we find that magickal energy follows the flow of our thoughts. Thinking about something invokes its presence on some level; it's simply a matter of what we do with those thoughts. As a general rule of perspective, fearful thoughts attract a fearful experience. Loving thoughts attract a loving experience. In many ways, we magickal folk get to choose our experiences by intentionally directing our subtle energies on a daily basis.

I tend to think of spellcasting, prayer, meditation, and ritualized intentions as "peaks," if you will, of our ordinary trains of thought. We often find ourselves preparing for hours, days, weeks, months, or even years for a specific ritual that launches a specific vibration into the fabric of the Universe at a designated time (one may call this the Cone of Power). Regardless of the nature of the magick—or its setting or context—we take some amount of time to plan our activity, ritualize it through action, and conclude by winding down, cleaning up, journaling, and otherwise reminiscing about the experience. In this way, ritualistic magick can be likened to a mountainous climb, including the ascent (preparation), goal (ritual), and the descent (decompression). Even though our time spent at the mountain's peak may feel timeless and mystical, the whole process was originally created through a conduit of routine thinking: our everyday minds.

Cognitive & Emotional Influences

Because our daily thoughts and actions are directly linked to our emotional responses, having acute awareness of our emotional reactions allows us to trace our thought patterns and distinguish illusion from objective understanding. Our thoughts influence our emotions and our emotions influence our thoughts. In our efforts to gain emotional awareness, we can begin by actively choosing to focus on how we think. An easy way to do this is to regularly take a step back so that we can examine how we perceive life, including ourselves, in any given moment. It's also worth considering that spellcraft is very much accomplished by way of emotional energy. We are much more able to influence reality through intentional emotional projection than we are by simply "thinking" a spell or going through the motions without the emotions. Drinking a single drop of rosemary tea with the emotional intention of healing and protection is miles more effective than drinking a whole gallon of the stuff without any intentional focus behind it.

Have you ever heard that old saying "Cast a spell and then forget about it?" It seems clear enough: weave your magick into reality and then stop feeding it your energy. The reasoning behind this idea is simple: if we forget about our magick, we leave it in the hands of the gods and spirits and what have you. In theory, this ensures that the magician won't agitate or nitpick the energy that has already been projected; it's been put it out there and doesn't need to be influenced any further. Thus the mere idea of "forgetting" about a spell implies that a person's everyday thoughts have an effect on previously cast spells. I believe that most practitioners would agree with this perspective. But at the same time, does "forgetting" about a spell really work as well in practice?

If I cast a spell of emotional healing for a friend, I could never bring myself to just forget about it. Instead, I'm going to check in with my friend regularly and do some follow-up work; that sort of thing is not something that's easily forgotten. If I cast a spell to banish my own pessimism, I'm most certainly going to keep my perspectives in check on a regular basis. If I cast a spell for love, I'm not going to allow myself to live in a perpetual state of fear or hopelessness every day; I'm going to trust myself, trust the Universe, and trust my magick. To try instantly forgetting about a spell is to be dishonest and, quite frankly, impedes our magickal work. Follow-through is part of the magick. This is where magickal responsibility comes into play. We must be consistently honest with our thoughts and emotions, understanding the effects our daily perspectives have on our lives. To forget about a spell is to pretend like it never happened, and this is dangerous territory both emotionally and psychologically. Perhaps spells are better approached by keeping them in the back of our minds while choosing not to obsess about the outcomes.

A Witch's thoughts and emotions can either reinforce or unravel their magick. That's a huge thing! We can be our own best cheerleader or our own worst enemy. As our thoughts and emotions interplay in our daily lives, we can choose to have them reinforce our magickal work or we can choose to have them undo it. Truly, this is not something to be taken lightly. If we actively channel our daily thoughts and emotions concerning our magick, we can add a boost of daily power to spells and rituals that we have already performed—this is why we see things like seven-day candles in Santeria and similar traditions. Daily reinforcement goes a long way. If we want to empower our magickal work, we need to channel our thoughts and emotions as they arise, whether they are attached to our current magickal work or otherwise. As many readers are aware, magick is not about doing but about being.

Mental & Emotional Overload

In my teens and twenties, I would sometimes find myself overwhelmed with emotion to the point that it would disrupt healthy functioning. My responses sometimes included oversleeping, social anxiety, unhealthy eating, overdrinking, and even self-harm. While many my emotional overreactions were undoubtedly related to youthful hormones, I discovered that certain lifestyle changes assisted with coming to a place of emotional balance.

Life is tricky. It's easy to become emotionally overwhelmed to the point of hopelessness, but many of the tormenting thoughts that inspire these emotional states are illusory. It can be challenging to work ourselves out of emotional overload, especially if that state has become routine, but where there's a will, there's a way. Sometimes this means making lifestyle modifications and working more diligently with techniques aimed at boosting self-awareness—and self-confidence! The following are a few options to consider on your own journey to mental and emotional well-being.

> COUNSELING: As mentioned earlier, I believe that everyone deserves to have counseling and therapy when they need it. When life is just too overwhelming, individuals who are professionally trained in the workings of the mind can be of great assistance. There are many different styles of counseling, therapy, and life coaching to choose from. Many professionals have online bios that can help potential clients get a better idea of their counseling styles, specialties, and personal values. (Please also note that free or discount therapists *are* available in most cities, as well as free online and phone-based services.)

Journaling & Art: Possibly one of the most underrated psychological activities, keeping a journal or diary can greatly assist in getting thoughts and emotions "out there." When we express our thoughts and emotions in this private manner, the energy becomes externalized, so it doesn't have to run amuck-amuck-amuck in our heads. Similarly, artistic expression of any type serves to creatively channel our innermost feelings. Not to mention that both journaling and art can be powerfully transformational acts of magickal intention.

Medicine: Although it might be obvious, I should note that none of the advice herein is a substitute for medical advice. For many emotionally sensitive individuals, a combination of medication and behavioral changes can produce dramatic healing effects. This category of "medicine" is not limited to Western pharmaceuticals; many people find that naturopathic and herbal medicine to be extremely effective. Everybody has a different constitution so there is no "right" medicinal answer for everyone. If you feel that it may benefit your daily life, I encourage you to speak with a physician and other healthcare professionals to determine if medicine would aid in your own mental and emotional balance. (As an aside, I do *not not not* recommend *homeopathy* or any homeopathic "remedies." These sugar pills and sprays have *no remaining molecule* of the original "medicine" from which they originate and are, like a proper snake-oil, purported to be "energy medicine." Yeah, no.)

Mindfulness: A term frequently used in both Buddhism and psychological circles, mindfulness implies self-awareness. To become mindful is to take a step back from our thoughts and emotions in order gain greater psychological equilibrium; in this way, we can take a moment to detach from our mind and emotions without actually disconnecting. Mindfulness encompasses the idea of present-moment awareness: to focus on the events of the now rather than any stress surrounding the past or the future. If we can train ourselves to observe our thoughts and emotions as frequently as possible, we can more easily take a step back at any given moment. We are not our thoughts. We are not our emotions. These are components that help create this thing we call *self*, and with the aid of daily mindfulness we can take a step back and choose to be the ones in control.

RITUAL: Who doesn't love a good ritual? Solid ceremonial standards like the Lesser Banishing Ritual of the Pentagram (LBRP) can balance our cognitive and emotional bodies while simultaneously invoking the spiritual realm. The same can be said about the recitation of mantras and other chants. Even a powerful recitation of the Witches' Rune, Wiccan Rede, or another magically poetic text can have instant calming effects. If creating your own ceremony, consider incorporating visualizations focused on dumping excessive energy into the earth. Similarly, it's wise to practice grounding by performing visualizations such as tree rooting. And for those who are especially emotionally sensitive, you may wish to perform a self-made ritual or spell in the bathtub, shower, or a body of water.

SLEEP, DIET & EXERCISE: One cannot underestimate the power of good sleep, regular exercise, and a healthy diet. Our bodies are the sacred temples in which our spirits have the pleasure of incarnating for this instant in time; taking care of the body is tending to the soul. It may take time to discover your unique needs and preferences in all of these realms, but the mind and emotions can greatly shift toward the positive once a personal balance is realized and diligently followed.

YOGA & MEDITATION: Highly advocated in Eastern spiritual traditions, Yoga and meditation have profound benefits psychologically, emotionally, physically, and spiritually. There are numerous styles, schools, and philosophies of both Yoga and meditation; in fact, the two practices are inextricably interlinked—they are one and the same. Integrating any measure of these practices on a regular basis can help emotionally and mentally balance any spiritual seeker. While various types of Yoga and meditation can seem intimidating to a newcomer, they are much easier to practice than is commonly believed. In many ways, these practices are inherently wired into our brains and bodies; it's just a matter of learning the techniques. It's no wonder that the various styles of Yoga and meditation have been practiced from time immemorial, and will most certainly continue to be practiced until our very end.

Sadness & Grief

"Art thou willing to suffer to learn?" These are key words in the first-degree initiation of traditional Gardnerian Wicca. They are not to be taken lightly. Life is a process of learning, and oftentimes pain is our greatest teacher. Witches understand the fact that spiritual initiation is not limited to ritual training. Life has the grandest of lessons to teach and, if we strive to overcome the pain and torment of various stages of being, we ascend to higher levels of learning, facing new challenges (opportunities) at every step. If Spirit permeates every aspect of our lives, it's only right to believe that lessons sometimes come to us through turmoil.

It's okay to feel sadness. We have to be depressed at times. It's okay to feel like life is falling apart, like there is no hope. To feel absolute misery, wishing nothing more than to escape this reality and all things in it. To feel dead inside, rendered powerless by a constant stream of tears, finding it near impossible to even wake up in the morning. To be numbed by the world and feel worthless in it all… Seriously, it's okay. But not for extreme lengths of time.

Feelings of grief and desolation are nothing to be ashamed of and are in fact necessary at times. If nervous breakdowns didn't happen, there would be no real growth in the spiritual realms. If we suppress tears and don't allow ourselves to feel pain, life is incomplete. If our emotional centers aren't allowed to flourish, we are not progressing in our spiritual paths.

In many ways, sadness can be comforting. The lulling uncertainty it brings makes a person feel alive. To experience strong emotions is to feel the experience of life at its fullest. It's only when a person gets stuck in a rut of habitually entering melancholy that there becomes a problem. As Pagans, we must strive for full recognition of our emotions and how we utilize them.

Though the Craft does not require perpetual happiness, it does require magickal practitioners to take accountability for the lessons in their lives and realize their own influence in the creation of emotional experiences. Magicians must not only learn from the lessons that life is continually teaching, but to move on to higher planes, discovering the means to a more vibrant life: one filled with hope and understanding.

Sadness and grief present two options. We can either fall victim to the emotions, letting them consume us, or we can choose to accept them and learn by facing them head-on—that is, becoming proactive to cope with and heal from such experiences. It is a process.

Sadness doesn't always need to have a direct reason to surface—no more than happiness or simple contentedness does. Emotions often force us to experience them because we need to face them at the time, even if external influences are not immediately apparent. Then again, more often than not, we can usually understand the reason for sadness when it arises. Sometimes it just takes the pressure of one more negative occurrence to cause a number of pent-up emotions to explode. The risks associated with emotional repression are vast and should be taken into consideration. When a person suppresses negative emotion for an extended period of time, the pressure naturally builds and may eventually explode. This can be a worse experience than simply dealing with the emotions in the first place. Mood swings are a part of life. The Craft does not require its adherents to be joyous and happy all of the time. The world, at least as it stands, is not pure love and light. We must process our emotions on a consistent basis to avoid this.

The world is filled with many, many evils. This can be observed by reading the news or getting any exposure to the public. Evil exists both locally and globally, and is very difficult to avoid. Just knowing the impurities around us, not to mention experiencing them firsthand, is enough to tempt us to shut off our emotional centers and make us apathetic to life, even nihilistic.

In times of sadness, we shift our energies from external to internal. We become equipped to face our shadows and deconstruct the ego. We question what is real and what's illusory. Everyone has a different way of dealing with intense emotions. Ongoing clinical depression leads to tunnel vision, wherein sadness is all that is focused on. When sadness gets to this point, someone either gets so comforted by the feeling that it serves as a tool of attention-getting and emotional codependence, or the person honestly feels that there is no hope in life. Both views are so easy to take because we are highly emotional beings, but both views also keep a person imprisoned in what Buddhists call the vicious *Wheel of Samsara*: suffering.

When overcome with depression, it can be easy to throw this negative emotion outward, shifting blame outside the self and onto others. This is a form of negative projection. In doing this, the person feels momentary comfort by placing the pain externally, usually onto someone else. Naturally, this manifests in the appearance of anger. Such anger is rarely justified and serves as a mask for sadness and internal pain. This reaction is drawn from the ego and is a form of instinctual self-preservation. Pointing the finger outside the self rarely solves issues. Rather, it perpetuates the blame game and harmful interactions. This downward spiral is difficult to unwind, but it *is* possible with constant awareness. Everyone projects their pain in a different manner. When we project our internal pain onto others, however, it comes back to us in the end.

Ultimately, we control our actions and reactions and ultimately our life's path. We can create a healthy and balanced life for ourselves and others, and sometimes it takes *time* to gain a perspective of what we are meant to do here in this lifetime. Allow this time and trust in the process. There is *always* a reason to carry on, even in the most seemingly desolate of times. Again, I urge readers to pursue compassionate therapy and counseling from trained professionals if feelings of hopelessness persist: this is not the emotional space in which we deserve to exist. At the very least, we all deserve to have baseline perspectives of *contentment*.

THE DARK NIGHT OF THE SOUL

When we are emotionally hurt, a certain numbness takes over. A feeling of hopelessness and misery overrides logical thinking, and insecurities tumble into the forefront. In the times of our deepest misery, all the demons we have hidden away break their chains to face us head-on. Life seems altogether meaningless and reality seems to crumble on all sides—nothing seems real...nothing is real. All is lulled, nulled, and bleak. Only hopelessness exists—a sense of dread and emptiness. While no words can accurately convey the intensity of the experience, this process is often termed the Dark Night of the Soul. The Christian mystic St. John of the Cross was the first to use the term in the sixteenth century, recognizing the experience as the feeling of the loss of God and the absence of any mystical experience.

We all must endure periods spiritual desolation at various points throughout our lives. The experience should be recognized as part of the natural process of metaphysical growth. Just knowing this can add a bit of padding to the pain, making the experience a bit more endurable. The Dark Night of the Soul is not a trivial experience, for it reaches into the innermost depths of the soul, forcing it to be pulled inside out for examination. Every bit of the self is drawn into question and everything one knows as truth is disbelieved. Everything is stilled at this crossroads, which forces the practitioner to choose between giving up and trekking on.

Periods of despondency are signs of spiritual growth. If the Magickal Arts and life itself were never questioned or doubted, we would be nothing more than blind followers. During the Dark Night's process, a psychological death takes place. It can be a frightening and uncertain experience, but this deconstruction must take place for rebirth to occur. We must go below before we can rise above. But: we must *choose* to rise above. And lemme tell you: it is well worth every bit of misery in the end. We get to be our own advocates, and we can *choose life* even when we believe the spark has gone out. In reality, the spark never goes out and there is *always hope*.

When we begin to return from the depths of sorrow and spiritual numbness, we become more aware. As the internal chaos of disorientation begins to wane, wisdom takes its place. Pieces of the formerly unseen begin to make themselves visible in the blurry whirlpool of lamentation. Once we can see our shadows for what they are, and once we choose to examine and decipher the experience, we find that positive aspects of life make themselves clearer.

There are times we must *break* before we can truly find the path we are meant to follow. When we choose to be compassionate toward our emotional struggles, we see that pain one of our greatest teachers and is an experience we must honor as a guide. We mustn't get trapped in dark emotional states; we can flow with life because life is constantly in flux. Recall the ancient Greek philosophical saying *panta rhei; ouden menei* (everything flows; nothing is stagnant). Even during times of desperation and grief—which I pray are few and far between for us all—we must remember that the spiral of life continues to function; it's up to us to get up and dance the spiral, even if it hurts like hell. Dark Nights of the Soul deconstruct our spirits and psyches in order to give us the opportunity to reconstruct our path…and slowly…eventually…we gather the courage to pick ourselves back up…we rebuild our perspectives and once again learn what it is to smile—and to be in awe of life itself.

Effigies & Emotional Channeling

When we allow ourselves to cry—and not to be overtaken by the feelings for too long a time—we find that tears can offer cathartic relief. If you cry regularly, it's a good idea to keep a channel for these powerful internal energies. For example, it could be a poppet or effigy you've made to represent the pain, which gives it a tangible physical form. In this case, the doll or symbol does not represent any particular person, but rather the emotion as a whole. If you make a doll, the best color of cloth to use is black (for banishing), and it would be best to fill it with herbs for banishing and releasing. Use your intuition. Smear tears on the effigy, grip it in your hands as you weep, seeing the pain flowing into the item, not to return. Smear it with your tears and snot, scream at, stomp on it, it and just…release. Dig deep within yourself and pull out old, painful memories. Allow them to surface and be directed into the object as much as possible. This is heavy internal shadow magick. When you're through, ceremonially burn, bury, or sink the effigy. Keep in mind that performing this doesn't mean you'll never feel sadness again; that would be even more reason to worry! It means you are actively going about finding the way out of emotional pain in order to reclaim your power as a human, as a soul, and as a Witch.

As dark artists, creativity comes naturally. Find or rediscover your unique niche of creative expression, be it painting, sketching, sewing, sculpting, performing, photographing, writing, creating music, or any other "out." When we have channels for our pain, the intense energetic states we experience are allowed to cycle *outward*, beyond ourselves and into external sources, thereby providing a very real energetic release.

When doing magick concerning emotions, bathing is essential. Water is the element of emotion and change. Immersing oneself in a cleansing bath or shower aids in bringing a person to a more complete level of emotional awareness while cleansing their body of energetic debris at the same time.

On a cross-cultural note, I'll make mention of the people of Samoa. Because of extreme expectations around how to properly go about life, Samoans have long understood the reason and necessity of "letting it all out." Traditionally, when life becomes too intense, a person has a nervous breakdown and temporarily withdraws from society. They are allowed a period of time to halt their family and employment obligations so they can hone their focus entirely on personal wellness and mental health. The individual's friends and relatives will pick up where they left off, taking over responsibilities so that the person can have ample space to sort things out. Friends and family will also deliver food to the person going through the experience and will monitor them regularly during the process until they can gather themselves and reenter into society.

As Witches, we can learn from the ways of our ancestors and from other cultures, both ancient and modern. When sorrow is recognized and we permit ourselves time to come to terms with it (through magick, meditation, reflection, professional therapy, energy healing, and so on), it will allow a more full, healthy, and realistic self-understanding to arise. In the end, emotions are an incredible roadmap for spiritual and magickal progression.

Ritual Meditation:
Cultivating Love & Compassion

Although I very much consider myself a Witch who is also an American Hindu, I have a special affinity toward Buddhism, finding that its general philosophies integrate superbly with Pagan spirituality. Buddhism uniquely places emphasis on training the *mind*. A number of Witches I know, myself included, have benefited from Buddha Dharma and have been able to successfully incorporate many of the path's teachings into our own Witchy ways. Buddhism is more of a philosophy than a religion…in fact, there are even atheist Buddhists! The many expressions of Buddhism worldwide *all* focus on peace and compassion for all beings. Compassion does not, however, mean that we must overextend ourselves or become subservient to someone else's will. It means that despite unavoidable differences, everyone deserves the opportunity to heal and cultivate the light of peace.

The exercise below is called a *metta bhavana* meditation. The word *metta* is Pali for "loving-kindness." *Bhavana* basically means "to develop into being," or simply "spiritual practice" in the broadest sense. Pali is an ancient Indian language similar to Sanskrit and is nearly identical to the language spoken in the time of the Buddha Siddhartha Gautama (c. 500 BCE), called Magadhi. Metta is akin to compassion in that its essence is all-encompassing and given unconditionally.

My Buddhist teacher Saramati taught me this meditation for cultivating metta. It is designed to help bring about acceptance of oneself and others, as well as to invoke a higher level of compassion, acceptance, and love in one's daily routine. Many Buddhist practitioners even perform this meditation on a daily basis!

In this, you will focus on four different people whose influences evoke a varied reaction in you, including yourself. The people you think about in the meditation can be different each time you practice this (aside from yourself, of course), or you can focus on the same individuals each time until you feel it is right to change. It's best if the person is living, but if there are unresolved issues with a person who has passed—or simply left your sphere of interaction—there's no reason not to include them in the visualizations.

This is one of the most comprehensible and direct forms of meditation. Metta Bhavana is a form of samata (or samatha) meditation, which encourages a focus on the breath. This ancient Hindu method of concentration meditation is mentioned in the sacred *Upanishads*. I have slightly modified the exactness of the original method, adding a bit here and there, yet still maintaining the essence of the traditional exercise.

You may pre-record the meditation or have a friend read it to you in a soft, slow monotone voice, inserting plenty of pauses between each step. You can also memorize the steps by reading them many times over or jot down short notes to glance at throughout.

1. Enter your temple room or ritual space if you have one. If you feel comfortable meditating outside and you know there will be no distractions, find your place there. Any form of light will do as long as it's not fluorescent or overpowering artificial light, as they distract from the energy at hand. Some prefer to work by sunlight or moderate backlighting, but the readers of this book will most likely prefer subtle candlelight, moonlight, or total blackness.

2. Once in your sacred space, find a comfortable posture that aligns your energy and allows your mind the clarity of focus. After grounding and centering, become aware of your physical body. Look at your hands, wiggle your toes, feel your hair: this is the body you're in and the shell that maintains your spiritual progression, grounding your mind to the physical plane. Looking at your physical body, become aware of your six sensory faculties: touch, smell, taste, sight, hearing, and mental process. These are the functions that serve as filters for spiritual experience. Observe your physical body even more deeply by seeing beneath your own skin. See your organs, muscles, and skeletal system in your mind's eye and try to understand their roles in your daily life. Mentally examine your body and all its parts.

3. Having become aware of your physical frame, close your eyes and enter the liminal territory of mind and imagination. First, monitor your breathing. Take regular breaths, not too deep or too shallow, preferably in and out of the nostrils. Witches prefer the sacred number thirteen, so let's use that for counting. Visualize the oxygen entering your body as a soft white, blue, or other calming color of your choice. Begin counting your breath to counts of thirteen. Bring your attention to where the air meets your skin with as you inhale; let this be the first count. Immediately after counting thirteen inhalations, count out the same number of exhalations, focusing on the point where the breath leaves your body. Immediately after this, finish with another set of thirteen counts, this time not focusing on your physical body at all. Simply count and know that your regular breathing is supporting your being. After you have put yourself in a heightened state of awareness, the core of the work begins.

4. FIRST PERSON: Before working on cultivating metta toward anyone else, we must first work on ourselves. Envision *yourself* sitting in front of your physical body, appearing exactly as you do now. Your eyes are closed and your back is erect. See the clothing you're wearing now and try to form the clearest and most realistic image of yourself as you are in the present moment. Let your mind construct the most realistic image of

yourself that you can. See yourself (both your physical body and your envisioned self) surrounded in the pure, limitless light of metta: glowing and serene, illuminating the aura. Do not move on to the next step until this has occurred and you are content looking at yourself. If you are judging yourself, release those thoughts like a passing cloud, and allow yourself to focus back on loving-kindness. Once you are content, let your image fade away and your mind slip back to blackness.

5. SECOND PERSON: Next, envision someone *near and dear to you* sitting in front of you in meditation. This should be a person for whom you already feel compassion and in whose presence you are comfortable. See them sitting just as you are sitting, practicing the same exercise. Envision them surrounded in the same light as you surrounded yourself in moments before. They are at peace and you are at peace, aligned and balanced with the light of metta. Once you feel the same alignment come about them, allow their image to fade to black.

6. THIRD PERSON: The next person you are to visualize should be a *neutral* person: someone who is real but whom you have never spoken to, only seen in passing. It could be a clerk at a grocery store, or someone you've seen on campus, at a club, or when taking a walk; it doesn't matter as long as they're someone you know *of* but are not directly acquainted with. Though you don't know them, understand that they are a human with the same needs and desires as yourself—someone who deserves to be surrounded with the light of metta regardless of who they are. See them as you did the others: meditating before you, surrounded in the light of loving-kindness. Once you feel their energy aligned to the same peacefulness as the others, allow the image to fade away.

7. FOURTH PERSON: This is going to be the most difficult visualization of them all, but is also the most beneficial. The person to be visualized is someone you have an *aversion* to. This doesn't need be someone you totally despise, but someone you are having problems with on some level, at least at the

moment. This could be a number of people: old friends, family members, or even someone you encountered online. See them sitting before you in meditation, knowing that they too exhibit human traits and are bound to a physical body. Realize that you actually have more commonalities than differences between you, at least in the sense of both being human. Attempt to see their "lighter side." Cast away negative thoughts you have for them; let these thoughts be placed aside for the moment, choosing to emotionally detach for the time being. Feelings of loving-kindness may take longer to arise than they did with in other steps, but eventually you will see the person surrounded in the light of metta, understanding that they need this light as much as you do. Allow them to be surrounded in cosmic love, because this is something we all deserve to feel. Once content, allow their image to pass and fade.

8. You should now visualize each person you reviewed in meditation. They should all be lined up and equally surrounded with the light of metta. See the image of yourself sitting next to the person you love, next to the "neutral" person, next to the person you are having problems with. See the light glowing, surrounding all four figures. The very same light emanates off each person, and it now surrounds everyone as a singular unit. All are surrounded with loving-kindness. When you feel ready, allow their images to fade while you come back to center.

9. To conclude this act of meditation and magick, slowly open your eyes and take a series of deep breaths. Look at your physical body and visualize yourself surrounded in Spirit's infinite light. See the light expanding from your own body to the whole of the room or environment you're currently in. This may take seconds or minutes to accomplish. Next, see the light growing to the rest of the premises, far beyond you, in the form of a gigantic sphere. See it expanding to the whole neighborhood, then to the community, to the town, the country, and then the world. Let this exercise take as long as needed. Once you have visualized Mother Earth surrounded with metta, let the light

expand even further, through our solar system, permeating all planes and outward to infinity, faster than the speed of light.

10. At this point, you're going to feel a bit high. You may feel hardly connected to your body, having traversed the Universe and all. Take your time to slowly ground and center your energy. Bring your conscious awareness back from the stars, back down to your geographical area, and finally back to your body. Breathe deeply, letting air enter your lungs and rejuvenate your blood. Wiggle your fingers and toes, becoming aware of your physical frame, and let your eyes slowly open. Odds are you'll have a nice grin across your face, knowing that you have just gifted a bit of enlightenment to yourself and to the world.

Chapter Two
The External Shadow

"Since most wisdom traditions are externally focused, they couch most metaphysical concepts in external themed metaphors. However, since Dark Paganism is an internally focused spirituality, I believe it's time to use different metaphors. While the ideas used in Dark Paganism are similar to those found in classic Western esotericism, we should reimagine many of the tropes and elements so as to be consistent with the internal spirituality at the heart of Dark Paganism."

— Frater Tenebris
from *The Philosophy of Dark Paganism: Wisdom & Magick to Cultivate the Self*

INVOCATION & GODFORM ASSUMPTION

Invocation refers to the act of drawing certain energies from outside oneself into either one's own body or, by some interpretations, the magickal vicinity. I believe that shadow magick is particularly relevant to this art: invocation is ultimately a mystical act of merging with the unseen as one calls forth a deity from the astral plane and invites them into their own body. The process of deital channeling is that of reaching through the veil of reality and tapping into the external energies of human archetypes.

Often, Witches simply use the term invocation to refer to the act of calling upon energies. This is just a matter of terminology. Technically, invocation only refers to inviting energies, such as a deity or ancestral spirit, into oneself. The act of calling forth energies is also called summoning, such as when asking a deity or spirit for assistance, or when calling the Watchtowers. Summoning an entity into manifestation is called evocation, as is the case with many forms of angelic and demonic magick.

The term journeying, on the other hand, refers to a person traveling astrally, in some manner, to a spiritual terrain. The practitioner goes into a deeply meditative state and meets a deity or spirit on the astral plane. Once aligned, the journeyer relays messages from the being. These messages could take the form of entire streaming sentences, or they might be random phrases, sounds, and foreign speech including colors, names, and cryptic words that are seemingly nonsensical. A person who practices this frequently, especially with one particular deity, is a good candidate to advance to full godform assumption. If you wish to practice invocation but have no experience in the field, it's best to become comfortable with and adept at journeying first.

For clarity's sake, I will use the terms godform assumption, aspecting, and Drawing Down synonymously with invocation, referring to the act of pulling an actual deity or spirit into your person. It is an act of oracular mediumship that is usually reserved for highly trained Priests and Priestesses in modern Witchcraft.

A number of shamanic and Indigenous cultures invoke ancestors and deities regularly, incorporating such practices as drumming, yelling, and ecstatic dance into their ceremonies to strengthen the process. The results are profound. Successful invocations will push the channeler aside, allowing the spirit to fully take over the body. Spirit possession is also seen frequently in Vodou, in which practitioners invoke the ancestral Orishas or Lwa, depending on tradition.

Many cultures still practice invocation as part of their common ritualistic observances. In Nepal, for example, animistic tribal Hindus called the Newa practice spirit possession. During a Full Moon ritual, a Dhamini invokes an ancestor, addresses the crowd, and performs shamanic healings individually. The individual will feed or place cooked rice on ritual attendees in an act of bestowing blessings. In the invocation, the Dhamini crouches, so as to "carry" the deity or spirit on their back. A ritual assistant accepts offerings to gift the spirit and is there to help the Dhamini throughout the possession.

Some Witches who practice godform assumption don't remember a thing about what was said afterward, having been a trance-channel the entire time, their waking self pushed completely aside by the deital or spiritual energy. Priests and Priestess are consciously removed from themselves. Their speech patterns, movements, and behavior noticeably change to fit the deity's or spirit's, which may be entirely separate from the invoker's typical behavior. When this happens, the invoker doesn't remember anything about the experience. This most extreme version occurs only when the person has practiced invocation or possession for many years (or at least has a natural disposition for oracular powers). Most practitioners remember portions of the experience but not the whole. Others remember all of it, though this is rare.

While invoking, practitioners tend to take a backseat to the energy called in; it's much like watching a film. It can also be likened to dreaming. Most practitioners call this "stepping back," and it seems to be the most common experience when practicing invocation. It's also good to keep in mind that every experience is different, affecting each practitioner uniquely.

I recall one of my first experiences with deital invocation when I was acting as High Priest for a Beltane ritual. It was a circle of thirteen practitioners out in the woods at a friend's cabin, and I was to invoke Cernnunos. I was wearing the appropriate robes, veils, crowns, and makeup to align with his essence, and was also carrying the adorned skull of a deer. The ritual assistant recited the Words of Power to help with the invocation while the rest of the group marched around the circle *deosil* (clockwise) chanting, "Cernnunos, Cernnunos, Cernnunos…" My eyes began to close and I saw my friend's dog Herkie trotting along with the rest of the group in circle as if he was just another practitioner. It was as if he was invoking Cernnunos along with the rest of them, and the surreality of seeing this helped me enter a trancelike state. From there, I began to perceive faeries and astral beings circling the space. My eyes closed and a surge of power rushed through me as I surrendered to the energy with Perfect Trust. Upon closing my eyes, every part of my body began to tingle. Ego-thoughts ceased to be, and all that existed was sensation. I could feel the souls of the beings walking around me while I transcended normal time. Cernnunos was there, inside me, taking over my normal self and shining through like a beacon of pure sunlight. "My" eyes opened and, with an enormous grin, the Horned One began to address the crowd, following that with individual consultations. I don't remember too much about what was said, but I was told afterward that it was profound and meaningful. For me, each invocation since then has become easier and more comfortable.

Personally, after practicing deital invocation, I cannot function for the rest of the night as I normally would. I need a series of grounding exercises and meditations, food, a bath, and a ridiculously long night's sleep. This is true for many practitioners, but over time, coming back from a trancelike state to waking life becomes less difficult. It becomes easier to separate the self from the deity or spirit if proper chakra exercises are done beforehand and energy is worked to secure a separation between the practitioner and the entity.

During a rite of invocation, each member of a Coven or group of practitioners should address questions and responses to the deity or spirit, *not* to the individual who is acting as the conduit. During the experience, the person often delivers important messages to the group or the Coven, communicates symbolically (depending on the deity or spirit), and gives insight and prophecy to individual seekers. I've learned from my experiences that preparing appropriate offerings beforehand is a must.

When a deity or spirit is invoked, the invoker mustn't be held responsible for what happens next. Usually, that person has little to no say in how the deity or spirit is channeled. Still, this is not an excuse for the individual to exaggerate the level of invocation, do inappropriate things, or put off bad behavior as the entity's doing. Not only is that incredibly disrespectful to the entity, but those with a discerning eye can see what belongs to the invoker—and what belongs to the invoked. At the same time, the practitioner shouldn't hold back if they are legitimately invoked, especially if a ritual assistant is there to guide the process.

If you practice the invocation of deities or spirits within your own tradition, it can be wise to invoke those whose essence is greatly *unlike* your own, such as one of a different gender or one whose qualities are separate from your own personality. In his book *Magick in Theory and Practice*, Aleister Crowley says this about godform assumption: "The danger of ceremonial magick—the subtlest and deepest danger—is this: that the magician will naturally tend to invoke that partial being which most strongly appeals to him, so that his natural excess in that direction will be still further exaggerated."

Aspects of Aspecting

Invocation may also be called aspecting. The biggest danger is that if the deity or spirit is not properly channeled, the invoker will have trouble coming back to their own body and may suffer for days trying to realign. The best way to prepare for invocation is, of course, to study and fully investigate exactly who will be channeled. All who will be present should also study. It's reckless to draw an entity into your person without knowing who or what it is.

It takes time to work through the stages of light to heavy invocation. If you are attempting this magick, begin by working in small doses with a deity or spirit you have already familiarized yourself with for years, perhaps through journeying, as discussed above, or through personal devotion and ritualistic work. The invoker must be familiar with the entity's energy pattern, as it will be merged with their own. In a more immediate sense, before invocation is attempted, the chakras must be opened in sacred space so that the person is entirely receptive to the entity. This is particularly true for *Muladhara* and *Sahasrara*, the Sanskrit terms for the base and crown chakras. When the chakras are opened, the invoker becomes an open channel of energy, allowing the entity to become more secured in the body. After the process is completed and the entity has either up and left or has been thanked and dismissed, the invoker's chakras must be gently closed so that their own energy doesn't "leak" for any amount of time.

Godform assumption is usually done with the help of a Craft-experienced assistant. This person may read, chant, or otherwise raise energy to better call the deity forth. The assistant also closely monitors the partner who is invoking, and can dismiss the deity if for some reason they refuse to let go or things get a bit too intense. In most cases, this isn't a worry, but is certainly a possibility.

When it comes to gods and goddesses in particular, one can either invoke specific deities or "greater deities." It's a good idea to begin the practice by working with a deity who is an embodiment of Nature—a generalized form of the Great God or Goddess. (This practice is actually traditional in Gardnerian and Alexandrian Witchcraft.)

Of course, the deity should be properly attuned to the season: for example, the archetypal Holly King should not be invoked at the height of summer! Nature deities often embody properties of the seasonal tide; they may not have the well-defined characteristics that individualistic deities do. Therefore, working with them can be easier and more comprehensible, especially for those beginning the practice.

There are many ways to connect to a deity successfully. Aside from the necessary precautions and dedication, attendees can help draw the deital essence forth by chanting, drumming, and making music, for example. The invoker may wish to dress up as the deity of choice, using masks, veils, jewelry, and garb. This is called *guising*, and it offers the deity an environment closer to their own natural or mythologized structure while also attuning the invoker more deeply. The surrounding decor can also be modified to the deity's mythology to better conduct them into the ritual space and make it a more comfortable setting for the magickal act.

Drawing Down

A common form invocation within traditional Wicca is Drawing Down the Moon. The term is rooted in the Italian *Aradia: The Gospel of the Witches*, a book essential to any student of the Craft, whether Stregheria or otherwise. *Strega* is an Italian word for Witch. Within Stregheria, it is believed that the goddess Aradia was an actual human Priestess who ascended upon her death, much like the Buddha or the Christ, and who became deified over time. The Aradia manuscript, which has an unknown origin, was published by Charles Godfrey Leland in the late 1800s. A portion of that text later formed the Wiccan Charge of the Goddess, which is recited by many practitioners upon drawing in a goddess (or the Great Goddess). The poetic Charge of the Goddess, originally compiled by Gerald Gardner in the 1940s, took phrases verbatim from both Charles Leland's and Aleister Crowley's work. It was later modified and edited by Gardner's High Priestess Doreen Valiente.

Irish Witch Janet Farrar, with her late husband Stewart, published the Charge of the God, also called Drawing Down the Sun, in *A Witches' Bible*. It was designed to enact a balance, so that a Priest would also have text to be read while helping a Priestess invoke.

Both texts are highly effective and serve their purpose in godform assumption. Many Witches begin invocation of the gods by reading the appropriate Charge either just before the invocation is attempted or just after the spirit is drawn into the practitioner, especially if the invoker doesn't notice the shift immediately. However, many invokers either do away with the Charges or use them in noninvocation rituals.

FASTING & SELF-SACRIFICE

Cross-cultural practices of endurance and spiritual cleansing include fasting and other forms of self-sacrifice; these can benefit any person practicing magickal spirituality. With the act of abstinence comes a recognizable sense of emptiness; a cycle of fulfillment is replaced by a void. This space can be filled with Divine Light, thus replacing the ordinary with the sacred. Disciplining oneself through fasting or something similar can easily be a practice of spiritual devotion. Self-discipline is a dedication to the higher planes by a willfully denying desires. What material dependencies do we put ahead of our spiritual focuses? Fasting can illuminate many important issues.

Fasting is indeed a form of shadow magick: by restricting external stimuli, it forces practitioners to face themselves and their habits. Mental states and issues that were once unseen tend to tumble into focus during a fast. Portions of the self are questioned, and meanwhile the surrounding world seems to take on a new hue. Perspectives on the external world change drastically as the self is alchemized through the experience. As with taking a drug, one's perceptions change permanently, even if only to a small degree. Fasting brings a person out of an ordinary state of consciousness by restricting or altering familiar routines. It's no wonder that fasting and other forms of self-sacrifice have long been practiced for cultivating self-awareness.

Fasting is a form of abstinence that has been practiced worldwide for countless centuries. Though each culture has used fasting for a variety of purposes, the most common ones are to gain self-awareness and communion with Spirit. This mystical connection is often gained through psychic vision during a fast. Any type of fasting forces a person to abstain from a regular cycle in order to let go of attachments. Fasting affirms one's placement in the Game of Reality by reassuring the practitioner that this plane and its comforts are but temporary stimuli.

Physically, the body is attached to a number of things necessary to function, such as air, water, food, shelter, and often sexual release. In Western culture, excess is often socially encouraged, if not demanded! Limiting and rationing our physical needs can be extremely trying in a hedonistic society. Spiritually, challenging our dependence on such things is one of the most beneficial things we can do. The body—or I should say the mind—is also attached to sensory experience beyond physical necessity. We may find ourselves addicted to certain modes of behavior, mindsets, or substances that may not exactly be beneficial in the long run. Fasting regularly from such dependencies shocks the mind and body out of habitual patterns that could gain unhealthy momentum over time. It is essential that we examine and bring to light our attachments, and anything on this plane that we may cling to, so we can see whatever is inhibiting our spiritual potential.

When fasting, we must remain steadfast and keep focused on the spiritual goal at hand. Constantly complaining about the difficulty of a fast takes energy away from the sacrifice. When an overabundance of negativity arises during fasting, much of it is subconscious darkness reemerging, just aching to be released. Anger and sadness are easy filters, or covers, for energy that wishes to depart, and these emotions must both be recognized and analyzed. What are their roots? How are they connected to the fast itself? How can these energies become constructively released without being allowed to spiral out of control?

Each type of fast produces a different effect; for example, abstaining from food may produce lightheadedness, while abstaining from sexual release may produce frustration. One may feel anything from agitation and upset to increased energy and optimism—it entirely depends on what is being sacrificed and the practitioner's approach, both of which influence the intensity of the fast. In my experience, common effects are cravings (obviously), mood swings, spiritual visions, sensations of disconnectedness from the physical body (a "lightness of being"), sorrow, ecstasy, mental flight, awareness of the energetic body and the etheric planes, lethargy and weakness, increased dream activity, headaches, borderline emotional breakdowns, heightened senses, awareness of mental clutter, and moments of mental clarity.

In some of the longer and more tedious fasts, the line may blur between the feeling of temporary "insanity" and the feeling of Gnosis or union with Spirit. The contrast between "pleasants" and "unpleasants" becomes less apparent. After experiencing a fast, a sense of holistic renewal and spiritual accomplishment results.

Cross-Cultural Fasting

Fasting is a worldwide religious practice. It is perhaps best known in association with Hinduism, as it is interwoven heavily into India's rich spiritual tradition. Traditional Hindus observe a number of food fasts throughout the year. The Vedic year has twelve lunar months, each with additional solar correspondences; there are many variations on the traditional Indian calendar. Hindu fasts are frequently associated with various deities and serve to honor them. Often, the decision to observe a deity's holy day depends on personal preference or on the customs of each individual Hindu sect. There seem to be many fasts and *vratas* (vows) associated with deital celebrations in the four lunar months called *Chaturmasya*, during which Lord Vishnu is said to sleep. This correlates with the rainy season in India, also called the monsoon season. The last of these four months is *Kartika*, which occurs either on the seventh or eighth month of the Gregorian year. Many Hindus restrict themselves to one vegetarian meal a day during Kartika, and practice various specific fasts during the whole period of Chaturmasya.

Hindu ascetics are also called *saddhus*: wandering holy people. These ascetics have always been out-castes in India, and their extreme lifestyles tend to keep them in such a social category. (Indian social systems are less strict than they used to be, but more legal equality in theory does not necessarily translate to practice.) These ascetics have renounced worldly pleasures in trade for a life of self-discipline, with the aim of growing closer to godhead. Buddhism and Sikhism also have their ascetic followers. Many, like the Buddha, were born in "higher" castes and renounced their former social status for asceticism.

Because Buddhism originated as a response to orthodox Hinduism, most Buddhist disciplines still include various fastings and vows in their regimes. Probably the most noticeable Buddhist self-sacrifice is the tonsure, or shaving of the head, which many monks and nuns undergo as a Rite of Passage and a declaration of sacrificing the ego for the sake of greater spiritual union.

Another religion heavily associated with fasting and self-sacrifice is Islam. In traditional Islamic religious practices, adherents observe full food fasting during the month of *Ramadan*. Ramadan occurs in the ninth month of the Islamic lunar calendar; as a result, its date in the Gregorian calendar shifts each year. During Ramadan, Muslims practice various strict forms of fasting and purification as devotional practices to Allah. For the entire month, Muslims are required to fast and purify from sunrise to sunset, traditionally abstaining from both food and sex. Fasts are broken at sundown each day of Ramadan.

Many Muslims fast on other holy days, though these disciplines vary from group to group. Traditionally, orthodox Muslims vow to abstain from alcohol throughout their lives. Many take this a step further by vowing to abstain from any sort of harmful behavior including anger, jealousy, lust, and greed, as much as possible.

Various schools of Christianity also practice fasting: not only abstinence from food on some occasions, but also through extended vows of celibacy for monks and nuns. The Bible tells of Moses fasting for forty days and forty nights; Jesus, too, underwent such a fast. In other verses, such as Luke 6:12 and Matthew 14:23, Jesus engages in solitary prayer and meditation, refusing sleep and devoting himself to Spirit. Fasting is also discussed in Matthew 6:16–18, wherein Jesus explains that abstaining from food is a personal act between oneself and the Divine rather than an attempt to win the approval of others. The many references to self-denial in the scriptures of Matthew suggest that its importance was well understood. Many followers of the Christ also engage in self-sacrifices as acts of dedication. Abstaining from sleep for religious purposes is often called "watching."

In Catholicism and Protestantism, Lent is observed during the forty-day period between Ash Wednesday and Holy Saturday (which follows Good Friday and precedes Easter Sunday). Traditionally, meat, wine, and festivities were abnegated during this holy time. But most modern observers choose to abstain from specific pleasurable activities to show penance before God; today, there is also a focus on acts of charity. A number of churches additionally require the faithful to adhere to a strict vegetarian diet, though this is not a worldwide phenomenon. (The word Lent is Old English for "spring." Less food was eaten at this time because the rations of autumn were running short. It was necessary to consume less, so a virtue was born of necessity.)

Many other religions have codified fasting in various ways. Traditional adherents to Judaism observe a number of days of sunrise-to-sundown fasting in the year (with water also proscribed). Judaism and other religions also make use of fasting when in mourning, or to mark particular Rites of Passage. Many schools of Taoism also recognize fasting, and some translate verses in the *Tao Te Ching* as referring to it. The practice is mentioned in the *Book of Mencius*, a text that greatly propelled the influence of Confucianism in China. Over time, Confucianism, Taoism, and Buddhism came to influence one another in many forms of Chinese philosophy.

Restricting one's food intake, sleep cycles, or speech; depriving oneself of sexual release or other sensations…these are all aspects of ascetic practice. Self-mortification, or torturing one's own physical body, is also common. All acts of self-sacrifice are undertaken with the goal of achieving spiritual illumination; it is thought that restricting and tormenting the physical body will push the soul to higher levels of awareness and union with Spirit. Asceticism is a lifelong path for many, and as such it certainly dwarfs the small bursts of self-sacrificial devotions and fasts that nonascetic spiritual seekers may attempt. However, no act of self-sacrifice should be underrated. It takes great determination, especially for those who are new to it. Though I imagine that nearly everyone reading these words is not an ascetic (myself included), integrating a bit of self-sacrifice on special days can be a tremendously beneficial spiritual practice.

For us, the goal is to step out of our normal modes of operation and allow new spiritual vibrations to enter our sphere. Restricting food and other forms of denial are not a punishment, but an opportunity to tap into that which may otherwise remain hidden. In her Christianity-centered book *Fasting: Spiritual Freedom Beyond Our Appetites*, Lynne Baab notes, "Fasting as self-punishment denies the freedom God gives us in Christ. Fasting as self-punishment does not create space for prayer, give us energy to our prayers, or enable us to listen to God." Regardless of one's religion—Christian, Pagan, Buddhist, Hindu, Jewish, Muslim, or anything else—fasting is one of the most spiritually beneficial disciplines a person can undertake when it is done not in the spirit of self-punishment, but as a way to open doors of spiritual revelation.

Planning Fasts

Fasting can be reasonably healthy if approached with awareness of the body and mind. Careful planning is necessary for a healthy and successful experience. Before attempting any sort of *food* fast, think sensibly about what you will be doing to your body. Fasting must be approached with caution and awareness of the individuality of body chemistry—everyone is different and has different limits.

Just as our biological needs and limits differ, the same holds true for the mind. If a person has never before experienced any sort of fast, immediately attempting hardcore self-denial would be like jumping into the deep end before learning to swim. It's always best to start with a "small" fast and work your way up gradually.

A three-day fast is great for one's first experience. Three and seven are auspicious numbers in magick, as three represents the phases of the Great Goddess or God (and is the number of the Holy Child), and seven is the number of primary planets and the days of the week. If you decide to abstain from food, it's a good idea to start with a gradual fast or a rice-and-juice fast, rather than completely halting your nutritional intake (this is discussed further on). If you allow yourself some experimentation and remain devoted to observing the body's reactions, you can gain a greater wisdom regarding the limits of your own body and mind. Discomfort is a natural reaction to fasting, and it isn't always an invitation to give up partway through. During a fast, if you feel you should "quit while you're ahead," analyze the feeling and look for its origins. Is it the mind expressing discomfort or is it actually a matter of health? You be the judge, and take care of yourself while pushing your limits.

If you are fasting from food and realize that you're growing too weak to continue or that your health might be at risk, do not immediately cease the fast and reenter your normal mode of operation. Food fasts must be eased out of, as the digestive system (in particular) can be shocked and thus injured if, after processing nothing or next to nothing, it is suddenly digesting regular meals again. You may have concerns as to the health risks of fasting; perhaps you take certain medicines that may not interact well with a decrease in food intake (for example). If your concerns are legitimate and medically based, rather than exclusively psychologically based, don't hesitate to discuss the risks and benefits with your healthcare practitioner.

When planning for fasts, pay strict attention to your work and/or school schedule. It's best to fast on days when it won't interfere and distract from any other tasks at hand. (It's also best to avoid driving a car on those days, as the mind is almost always in an altered state.) For a three-day fast, I've found it beneficial to begin on a "day off," still going about daily obligations. Of course, this option depends entirely on the nature of the fast and the practitioner's reaction to it. For example, a vow of silence while at work or school may be possible for some people, though it would unfeasible for others.

If a person decides to undertake a fast, it must be carefully planned. The goal of the fast must be crystal clear; this will both strengthen the devotion and provide fuel for the fire of motivation that keeps a person going in the sacrifice. Doubt and frustration most definitely arise in the fasting process. Depending on the fast, that can be a heavy yet necessary thing to overcome.

When enduring any type of fast, I like to keep a journal to monitor my mind and body's reactions. It may be a "chaos magick" thing to say, but during the fast, do whatever works for you. Set your own boundaries and limits, determine your current comfort-versus-discomfort threshold, then push that level accordingly. How you conduct a fast is entirely your call. If a full food fast is too difficult, consider eating only white rice or fruit during that period instead. If fully fasting from technology isn't feasible, consider allowing yourself to operate a car but nothing else. If fasting from tobacco is extremely difficult, consider using an herbal smoking blend as a tobacco-free substitute. At the same time, be very careful how much leeway you allow yourself; with too much leeway, the purpose of the fast diminishes. It's all about pushing yourself to your limits (and a little beyond them) to allow a small rebirth to occur as a result.

Furthermore, I recommend doing whatever works for you ritualistically. Meditation is a great asset during any type of fast. Sitting in silence and stilling the mind for an extended period brings greater focus and peace. Using visualization techniques, whether recommended by others or self-created, sharpens particular vibrations and makes waking life a bit smoother. Taking a bath also aids in calming the mind and body. Bathing can itself be an amazing ritualistic experience. I also recommend a healthy amount of reading; spiritual and occult studies can be great points of grounding and reassurance when fasting. Undertaking a metaphysical project during this time can also be a constructive way to ground spacey energies that can lead to discouragement. For example, during one of my seven-day fasts, I created "*materia magicka*" and "*materia medica*" reference cards for all the herbs I own. During others, I made it a point to learn as much as I could about one particular occult subject or another. Fasting is also one of the most ideal times to create any sort of art. The possibilities are endless!

During a fast, dedicatory actions are of immense benefit. If you are familiar with your spirit guide(s) or animal spirit(s), work with them. Meditate with them, invite their energies into your experience, and align yourself to their wisdom. If you're close with a particular god or goddess, dedicate the fast to that deity from the outset and continue to ritualistically commune with them. If you have a penchant for working with elemental energies, surround yourself with Nature as much as possible and perform personally meaningful elemental magick. In other words, take advantage of your own spiritual findings, leanings, and curiosities to make your fast a totally personal spiritual experience!

A common metaphysical exercise that is profoundly effective for letting go of emotional attachment is that of "stepping back." During a fast, this exercise can increase dedicatory determination. It takes practice, but many of its effects can be felt immediately. If preferred, this may be performed within a ritualistic environment. I strongly believe that such exercises in awareness should be practiced regularly, both during fasting and in regular, nonfasting life. The goal is to simply step back from yourself to see a greater picture. Let's try it now: become aware of yourself at this very moment. You might first observe your present activity: reading. Simply know that you are reading. From there, take a step back: where are you sitting, how are you positioned, and what is the surrounding environment like? From here, you may take another step back: you are reading these words, but who does this "you" refer to? Become aware of the body as a simple vessel for the soul (or "spirit" if you prefer). This soul is perceiving and absorbing its current experience through the six sensory faculties of the physical (mortal) body. The body and all of its sensory faculties will perish, given time. It will change, it will die, it will return to the elements. Now become aware that all things around you, from the book you are holding to the clothes you are wearing to the seat you are positioned on, are only temporary structures that will eventually cease to be. Nothing is without change. From here, contemplate the division between the soul and physical reality. Come to think of your perception as an emanation of the soul: you are observing your body experiencing stimuli. You are not your body, but have chosen to inhabit this shell temporarily. Allow yourself to detach from the idea that the mind is subject to the body, realizing that the body is in fact subject to the mind.

This is one example of "stepping back," and can be performed at any time that circumstances permit. As we are incarnated in these bodies, it's easy to forget that the soul and the physical frame are separate paradigms, only working together for a brief period of time. Should this type of work become overwhelming—and it should, as undeniable questions of existence naturally arise and seek resolution—proper grounding techniques should be performed to center the Higher Self and Lower Self as one. This dance of two bodies is the dance of life.

FOOD FASTING

Food is linked to creation. Food allows for survival and is a link in the chain of life, death, and rebirth: a concept illustrated in the classical Hindu view that food itself is a direct reincarnation of human essence. Cremation is an ordinary procedure in India, and many believe that a person "becomes" smoke when cremated. The smoke is then integrated with the atmosphere and sky, and is partially brought back to the earth through rain. The rain nourishes plants, which are eaten as food, and thus reabsorbed into the living.

Many assume that fasting must involve denial of all food, and possibly water as well. This is undoubtedly the most jarring type of fast, and can also be the most dangerous. I would never advise a person to go without water, as such asceticism can be more damaging than rewarding. I also have a difficult time advising people to go for more than a day or two entirely without food. Full fasts are noble but must be approached with extreme caution. For a person who has never fasted, I would recommend numerous partial fasts over time before jumping into what may be treacherous waters.

In his book *New Aeon Magick: Thelema Without Tears*, author Gerald del Campo recommends an every-other-day form of fast: eat normally on alternate days, allowing juice and herbal tea only on the fasting days. I agree—playing with this method can be a balanced way to introduce oneself to this spiritual art. To keep natural vitamins and minerals flowing, keep various fruit juices on hand. I would advise against too much juice that is acidic in nature, such as orange, lemon, and grapefruit. I prefer apple, cranberry, and pear. Organic juice that is not made from concentrate is undoubtedly the best. There are tons of options!

One can also try a juice-only fast for a few days. These generally include both fruit and vegetable juice, and are extremely detoxifying. Juice fasts allow nutrients to still enter the body even when nothing is actually being eaten. With vegetable juice, ensure that it's not full of sodium and is, ideally, organic and not from concentrate. Additionally, should one choose to permit it, fennel seeds are great to munch on when enduring any type of food fast, especially a full fast. Fennel seeds were eaten during church fasting days in the Middle Ages both to curb the appetite and to freshen the breath.

Also, I've found that bentonite clay is an incredible asset to the process. This type of clay is sold in herb and health food stores in powder form, and is also known as calcium bentonite. It is also sold under the name Pascalite clay. It has extreme cleansing properties and is surprisingly versatile. It can be used to relieve a wide array of digestive ailments, and consuming this during a food fast of any sort will help cleanse and purify the body internally, not to mention energetically. I've had astounding success with this clay both within and outside of fasting. The Native American nations of the Wyoming Big Horn Mountains called it *ee-wah-kee*, "the mud that heals." Not only does it leach toxic materials from the digestive system (especially the colon), but it can be caked on wounds to prevent infection, and on scars or external marks as a topical healing ointment. Some accounts even speak of the clay healing more long-term skin ailments such as candida, psoriasis, and acne. If you're a Witch or herbal healer, this healing clay is a must for your cabinet!

THE RICE FAST

When consuming only rice, some people allow themselves only white rice while others use brown. Some permit the addition of soy sauce, chili sauce, sesame seeds, seaweed, and/or olive oil, in which the rice is fried. These ingredients can add flavor to the "empty" quality of white rice in particular, as it is relatively flavorless and has little nutritional value beyond its calories. As an "empty filler," cooked rice is ideal for our purpose. It lets the digestive system keep operating while at the same time denying the body most nutrients. It's a good idea to thoroughly rinse rice before cooking it in order to remove excess starch and any synthetic vitamins and minerals sprayed on it before packaging. Rice can also be consumed in a variety of other forms, including rice noodles, rice puff cereal, rice cakes, rice crackers, and rice milk. Read ingredients lists closely to avoid consuming more than is desired. Water is essential during a rice fast, and many people like to consume non-acidic juice as well. Either way, I recommend eating small amounts frequently—at least once every hour, even if only a small amount—to keep the digestive system in regular operation. Although the body is processing food with almost no nutritional value, the discomfort of hunger is greatly eased. Rice is the perfect fasting food; it doesn't shock the system too much, but it takes a person out of the ordinary eating cycle just enough to alter consciousness and bring certain issues to light.

THE GRADUAL FOOD FAST

Here the practitioner tapers off certain foods down to a certain fasting minimum, then tapers back up again. A seven-day gradual fast is ideal, as it allows one to go through the full week both spiritually and mundanely, experiencing the sacrifice. The ordinary grind of work, school, and so on, is experienced during the fast, and the planetary rulership of each day is encountered in the duration of one fast. Each day of the week is ruled by one of the primary planets of classical

Hermetic astrology. Devoting each day of the fast to a planet is ideal for a Witch or magician, following this pattern:

> Sunday: Sun
> Monday: Moon
> Tuesday: Mars
> Wednesday: Mercury
> Thursday: Jupiter
> Friday: Venus
> Saturday: Saturn

Three seven-day gradual fast plans are outlined below, geared to meat and dairy eaters, vegetarians, and vegans, respectively. Depending on one's dietary habits, these variations help disperse protein and other vital nutrients and help prevent wear and distress on the body. Nuts and seeds carry a particular vibration (and protein content) that are permitted on some days and not on others. All three plans include fruits and "surface" vegetables: those that grow above ground. ("Buried" vegetables that grow underground, such as carrots and potatoes, are dense and carry a certain heavy earth vibration, so they are not incorporated in these fasts.) Remember to drink non-acidic juice every day of any fast outlined below, so as to keep the vitamins flowing. Remember to eat the permitted foods often, at least a small amount every hour during each fasting day. Please note that I am not a nutritionist, so please consult a healthcare professional before attempting fasts of any sort, and always use common sense.

If you currently eat meat and dairy:

- Day 1: Allow fruits, surface vegetables, rice, and dairy. No meat, nuts, or seeds.
- Day 2: Allow fruits, surface vegetables, and rice. No meat, dairy, nuts, or seeds.
- Day 3: Allow only nuts, seeds, and rice.
- Day 4: Rice (and juice) only.
- Day 5: Allow only nuts, seeds, and rice.
- Day 6: Allow fruits, surface vegetables, and rice. No meat, dairy, nuts, or seeds.

- DAY 7: Allow fruits, surface vegetables, rice, and dairy. No meat, nuts, or seeds.

If you are currently vegetarian:

- DAY 1: Allow fruits, surface vegetables, and rice. No dairy, nuts, or seeds.
- DAY 2: Allow fruits and rice. No dairy, nuts, seeds, or vegetables.
- DAY 3: Allow only nuts, seeds, and rice.
- DAY 4: Rice (and juice) only.
- DAY 5: Allow only nuts, seeds, and rice.
- DAY 6: Allow fruits and rice. No dairy, nuts, seeds, or vegetables.
- DAY 7: Allow fruits, surface vegetables, and rice. No dairy, nuts, or seeds.

If you are currently vegan:

- DAY 1: Allow fruits, surface vegetables, nuts, seeds, and rice. No cooked food besides rice.
- DAY 2: Allow fruits, nuts, seeds, and rice. No cooked food besides rice, and no vegetables.
- DAY 3: Rice and (uncooked) fruits only.
- DAY 4: Rice (and juice) only.
- DAY 5: Rice and (uncooked) fruits only.
- DAY 6: Allow fruits, nuts, seeds, and rice. No cooked food besides rice, and no vegetables.
- DAY 7: Allow fruits, surface vegetables, nuts, seeds, and rice. No cooked food besides rice.

In the latter half of a gradual food fast, when reintegrating each previously subtracted food, "celebrate" that item. And at any time we can deepen our appreciation for rice by honoring and contemplating the grain that has for centuries sustained people across the globe.

A less intense dietary variation is to simply abstain from unnatural foods for a period of time. With all the "food" products available on the market that are genetically modified or include toxic ingredients like partially hydrogenated oil and high-fructose corn syrup, most spiritual seekers habitually tend to select all-natural or organic foods whenever possible. If you are not in the habit of eating only natural and organic foods, this type of dietary shift may be a good introduction to fasting—or a dedication for life!

VEGETARIANISM & VEGANISM

Another type of food fast is to immerse oneself in a vegetarian or vegan diet for a period of time. For non-vegetarians, the effects of subtracting meat from the diet often include feelings of "lightness," a greater sense of mental and physical purity, and expanded spiritual awareness.

Indeed, metaphysically, the death energy latent in factory-farmed animal corpses is heavy with misery. Perpetuating cycles of animal abuse and the absorption of such energies into the body is, I believe, antispiritual. Personally, I think that everyone who is physically able should be either vegetarian or vegan for life, or at least eat *only* humanely raised meat and hunted game. The horrors and tortures of factory "farming" are unspeakable; it is hell on earth for literally billions upon billions of animals who deserve to be treated as sentient beings rather than financial "product." Our generation is blessed with choice, and consuming flesh is not, quite honestly, necessary for our health and well-being. Additionally, we are not our ancestors; rarely do most of us hunt and gather.

To those unfamiliar with factory farming, this point of view may sound overly compassionate or idealistic, but in truth, no being should be treated in the ways that countless animals are constantly treated, unseen and unregulated. Every time we take a bite of factory-farmed meat, we both contribute to and endorse a brutal and inhumane cycle of anguish for other beings in our immediate reality. The gruesome truth of this slaughter mustn't be brushed aside or conveniently ignored or justified by spiritual seekers. Simple research into the reality of factory farming and the health risks of meat and dairy are worth investigating.

Although fasting is mainly discussed as it pertains to food and dietary intake, there are countless methods of sacrifice that we can implore for spiritual uses. Any method of fasting can make a person confront their darker self and present an opportunity for healing; after all, if something is taken away, we *must* invite another energy to take its place. Let's examine some of these alternatives to fasting from food.

VOWS OF SILENCE

As a teenager, I once had a dream about refraining from speech for a period of three days. Perhaps it was a result of seeing the film version of Marion Zimmer Bradley's *The Mists of Avalon*, in which a character (also called Raven!) has taken a lifelong vow of silence. The dream was a spiritual message nonetheless and, for me, the results were awesome. Since then, I've performed other vows of silence and have discovered the same spiritual success. I also practice three-day vows of silence on a semiregular basis, usually aligning them with specific Hindu or Pagan festival days.

Vows of silence are beneficial in numerous ways. As humans, we are accustomed to communicating verbally. Removing that element from our lives for a period of time helps us become more aware of our methods of, and motivations for, verbal communication. A vow of silence allows us to catch instinctual vocal reactions, many of which accompany hand or body gestures. We also see exactly how often we inadvertently mumble or mutter to ourselves, so we're forced to bite our tongue!

The extent of the vow is up to the practitioner. Will you let yourself write notes or do visual charades whilst remaining silent? Will you let yourself respond to emails, texts, and other written messages? Will you cease all forms of communication altogether? Whatever the case, I recommend carrying a notecard reading, "I am undergoing a vow of silence for [however many] days as a devotion to [Spirit, the gods, or your patron deity]," or something similar.

Vows of silence bring us a greater awareness of nonverbal communication and let us see how normal communications are conveyed through a combination of action, facial expression, motion, and voice. Simply observing other people's ordinary behavior during this fast brings many aspects of the realm of communication into clarity. When we are forced to become the observer, we truly observe. (Undertaking a vow of silence is often much more entertaining than it is stressful, making it a fast that's both fun and enlightening.)

Vows of silence can help a modern magickal practitioner to better actualize the four Laws of the Magus, which are "To Know, To Dare, To Will, To Keep Silent." This is also called the Witch's Pyramid or Magician's Ladder.

A number of occult systems require that a person undertake a vow of silence or simply remain silent in regard to idle words, gossip, or negative speech, all of which are a variation of the vow of silence. Occultist and chaos magician Robert Anton Wilson was a fan of removing the word "I" from one's vocabulary. In the early twentieth century, Indian-born Bahmanji Pestonji Wadia endorsed various forms of silence and helped to integrate the teachings into the budding Western movement of Theosophy. The mystic, scientist, and mathematician Pythagoras is also documented as having endured a five-year vow of silence in the sixth century BCE.

VOWS OF CELIBACY

Particularly prevalent in Christianity, Buddhism, and Hinduism, vows of celibacy call for a person to refrain from sexual activity. Some people and traditions disallow non-intercourse sexual pleasure and masturbation, while others permit either or both. Like the concept of chastity, celibacy is linked to notions of sexual purity, but it does not imply virginity like the term chastity does.

Some people take lifelong vows of celibacy in accordance with religious requirements. Many Eastern religious sects practice celibacy, as do monks and nuns of some Western religions. The goal is to eliminate desire and the attachment to worldly pleasure that can easily arise. Some Christians, especially Catholics, and in particular Catholic clergy, take lifelong vows of celibacy as an act of dedication before God.

For the average Westerner, voluntarily abstaining from any sort of sexual activity for a period of time can be quite a trial, since most people sexually release on a regular basis. For the most challenge and the most benefit, disallowing both sex and masturbation is particularly effective. Refraining from orgasm forces us to examine our own sexual tendencies and observe which thoughts induce arousal. This can allow us to reflect on our sexual motivations, think about sexual experiences of the past, contemplate sexual energy and orientation, and come to a more balanced state of mind regarding sex and sexuality.

FASTING FROM DEPENDENCIES

So…what's your crutch? Alcohol? Tobacco? Caffeine? Ganja? Food? Gaming? Television? Gambling? Chill pills? Something else? Admittedly, most of us have one type of crutch or another. This isn't to say that every substance or habit is harmful, or that it's wrong to use recreational substances now and then. But we do often tend to develop psychological dependencies on things that have mood-altering effects on us. (My use of the terms "substance" or "drug" includes excessive eating, television, video games, and other habits.) While one person may use a drug recreationally, another may develop a dependency. While one person may experience no ill effects from the use, others may injure their bodies and cause harm in the long run.

Either way, it's wise to examine addictions and potential addictions, and learn to operate with or without one's substance of choice. Witches and magicians are pretty liberal about substance use. If using a drug causes no harm to oneself or others, it's generally considered okay to use. The desire to use substances to alter one's consciousness, whether to a small or significant degree, is quite natural. I would even argue that most people live a more productive and holistically healthy life if they have something to take the edge off now and then—so long as it's used sparingly and doesn't excessively harm the body.

What about fasting from pharmaceuticals? Western prescription drugs can have positive or negative effects, or there may be tradeoffs of pros and cons. Some medicines are prescribed for physiological reasons, and others for psychological reasons. If you are considering a fast from a prescription medicine, whether for physical or psychological health, first consult the doctor who prescribed it. Taking a break from it without understanding the implications can be damaging. Is the prescription something you feel you can do without at this point, or is it absolutely necessary? If you feel that you may simply be psychologically dependent on a certain medication, it may be beneficial to try easing off it, under a doctor's supervision, and see how you operate.

Many people self-medicate with substances, which can have either positive or negative effects, depending on the person's reactions in the short and long term. Depending on one's physiological need for "self-medicating" with recreational substances, fasting from them can be beneficial. If a person self-medicates with caffeine, nicotine, alcohol, cannabis, or something similar, it can be spiritually rewarding to take a break from the substance of choice, allowing the body to cleanse and return to a more natural state. Do you feel that you can't start the day without drinking coffee or smoking a cigarette, or you can't relax in the evening without having a few drinks or smoking a bowl? What, for you, would be safe to cut out of your system for a period of time? What is the degree of your dependency, if you have one, and how can you safely and healthily subtract the drug from your routine? Is your drug of choice relatively harmless, or is it something you should cease using altogether? Would you, and are you able to, take a break from a substance for a week? A month? A year? The rest of your life? The choice is personal, but the decision should be made intelligently, and with the advice of others.

It's easy to become accustomed to using substances, which is why taking a break from them can be so helpful. We must be the ones in control, not the substance. Fasting from dependencies allows us to take a step back and realize that we can function without a crutch, even if it's difficult at first. If attempting this sort of fast, it's a good idea to slowly ease off a substance, eliminate it from your system entirely, and then ease back into it if you so desire. A cold-turkey approach isn't always the best option, especially in the case of pharmaceuticals, but it may work best for recreational substance users, depending on one's body chemistry.

TECHNOLOGY FASTS

As I sit at the computer writing these words, I realize how dependent I am on technology. The computer is the most obvious form of technology I'm using at the moment, but as I look around, I notice more. A light bulb is shining above me, the stereo is playing, a housemate is on the phone, a fan is rotating, an electric kettle is boiling, and soup is being heated on the stove. That's a lot of electricity!

Living in a modern world, we are constantly using technology for our daily needs. What if, one day, technology failed? Could we survive? This is something to consider when enduring a fast from technology. How truly independent from technology, particularly electronic technology, are we?

If you decide to undergo a technology fast, consider how strict you wish it to be. What is the scope of the term "technology?" Obviously, things like phones, computers, microwaves, and televisions are out of the question. Would you decide to stop driving or using public transportation? Would you use the stove? The oven? Lights? Electronic timepieces? The refrigerator? Would you allow others to operate electrical devices for you? Will you perform this in conjunction with another fast or two? It's up to you; just don't be too lenient on yourself! Imagine all the ways this sacrifice could be rewarding…books and baths by candlelight never sounded so good!

Eliminating technology from one's daily operation is, like all sacrifices, both difficult and rewarding. Such an endeavor illuminates our modern lifestyle and reminds us that humans operated without electronic technology for many aeons.

SLEEP FASTS

Before I attempted fasting from sleep, I had never pulled an all-nighter. For the longest time, I held on to the belief that I could not function without at least eight hours of sleep. Now I realize that if the need arises, I can function on less sleep and catch up at a later time. Though I still get loopier than the average Joe, confronting the long-held fear by undergoing a sleep fast proved to lessen its intensity for me. People vary in the amount of sleep they need to operate well. Some people manage fine on only four hours a night, while others function best on ten. Any type of fasting is a highly personal devotion, as everyone's constitution is different, and this may be especially true with sleep.

Sleep fasts must be carefully planned, as should any self-restriction. It's a good idea to start by staying awake for only one night. If that treats you well, try for two the next time. As a general rule, sleep deprivation produces effects of irritability, grogginess, forgetfulness, and weakness. It can make a person feel that life is a dream. I tend to become more apathetic with sleep loss, feeling a sort of "pleasant frustration." One's memory, sense of time, and communication abilities alter with sleep deprivation. Two or three days of sleep fasting can produce minor auditory and visual hallucinations. One's reaction time and attention span can both be reduced, which makes meditation a much wiser choice than driving a car. If you are planning a fast from sleep, please be careful. Prolonged sleep deprivation can cause a state called *oneirophrenia*, in which a person not only perceives life as a dream, but has strong delusions and hallucinations. Don't push yourself too hard; fasting of any sort requires utmost self-awareness. One option is to let yourself take a set number of forty-minute naps throughout the fast. This way we can brush up against the astral plane for but a moment, rejuvenating ourselves slightly before returning to this plane. A person usually enters the REM state (rapid eye movement, indicating deeper sleep) about thirty or forty minutes after falling asleep, so shorter naps will prevent much of the waking disorientation caused by interrupting REM. You may also wish to permit yourself stimulants such as caffeine, ginseng, and coca tea. I would, however, strongly recommend against using synthetic "uppers" such as energy drinks and drugs. The experience should be as pure as possible.

FASTING FROM SOCIETY

Also called isolation fasts, abstaining from contact with anybody but yourself (and pets!) is most definitely a form of self-sacrifice. Most of us interact with other people daily. When a person is undistracted by others, mental processes become more easily visible, allowing a better view of the mind and its workings.

If you live a highly social lifestyle, taking some time for yourself, and only yourself, can be an amazing, much-needed antidote. We so often integrate our lives with the lives of others. This is a natural part of human living, but forgetting to balance sociality with solitude (and vice versa) can be spiritually detrimental. For people who are highly empathic or simply energy-sensitive, restricting oneself socially can permit time for energy work, artistic expression, meditation, ritual, and healthy self-analysis. Foreign energies naturally attach themselves to our auras throughout the day, so we must take proper time to cleanse and come to center. Setting aside time for solitude creates an opportunity for this grounding and centering to happen without distraction.

Many people undergoing a social fast prefer to isolate themselves somewhere other than at home. Some go camping, which sets a natural atmosphere. If you perform this sort of fast from home, it's essential to turn off your phone and email systems, and probably the radio and television too. Alert friends and family of your self-isolation and stick a note on the door. If you live with a partner or roommates, tell them beforehand what you're doing, but don't let their proximity distract from your fast. Certainly, in the case of an honest emergency, the fast should be broken.

One much simpler modification of this fast from society is to simply refrain from purchasing anything. By not exchanging money with anyone, we temporarily remove ourselves from the extremes of our society's commercial sphere. If you're planning a full isolation fast, how long would you like it to continue? Depending on your lifestyle, a few days or a week may be the ideal time frame. Perhaps refraining from purchasing anything could last a longer period of time, such as a month. It's your intuition and your choice.

APPEARANCE FASTING

We live in a culture that's unhealthily fixated on physical appearance. As we present ourselves to the world, we're sometimes judged by what we wear or don't wear, and also judged by other aspects of our physical appearance. Our culture far too often equates a person's appearance with their worth. Many people spend their lives worrying about their appearance, constantly modifying themselves to impress other people and, unfortunately, end up relying on other people's shallow acceptance to feel valuable and worth loving. Empowerment comes from separating oneself from others' expectations and judgments enough to find security in one's own expression and appearance.

Physical appearance is, of course, secondary to spiritual living. At the same time, appearance can be a wonderful platform for artistic expression. For readers whose fashions often reflect either their subcultural interests or "alternative" modalities, I recommend wearing completely different clothing for this fast. Perhaps wearing ordinary pants, a T-shirt, a baseball cap, and no makeup would be a strong enough antithesis to your usual style that this fast would have strong effects. What would it be like to visually fit into the mainstream, instead of standing out?

For readers whose wardrobe is more "ordinary," perhaps just the opposite would be a noble change. I would recommend examining a subculture's common visual expression and dressing to the nines. To take it a step further, you may choose to immerse yourself even deeper in a subculture by going to a Goth club, punk rock concert, reggae show, electronic dance event, polka party, or what have you.

If choosing to fast from your typical appearance, it's a must to go out in public at least once a day in order to fully feel the effects of the sacrifice, and it's best to continue the fast for at least a week. Altering our visual appearance also alters the way people respond to us, both noticeably and energetically. Changing our appearance makes us look at things a bit differently; our perceptions can expand as we see what it's like to walk in different shoes.

Ritual Meditation: A Ceremony of Silence

Simply sacrificing one element of a ritual—speech, in this case—can do wonders in terms of changing the vibration, experience, and outcome of a ceremony. This is a ritual of silence. No words are to be spoken throughout the process.

So many rituals and spells place emphasis on speech. We may have been told that the words themselves create the magick, and Hollywoodization certainly doesn't help. Vocalization holds very intense power, but when an abundance of idle words is spoken in circle, the words become just as fleeting as the surrounding air.

On the other hand, when ritual is enacted with intention, words become secondary; they are but a guide for conscious will. Words are symbols and words are tools. In the following circle-casting meditation, we will see ritualism in a different light and work purely from the energetic plane, immersing ourselves in enigmatic silence. This ritual should get you comfortable with the idea of a silent circle for when the need arises in the future. (I don't recommend silence for all rituals; only for those for which it feels appropriate.)

Our intention with this ritual is pure experience, so it does not include any spellwork, but instead includes moments of communion and one strong apex of heightened spiritual awareness. This ritual may be the perfect conclusion to a period of fasting, particularly a vow of silence. If so, no word should be spoken until the very end, which then breaks the fast. Otherwise, if it's your practice, perform a vocal *or* nonvocal (visualized) Lesser Banishing Ritual of the

Pentagram (LBRP) beforehand, or any other protective exercises you deem appropriate.

For this ritual, have neither music playing nor any ruckus in the background. Prepare yourself, your altar, your tools, and your environment. Fire up candles and incense, turn off the lights, get naked or robed, and make sure your tools are properly placed, your statues anointed, and the dust swept. Taking a ritual bath or shower beforehand will also serve to cleanse the astral body in preparation for the rite. And, quite naturally, this ritual should be nocturnal because, well, *darkness* and stuff!

1. Sit comfortably to start the journey, then begin by clearing your mind. (Please wait until step 4 to begin casting the circle and calling the quarters.) Take three deep breaths in through the nose and out through the mouth. Let the thoughts of the day drift away like moving clouds. This is not the time to focus on what happened today or what you need to do tomorrow… allow the common world to dissipate as you enter the sacred terrain of the mind. For several minutes, sense the oxygen entering your nostrils and exiting your lips. Bring absolute focus to your breath.

2. Kneel or sit before your altar to begin the ritual, simply gazing at your tools. Look at each one for at least twenty seconds. As you do this, form an awareness in your mind of each tool's purpose. Is it frequently used or simply decorative? Rarely acknowledged or looked at daily? Physically, what materials is it made of? Energetically, is it highly charged or relatively empty? Consider these questions, taking as long as you need.

3. Reflecting on the tools, continue to meditate as long as you'd like, and for at least five minutes. This is important—as your focus slips to the mental plane, distractive images and sounds are given the opportunity to flee. Simply bring your focus back to your breath if you get lost in thought.

4. Raise your hands to the East (where most traditional circles begin) and, instead of "thinking" words in your mind, simply

feel the essence of the East, that of Air. Visualize all things that represent Air to you: rushing breezes, the breath of life, billowing smoke, clouds, or birds, for example. Envision any metaphysical associations the element has for you, too, such as intellectuality, study, knowledge, and so on, as well as any symbols you may associate with the direction. Mentally summon the element into the ritual space, slowly and with much intent and gratitude.

5. Move deosil to face the South, the quadrant of Fire, and repeat as above, using the elemental properties of this direction. Visualization suggestions: flames, candlelight, the sun, the desert, volcanoes, and so on. Metaphysical visualizations can include motivation, invigoration, sexuality, and so on, as well as any symbols you may associate with the direction. Again, summon the quadrant into the space.

6. Move deosil to face the West, the quadrant of Water. Visualization suggestions: rivers, streams, lakes, oceans, dewdrops, fog, emotions, change, empathy, and so on, as well as any symbols you may associate with the direction.

7. Complete the circle with the North, the element of Earth. Visualization suggestions: grass, trees, plants, ancient stone, fossils, minerals, grounding, stability, the material world, and so on, as well as any symbols you may associate with the direction.

8. Once the elements have palpably entered the circle, a relatively brief communion will take place with the fifth "element," Spirit: that which is All Things. Rather than communicating with an individual god or goddess (or even the Great God and Goddess), the emphasis here is on Spirit or *Akasha*: that which is both, that which is neither. Although Spirit is strongly in the circle already, it will also be invited as an individual force.

9. Sit comfortably at your altar or shrine and give yourself time to soak up the presence of the four elements. When you feel

centered and aware, raise up your hands to invite Spirit unto you. Close your eyes and envision a single point about four feet above your head. This point is spinning and spiraling deosil, becoming a larger and larger spiral. Its color is white. Lower your projective arm (the one you write with), keeping your receptive arm raised. With that raised hand, form a pointing finger and invite the spiral's tail to touch your fingertip. Keep this brief: when you feel an intense *pulse* or *shock* through your hand and body, drop the hand and envision the spiral's tail returning to the area above you. See your whole body bathed in whiteness as it fills your aura and alters your consciousness. Pay no attention to the physical plane, only to the energy around you. Give yourself time to soak this up before closing the spiral.

10. When ready, envision the spiral spinning *widdershins* (counter-clockwise) back into itself, back to a singular point, and finally vanishing. Open your eyes and take a deep breath, blowing upward to thank the Cosmic Consciousness. Clasp your hands in prayer position and bow, wordlessly thanking the Universe for this communion.

11. Dismiss the elements one by one. As you approach each direction, beginning with the North and ending in the East, see the energy you summoned (including the images, feelings, and symbols) being sucked in a widdershins direction, back into itself, and finally closing. Move your arms widdershins to gather the energy, spinning around a bit if necessary to help push it back. The doorway of each quadrant should be closed in the same way in which it opened on first appearance. At each quadrant, end the visualization with a forceful exhalation and a deep bow in gratitude for the energy's presence.

12. Once you feel the elements have been properly dismissed, take a moment to ground and center if need be, concluding by deconstructing the circle as you normally would (without vocalizing, of course).

13. End by tapping thrice, whether by tapping the end of a ritual tool three times, by loudly clapping thrice, or by knocking three times against a solid surface. This will diffuse the energy and declare the rite completed. Before closing the circle, break the silence by bellowing a resounding, *"So Mote It Be!"*

MAGICKAL JEWELRY & METALS

What can I say, so many of us Witches of darker persuasions tend to be attracted to jewelry and magickal bling. We *are* fabulous creatures of the night, after all. I include this section within this External Shadow chapter because, as with anything in the natural world, metals carry distinct etheric qualities that one should be aware of when wearing, activating, or using them in magickal work. This is especially relevant when performing a skyclad (nude) working, wherein the Dark Witch is wearing only jewelry. Metals shimmer and reflect light, becoming important pieces of focus in ritual, especially rituals held under shroud of night.

Jewelry has long been used in magick. Its most common historical use is protective: to guard against demons, malicious creatures, and adversarial attacks. With the rise of metallurgy, specifically designed pieces came to be used as amulets. This is prevalent in many societies, both magickal and superstitious.

Jewelry is relevant to any genre of magick, from Nature magick to ceremonial Arts. Many practitioners prefer wearing ritual jewelry in the form of charms, amulets, and talismans that are aligned to a particular vibration or intention. Each piece is a significant reflection of a practitioner's individual callings.

Jewelry can be a stylistic way to display your beliefs and alignments either inside or outside of ritual circle. Some magicians choose to eliminate all decorative wear, including jewelry, from the body prior to ritual. They believe the pieces detract from the energies raised, inhibiting the natural flow. On the other hand, most occultists feel that if a piece is properly charged, the magickal act is actually emphasized and the raising of energy can be more successfully directed for a specific purpose. This debate goes hand in hand with the ideas of body piercings being either beneficial or detrimental additions to magickal work. Some believe that metal is conductive to spiritual vibrations when used in ritual and that simply wearing it presents a suitable image of oneself to the gods and spirits, filled to the brim with sacred symbolism. This is especially beneficial when each piece has been previously charged with spiritual intent.

Bigghes

Jewelry pieces reserved solely for ritual and ceremonial purposes are called *bigghes*. This term separates ordinary jewelry from sacred jewelry. Bigghes originally referred to a High Priestess's ceremonial jewelry but is now used more to refer to any Witch's jewels.

Some choose to hide and physically protect their bigghes outside of circle in order to ensure that no external energies become attached to the piece. A popular method is to wrap the ornament in cloth, specifically black for protection, or keep it locked up safe and sound. Some choose to reserve certain jewelry for nocturnal rites and others for diurnal, keeping the jewelry attuned only to those specific ritualistic energies.

Chinese Mysticism, Taoism & Metal

Spirit is commonly referred to as its own element in Paganism and Wicca. This recognition places an emphasis on the Divine as the most important "element" making up reality. On the Pagan/Wiccan pentacle or pentagram, Spirit is placed at the highest point, understood as supreme because it unifies the elements and seals them all together. Though Paganism recognizes Spirit individually, no separation is seen in the Chinese system between Spirit and the other elements. All intertwine and interconnect perfectly, forming the Universe. The existence of *chi* is understood as connecting their conception of the physical elements. The recognition of the five Chinese elements came about before humankind drew a strict separation between everyday life and spirituality. Therefore, it was unnecessary at the time to consider Spirit individualistically. Some Pagans use the Chinese elements instead of the traditional Pagan ones, while most do not.

In modern Pagan systems, metals first and foremost correspond to the element Earth. In Chinese spiritual systems, the element Metal is said to encompass all forms of rock and mineral life. In the Taoist practice *Feng Shui*, metal represents inner strength, determination, and receptivity. Physically, metal expands when heated. This reiterates the energetic receptivity of metal—that is, if one understands physical reality (the metal itself) as a reflection of the spiritual. Within Chinese spiritual systems, its energy also dominates the autumnal season and draws energy inward for personal reflection, centering it on the subconscious mind. In Chinese astrology, Metal rules the birth signs Monkey and Rooster as a fixed element. In more detailed Chinese astrology, the element ruling each animal rotates continuously while certain attributions remain fixed, so that each birth year has an additional correspondence. Those ruled by Metal tend to be confident, aggressive, and assertive in nature. Metal is said to correspond to the body's lungs. The lungs hold the sacred breath of life. This is recognized in Buddhist *vipassana* (breathing or "insight") meditation which, though having originated with early *Theravada* Buddhism (which is a school of *Hinayana* or Early Conservative Buddhism), is common in the Chinese *Chan* (Zen) Buddhist tradition as well. The skin also breathes and is therefore also ruled by Metal. The nose and mouth are also included, as they are gateways of the breath. Finally, the large intestine corresponds to Metal, as oxygen in the diaphragm regulates abdominal pressure. Deep breathing is essential to keep the blood flowing and the body moving.

In the Chinese alchemical system (related to Taoism), seven metals are specifically emphasized: iron, copper, silver, tin, gold, mercury, and lead. Each represents a particular stage in the development of humanity. Each corresponds to a planet, having specific astrological correspondences (see the following chart). Planetary associations with metals came about entirely as a result of the development of alchemical sciences. The symbolism of "seven" is reflected in the Western seven-point star called the septagram, and in the traditional Hermetic hexagram, wherein six planets represent each point of the symbol with Sun resting in the center. The number seven is also significant in the Hindu chakra system, as the body contains seven main "light wheel" energetic vortexes along the spine.

Additional Pointers on Magickal Jewelry

When searching for jewelry, or crafting it oneself, one must be mindful of the piece in both a magickal sense and a physical sense. Magical jewelry should be an extension of the practitioner's internal spiritual being. Not only is a piece's symbolism significant, but its physical origin and placement on the body are of additional importance.

Sadly, due to corporatism, the majority of jewelry is mass-manufactured overseas. Most of these pieces are made of tin, pewter, or reconstituted silver. These kinds of metals hold a low concentration of energy, causing them to be more difficult to enchant or imbue with magickal properties. Though the price of "real" metal may be considerably higher than the mass-produced, it is magickally worth it in the long run, not to mention the aesthetic beauty that "real" metal holds. Naturally, handmade pieces hold more sentimental and actual value, even if the wearer does not personally know the creator. Each handmade piece is unique and can both conduct and hold a greater capacity of personal energy.

Please be a good Witch by asking about the source (supplier) for the gemstones and crystals you wear; if stones are not ethically mined, whether in terms of the ecosystem or the human labor involved, they won't carry good vibes for you or anyone else.

Jewelry should not be worn nonchalantly. I believe the wearer should have a good amount of knowledge about the symbol they bear and should carry personal sentiments for the piece. Far too many people walk around with flashy symbols while completely unaware of their meanings. And don't even get me started on tattoos!

In addition to having a personal connection to the symbolism of the jewelry, one should always be aware of the reaction it evokes from onlookers. How does the symbol affect other people; what emotions does it have the potential to bring about in the viewer based on what it might represent to them? Perhaps a Baphomet pendant or Seal of Saturn isn't the best piece to wear to the dentist's office or a parent-teacher conference.

Any item added to the body naturally influences the body's energetic flow. Metals have specific properties that can either inhibit or increase the energetic flow in the area in which it is worn. If a piece is worn near a chakra or bodily energy vortex, effects are sure to follow. The placement of magickal jewelry is of great importance…which brings us to this list!

RINGS

Fashioned as a perfect circle, the ring represents eternity, reincarnation, and the cycles of the Universe. It acts as a smaller representation of the magician or Witches' sacred circle. Because of the ring's shape, magickal energy flows very well through it when it's charged. Its smoothness symbolizes the smoothness of dancing life in all its cycles.

The ring has long been associated with love. It is a symbol of unity in marriage and handfasting ceremonies, solidifying the connectedness between individuals and the influence of the Divine in the ceremony. The ring is placed on the third finger of the left hand, which was once believed to have a vein or nerve in it connecting to the heart. This was actually a misunderstanding but was believed to be true by the Egyptians, then later adopted by the Greeks and finally by Europeans.

Rings can be imbued with any purpose the wearer desires. Because they sit directly on the flesh, the energy of the charged ring has a constant connection with the body. Rings worn on the projecting hand (the hand you write with) should be imbued with properties you wish to project to others, such as healing, awareness, peace, and so forth. Rings worn on the receiving hand should be imbued with properties you wish to invite into yourself. For some wearers, the finger on which the ring is worn is of extreme importance. Traditional Hermetic elemental attributions are as such:

> THUMB: Water
> POINTER: Fire
> MIDDLE: Spirit
> RING: Earth
> PINKY: Air

We can also channel the elements through the fingers when inviting them into ritual space. In some modern traditions, the associations between the ring finger and the thumb are switched.

This actually makes more sense to me than the former, considering that the thumb is more solid or earthy, and the ring finger is more undulant or watery. I do believe that the finger best associated with Spirit is the middle because it's the longest of the five. As my Georgian Priestess Zanoni Silverknife taught me years ago, think twice before flipping someone off…your spirit may be open for anyone to grab!

NECKLACES

Necklaces are a part of every culture and are included in many popular myths. A necklace called *Brisingamen* was worn by the goddess Freyja in Norse mythology. This necklace was made of gold, created by dwarfs, and was associated with the ability to bring out the beauty of the wearer. The enchanted necklace was later stolen by the trickster deity Loki—go figure!

A necklace surrounds the wearer with the energy of the piece, intertwining its essence with that of the wearer throughout the day. This is one reason the jewelry worn should be chosen with care! Necklaces can hang at the throat or heart chakra area. Therefore, such pieces work with energies of each: The heart chakra is green in ethereal color and contains the vibratory qualities of love, compassion, empathy, and understanding. The throat chakra is blue in color, connected to energies of communication and self-worth. The jewelry worn on each chakra point can be attuned directly to these associations, or it can simply carry its own magickal charge and use these chakra points as an entryway into the energy body.

BRACELETS

Fashioned in a circular form, bracelets hold similar properties to rings. Wearing empowered bracelets on each wrist is extremely effective for imbuing the magician with particular vibrations, either balancing one's energy or attuning it to an intended purpose. For this reason, bracelets are especially good for magick of a self-transformative nature. Bracelets made of gemstones or a series of threaded stones can be highly charged with magickal associations appropriate to the mineral. Metal bracelets carry many associations, as described in the list of metals to follow, while magnetic bracelets are reserved for a specific energy healing practice called magnotherapy.

EARRINGS

Ear piercings were once thought to guard against disease, head pain, and "sinful words." Considering that I currently have twenty ear piercings, I can't exactly vouch for the validity of that last part! (Still, each piercing is imbued with magickal intention, and some of the pieces are gemstones rather than just sterling silver.) Because earrings in pairs are oftentimes worn on opposite sides of the head, they may be empowered with balance and equilibrium. Throughout the day, energies bounce from one earring to the other and thus through the head and upper chakras. If enchanted as magickal polarities, earrings can lend an extreme amount of power to the wearer, especially if the symbolism, structure, and content of the pieces are considered.

CROWNS

Without a doubt, ceremonial crowns are *absolutely fabulous*. They are most commonly worn by women because of their historic usage. Witches who are women often prefer crescent moons on their crowns, while men often prefer pentagrams and God-horns in ritual. In traditional Wicca, the Coven's Priest and Priestess wear crowns symbolizing a direct link to the gods. Most crowns are made of sterling silver; the well-made ones tend to be fairly pricey. If the Lady chooses to wear her ceremonial crown outside of circle, she best be prepared to live in magickal consciousness the whole day through, standing strong and spiritually aware as a Priestess of the Goddess. Some people wear tiaras and crowns non-ceremonially, for fashion's sake; this is simply for decoration, but as with all jewelry, it may be used to top off an enchanting outfit.

Magickal Properties of Metals

I have always seen molded metal (including jewelry) as corresponding to both the elements Earth and Fire, regardless of the type. Metal is a natural substance that is melted, molded, and formed into shape through a process involving extreme heat from fire. The element Earth represents strength, grounding, and Gaia-connection. It is the rational and logical portion of the human psyche. Fire represents passion, motivation, and strength. Its flame is a guiding light to spiritual awakening. Beyond the concept of Earth-Fire connectedness, the various metals also correspond to different elemental properties that distinguish their unique energetic currents. Metal jewelry may be worn to draw upon Earth and Fire alone, or magickally worked upon to fine-tune the specific qualities of the individual metal.

The following is a list of generally recognized associations for various types of metals. I invite readers to reference this list when purchasing or creating metallic jewelry and other metallic items designed to be utilized in ritual.

METAL: ALUMINUM

PERIODIC: 13: Al, 26.981538
PLANET: Mercury
ELEMENT: Air
GENDER: Masculine
VIBRATION: Medium
MAGICKAL USES: Mental Powers, Strengthening Spells, Travel (See also Mercury)
NOTES: Aluminum foil can be used in sympathetic magick to fashion shapes and items. Aluminum is a great substitute for the lethal substance mercury (quicksilver), or any silver metal in a pinch. Aluminum is a great conductor of electricity as well as magickal energy. It can be placed on the altar to invoke celestial vibrations or fashioned into a particular shape—such as a moon, sun, or planetary symbol—to draw specific energies to the ritual space. This is a fun activity for young Pagans to take part in and can also be a lighthearted group project.

METAL: BRASS

PERIODIC: N/A
PLANET: Sun
ELEMENT: Fire
GENDER: Male
VIBRATION: High
MAGICKAL USES: Deflecting Harm, Fire Magick, Healing, Love, Luck, Mental Powers, Money, Protection (See also Copper)
NOTES: Brass is a much less costly substitute for gold; it is an alloy of copper, zinc, and other metals. It's still attuned to solar energy but has less strength than gold. Ringing brass bells or vibrating brass singing-bowls emits cleansing vibrations to an area—also attracting prosperity and good fortune, according to Eastern mysticism. Brass is used in defense and protection spells, surrounding the user with its shielding energy.

METAL: BRONZE

PERIODIC: N/A
PLANET: Venus & Jupiter
ELEMENT: Air & Water
GENDER: Masculine & Feminine
VIBRATION: Medium-High
MAGICKAL USES: See Copper & Tin
NOTES: Bronze is a mixture of copper and tin. It vibrates to properties of both metals and can be used when either or both are desired in spellcraft.

METAL: COPPER

PERIODIC: 29: Cu, 63.546
PLANET: Venus
ELEMENT: Water
GENDER: Feminine
VIBRATION: Medium-High
MAGICKAL USES: Amplifying Energy, Balance, Beauty, Calming, Clarity, Compassion, Conducting Energy, Confidence,

Cooperation, Creativity, Divination, Emotions, Empathy, Fire Magick, Friendship, Harmony, Healing, Intuition, Love, Luck, Lust, Money, Motivation, Newness, Passion, Physical Health, Pleasure, Preventing Illness, Prosperity, Psychic Development, Sexuality, Sociability, Strengthening Spells, Sustenance, Unity

NOTES: The Roman goddess Venus is akin to the Teutonic goddess Freyja and the Greek Aphrodite, the goddess of beauty and love. Copper is used to attune to her energies and influence. It also holds significance to solar deities and provides a reliable channel for their energies.

The energy of Venus is attuned to anything of personal value or worth. Copper can assist us in attracting what we desire in life. Copper is also used in love magick, which can be very risky business if not executed properly. Life's priorities must be in place before working Venusian magick.

Copper wands are excellent tools to focus and direct magick. You can also wrap handmade wands in copper wire to more powerfully conduct energy. Cooper wands should be reserved for very meaningful workings, as the metal is a conduit between the mind and spirit. It is also one of the most healing of metals, used throughout many cultures to assist in curative techniques like relieving pain. Additionally, copper is said to attract finances and material wealth, and used to be fashioned into scrying bowls for divinatory work.

Copper's energy is that of self-love and self-confidence. The metal is a motivator and exciter of personal power. It allows the user to see with more clarity and assurance, helping the user more easily identify personal barriers and developmental hang-ups.

METAL: GOLD

PERIODIC: 79: Au, 196.96655
PLANET: Sun
ELEMENT: Fire
GENDER: Masculine
VIBRATION: High
MAGICKAL USES: Acceptance, Affirmation, Art, Assertion, Balance, Calming, Courage, Creativity, Dedication, Direction, Energy, Esteem, God Invocation, Guidance, Happiness, Healing, Health,

Individuality, Inspiration, Life Choices, Male Mysteries, Mental Powers, Money, Power, Prosperity, Protection, Purification, Realization, Rebirth, Satisfaction, Seasonal Connectedness, Self-Awareness, Spiritual Direction, Strength, Study, Success, Wisdom

NOTES: As a "planet," the Sun rules the metal gold first and foremost, also having lesser influence on different golden-colored metals. Pyrite or fool's gold (not on this list) is the best substitute for gold in magick, as it is often found alongside gold underground. Brass and copper are also viable substitutes because of their color. Gold is considered to be the most magickally potent metal of them all, as it has many uses and adds a boost of power to any working. Also, its protective qualities are valued in many cultures, and it is worn on the body to both strengthen the aura and invite spiritual protection. Gold's energy is soothing, helping to calm anger, increase clarity, and cultivate optimism. It works its magick particularly on the mental plane, which is associated with learning, understanding, and comprehension. Cosmically, only gold and platinum were created as the result of the blinding flash of light known as a supernova: the death of a star.

As I mentioned, other metals similar in color may be substituted for actual gold. Adding a speck of real gold to a spell can, however, work wonders! In some ancient esoteric orders, gold was the highest substance one could offer the gods. It represents purity and spiritual strength, serving as a magickally versatile substance. Gold is the traditional metal of the High Priest, who wears it in circle to invoke the strength and wisdom of the Solar God. Numerous holy sculptures and temples throughout the world are also fashioned specifically with gold.

METAL: IRON

PERIODIC: 26: Fe, 55.8457
PLANET: Mars
ELEMENT: Fire
GENDER: Masculine
VIBRATION: Low
MAGICKAL USES: Action, Aggression, Balance, Change, Chaos, Courage, Cursing, Deflecting Harm, Determination, Emotional

Control, Extraterrestrial Communication, Faerie Magick, Facing Challenges, Grounding, Healing, Instincts, Justice, Motivation, Physical Health, Protection, Pursuance, Releasing Anger, Sexuality, Strength, Strengthening Spells, Success, Wealth, Willpower

NOTES: Iron can be used for physical health and healing. It is also a "kicker," adding an extra boost to spells. When utilized properly, Mars's energy magnifies intention. However, beware of possibly shutting off your psychic centers with its use, as shutting off your energetic receptivity is not recommended unless a situation is extreme.

One can even use a kitchen knife to imbue a spell with Mars energy—but don't use the knife again in the kitchen, as the Mars attunement can make it susceptible to random finger slicing! Mars rules iron and therefore rules blood. Mars is red, rust is red, and blood is red: all significant similarities when Mars's warring energy is considered. Ancient Greeks actually banned the use of iron in temples and sacred sites, knowing its power to attract warlike energy. Rather, it was reserved for purely physical and industrial work for its material strength. It is considered by some to be the "darkest" and most dangerous metal, so its use in modern time must be particularly well thought out. Some Pagans, especially those of a Greek persuasion, still refuse to incorporate any iron in ritual or allow its presence into sacred space. Whether or not these ideas are superstitious, Mars's energy is oftentimes difficult to conduct or control regardless. I must give fair warning not to use iron in magick when feeling aggression or anger because the results could be harsher than originally intended.

Conversely, iron may be the best metal for protection if utilized properly. It has long been used to deflect "polluting" vibrations such as death, plagues, sickness, and psychic attack. Iron wands may be used to combat harmful entities and spirits, as iron is a powerful conductor whose energy, like silver, easily affects the unseen planes. Iron has also been used in the past to protect against malevolent faeries or ghosts, as well as for interdimensional and extraterrestrial communication.

An easy and fun way to incorporate Mars's protective energy into practical magick is to form what is called a Mars Jar. Simply take a real iron nail (not silver or steel) and a clear, empty bottle. Fill it with water and plop in the nail. It will slowly rust in the jar, dissolving bit by bit, transforming the water into an amber-colored potion. The jar may be placed in a windowsill to absorb moonlight and sunlight. Various herbs, seeds, and stones can be added to the mixture for a boost of protection. Needless to say, please don't drink it to absorb the protection; the effects would be quite the opposite.

METAL: LEAD

PERIODIC: 82: Pb, 207.2
PLANET: Saturn
ELEMENT: Earth
GENDER: Masculine & Feminine
VIBRATION: Low
MAGICKAL USES: Ambition, Banishing, Binding, Boundaries, Business, Change, Chaos, Cleansing, Cursing, Death Magick, Deflecting Harm, Discipline, Divination, Exorcism, Fear-Based Issues, Freedom, Grounding, Habit-Breaking, Healing, Introspection, Introversion, Legal Issues, Magickal Petitions, Materialism, Meditation, Necromancy, New Beginnings, Past-Life Regression, Protection, Receiving, Recurring Cycles, Releasing, Restrictions & Freedoms, Self-Control, Stability, Strengthening Spells, Thaumaturgy, Transformation, Wishes
NOTES: Lead is attuned to Saturn's energy and can be used for both banishing and receiving. Saturn brings form to ideas, ruling the physical realm. Bringing about change in the physical realm through magickal means is called thaumaturgy, a term sometimes referenced in ceremonial magick. Lead is great to use in manifestation and for bringing ideas to physical fruition. Its results tend to be long-lasting rather than fleeting, so be sure to use it for important things like long-term healing and protection.

Lead strengthens spells and is used to usher in new beginnings associated with personal change. Lead is great for Coven work, as its energy helps solidify the connectedness of the members, serving to illuminate the greater goals of the group. Perhaps a Coven could share a lead wand or athamé among members, or pass the metal around during a meditation or chant. Keep in mind that lead is poisonous to the human system, so work with the metal carefully. An ideal substitute for lead in minor spells is graphite: pencil "lead."

Lead was formerly used to manufacture coffins and caskets; they were generally reserved for the burials of religious leaders and, of course, the elite. It was used as such for superstitious reasons, believing that harmful spirits (including worms) could not penetrate the substance and potentially desecrate the corpse or the soul of the buried. As a result, the metal gained associations with death and spiritual protection.

Hundreds of *defixiones* ("curse tablets") have been discovered in burial grounds in specific areas of the early Mediterranean world. Most defixiones are made of lead. There are various reasons for this occurrence, including the metal's durability and availability at the time. The discovery of these written spells solidified the knowledge that magick was practiced regularly in classical antiquity.

METAL: MERCURY (QUICKSILVER)

PERIODIC: 80: Hg, 200.59
PLANET: Mercury
ELEMENT: Earth, Air & Water
GENDER: Feminine
VIBRATION: High
MAGICKAL USES: Agility, Astral Projection, Balance, Beauty, Change, Clairvoyance, Communication, Contemplation, Death, Divination, Dreaming, Intellect, Learning, Luck, Mental Powers, Prioritizing, Realizations, Strengthening Spells, Study, Travel
NOTES: Mercury is both the "trickster" and the voyager between the worlds. The liquid metal quicksilver, now known as mercury, "tricks" us with its stunningly beautiful appearance, but is quite deadly in

actuality. It's poisonous to touch, breathe, or ingest, but not to look at! Some Witches call quicksilver the "belladonna of the mineral kingdom" for this reason. Numerous early alchemists experimented in depth with mercury, unaware of its toxic properties. This hands-on approach caused serious brain damage over time as the substance seeped through the skin, and was the reason so many alchemists are documented as going mad at some point in their lives.

The Roman god Mercury, also known as Hermes in Greek, is akin to both the Egyptian Thoth and the Teutonic (Norse) Loki. He functions similarly to Coyote medicine in Native American traditions, and his energy is influential to quicksilver. Also, the planet Mercury is the closest to the sun and is the quickest moving. Quicksilver or a substitute metal can help project intention to the Universe and add a quickening boost.

Rather than trying to track down the liquid mercury, you can use one of the many of valid substitutes, the best being aluminum. You can also invoke the essence of mercury by drawing the planetary sigil on parchment/aluminum foil, on yourself, or on candles. You must then align your energy with its properties. I would recommend doing additional research on its properties before attempting this. Please don't use mercury in ritual. No, seriously.

METAL: PEWTER

PERIODIC: N/A
PLANET: Venus & Jupiter
ELEMENT: Water & Air
GENDER: Feminine & Masculine
VIBRATION: Medium
MAGICKAL USES: See Copper & Tin
NOTES: Pewter is a common metal for pendants, but not so much in magickal use. It actually carries minor properties of copper and tin, as it is a combination of the two with antimony added. Pewter is a fairly weak material, making it somewhat difficult to harness energy. For pewter's magickal properties, see the similarities between copper and tin and decide how to utilize it from there.

METAL: PLATINUM

PERIODIC: 78: Pt, 195.078
PLANET: Moon
ELEMENT: Water
GENDER: Feminine
VIBRATION: High
MAGICKAL USES: Abundance, Balance, Channeling, Communication, Friendship, Growth, Health, Hope, Intuition, Love, Materialism, Memory, Mental Powers, Money, Optimism, Psychic Powers, Sustenance, Transformation, Upperworld Communication (See also Iron)
NOTES: Platinum is called "white gold" and is an expensive form of iron. It takes ten tons of iron ore to produce one ounce of platinum! It is valued for its rarity and the fact that it never rusts nor tarnishes. Three-thousand-year-old Egyptian tombs have been discovered with platinum hieroglyphics still in perfect condition. Platinum is relatively rare and pricey, and can be used to align to the Higher Self, as the substance itself is a "high" product of iron. It can also be used to align both the physical and energetic bodies, as well as to strengthen intuitive powers.

Cosmically, only platinum and gold were created as the result of the blinding flash of light known as a supernova: the death of a star.

METAL: SILVER

PERIODIC: 47: Ag, 107.8682
PLANET: Moon
ELEMENT: Water
GENDER: Feminine
VIBRATION: High
MAGICKAL USES: Acceptance, Alignment, Art, Astral Projection, Balance, Beauty, Care, Communication, Dance, Divination, Dreaming, Eloquence, Empathy, Female Mysteries, Fertility, Gardening, Goddess Invocation, Guidance, Healing, Hope, Inspiration, Intuition, Love, Lunar Attunement, Meditation, Menstrual Attunement, Money, Night Magick, Nourishment,

Nurturing, Optimism, Peace, Personality, Prosperity, Protection, Psychic Powers, Purity, Self-Reflection, Sensitivity, Study, Travel, Wealth

Notes: Silver is ruled by the "planet" Moon, which influences the soul's emotional centers. It guides intuition and helps us understand the necessary balance of nighttime, as well as the necessity of introspection. As Lady Luna shines visibly at night, silver's influence is Otherworldly, mysterious, and connected to sleep and dreaming. It helps in projecting the magician's energy to the subtle realms, aiding in trance-work, meditation, and easing into a transcendental frame of mind. Silver is probably the best metal to utilize for psychic and divination-based skills. Just wearing the metal alters a person's energy field, making them more receptive to psychic energy and insight. It is also believed to help clarify communication and allow for eloquence in speech.

Silver is the traditional metal of the High Priestess. She wears it to invoke the ageless wisdom of the Lunar Goddess and to align herself with her guidance. It is also the traditional metal of the buckles on a Witch's garter, along with other ceremonial bigghes like charms, rings, and crowns.

Incorporating silver into your life is a great way to honor the gods and declare your dedication to working magick on the inner planes. It is rare to find a modern Witch who does not use silver as a predominant metal. This is because of its lunar attribution, something Witches holds in high regard, especially those of us who are drawn to darkness and nocturnal energy.

The most common magickal use of silver is by way of sterling silver pendants, talismans, and piercing jewelry. Silver holds particularly strong power at the Full Moon and is wonderful to wear in Esbats. A silver wand is quite useful in working with (or even against) unseen forces because of its ability to conduct both physical and metaphysical energy. Silver is easy to imbue with a desired magickal intent because the mineral is naturally receptive and absorptive. For this reason, be careful not to expose silver to unhealthy vibrations. If you are wearing a silver pendant, I advise tucking it under your shirt if you happen to encounter any adverse situations or surrounding energies.

METAL: STEEL

PERIODIC: N/A
PLANET: Mars
ELEMENT: Fire
GENDER: Masculine
VIBRATION: Low
MAGICKAL USES: Deflecting Harm, Divination, Dream Protection, Grounding, Healing, Protection, Stability (See also Iron)
NOTES: Steel is a relatively new metal. It is a modification of wrought iron and/or cast iron, and is constructed for strength and durability. Therefore, it holds similar properties to iron but is not as powerful when used magickally.

Steel's main attribute is protection, and its success has been documented by many. It may also be used sympathetically to provide strength or endurance to a situation, or to add projective energy to a spell.

A great way to incorporate steel into a spell is to use a can. Nearly all "tin cans" are made of steel nowadays, as they are more environmentally friendly than tin. One can use a steel can as a burning bowl for parchment petitions and written spells. They can also be filled with metaphysical herbs and stones. Seal the can with appropriately colored candle wax and decorate it with marker-drawn symbols.

METAL: TIN

PERIODIC: 50: Sn, 118.710
PLANET: Jupiter
ELEMENT: Air
GENDER: Masculine
VIBRATION: Medium
MAGICKAL USES: Abundance, Balance, Creativity, Divination, Expansiveness, Generosity, Growth, Healing, Health, Hope, Ideas, Intuition, Justice, Learning, Love, Luck, Mental Powers, Money, Opportunities, Philosophy, Prosperity, Spiritual Awareness, Success, Travel, Wisdom
NOTES: Jupiter rules tin, which can help in self-expression and the clarification of ideas. Jupiter embodies generosity and patronage,

yet is also the idealist; using too much of its energy can lead to only temporary satisfaction. The Roman god "King" Jupiter (Zeus in Greek) is named after the largest planet in our solar system with good reason! The planet's influence is grandiose and powerful, passionate and motivated. Tin is a great metal for divination and psychic work, assisting in clearing of the mind.

DIVINATION: READING THE SIGNS

Divination…what a wonderful, mysterious practice. The purpose of divination is to gain metaphysical prophecy and insight through the act of scrying or analyzing certain physical objects or occurrences. Throughout history, some sort of divination has been practiced by most cultures and virtually all religions. This is especially understandable for animistic cultures, as the manifest plane is so often revered as a reflection of the spiritual plane or as a construction of spiritual forces. It only makes sense that the Divine would deliver messages to us through the medium of our immediately perceived reality. As a magickal practice, tool-based divination is "external" in that we observe signs and symbols outside of ourselves, relying on our own perception of the external environment.

Thousands of books that discuss divinatory practices are available, and many more focus specifically on one type of divination, the most popular methods being Tarot cards, astrological readings, and dream interpretation, closely followed by runes, palmistry, crystal ball scrying, geomancy, tea leaf reading, the use of spirit boards such as Ouija, and the pendulum. So, instead of repeating information that most readers have already encountered, I present a list of divinatory methods that are now considered archaic—maybe you'd like to experiment with some!

Obscure Methods of Divination

Listed here are some more archaic methods of divination. I include them mostly for curiosity's sake, since few of them are practiced nowadays, but this list can also serve as a reference for those wishing to expand and experiment with their divinatory practices. Because we can use virtually any medium that is remotely open to interpretation, I hope this list inspires readers to reach creatively into the subtle planes for answers and insight. I must warn you: some of the historical methods of divination are absolutely hysterical in a modern context!

AEROMANCY: Gazing at the clouds and interpreting their shapes

ALECTRYOMANCY: Having a rooster strategically peck grains of food placed on letters of the alphabet

ALEUROMANCY: Divining messages through flour or baked goods, as with fortune cookies!

ALOMANCY: Divination by way of throwing salt and observing the resulting shapes

AMNIOMANCY: Scrying in the caul around a child at birth (this happens rarely and is said to be a magickal omen)

ANTHROPOMANCY: Examining a person's intestines; also called *hepatoscopy*

APANTOMANCY: Paying attention to random signs from the Universe

ARITHMANCY: Reading the significance of numbers; also called *numerology*

ASPIDOMANCY: Trancelike oracular divination performed in a magick circle

ASTRAGALOMANCY: Examining the knucklebones; this can accompany *palmistry*

BELOMANCY: Observing the placement of (fallen?) arrows

BIBLIOMANCY: Divination by using a book, such as pricking it with a needle and reading the punctured words for prophecy, or simply opening a book to a random paragraph

CAPNOMANCY: Gazing at the smoke of a fire

CARTOMANCY: Divining with cards, such as the *Tarot*

CARTOPEDY: Reading patterns on the feet; similar to *palmistry*

CATOPTROMANCY: Gazing in a mirror (such as a black scrying mirror)

CAUSIMOMANCY: Throwing an object into a fire in order to answer a yes-or-no question based on whether or not it burns

CEPHALOMANCY: Divination by means of a donkey's head

CERAUNOSCOPY: Observing weather phenomena

CEROMANCY: Analyzing patterns in melted wax dripped on a flat surface

CHIROMANCY: Examining the lines and shapes of the hands; also called *palmistry*

CLEDONOMANCY: Observing the significance of random things people say

CLEIDOMANCY: Observing a string-suspended key, similar to *pendulum* divination
CLEROMANCY: Throwing runes, dice, or similar items
CROMNIOMANCY: Divination in onions
DACTYLOMANCY: Divination with finger rings
DAPHNOMANCY: Divination with twigs from the laurel tree, especially burning in a fire
EMPYROMANCY: Interpreting the char marks on an object that has been burned in a fire
GELOSCOPY: Observing the pattern of a person's laughter
GYROMANCY: Blindly walking in a chalk-drawn circle and noting the location at which you have stopped
HIPPHOMANCY: Observing the pace of horses
HOROSCOPY: Divination by means of the stars and planetary configurations; also called *astrology*
HYDROMANCY: Gazing in a body of water
ICHTHYOMANCY: Examining the intestines of a dead fish
LAMPADOMANCY: Observing an oil lamp (common in Egypt and Greece)
LECANOMANCY: Throwing stones into water and observing the effects
LIBANOMANCY: Gazing at the smoke of incense
LITHOMANCY: Reflecting on stones, especially precious minerals
LYCHNOMANCY: Gazing at the flame of a candle or lamp
MARGARITOMANCY: Divination in a pearl; unrelated to margarita drinks (unfortunately)
METOPOSCOPY: Examining lines on a person's forehead
MOLYBDOMANCY: Dropping melted metal into water, particularly lead
MYOMANCY: Divination by means of rats and mice
NECROMANCY: Divination or communication with the dead (see chapter VI)
NECYOMANCY: Examining the nervous system of a dead person or animal
OINOMANCY: Divination in wine
OLOLYGMANCY: Paying attention to the howling of dogs and wolves
OMPHALOMANCY: Divination by the navel or belly-button
ONEIROMANCY: Interpreting the symbolism of dreams
ONOMANCY: Interpreting the letters in a person's name; similar to forms of *numerology*

ONYCHOMANCY: Interpreting the pattern of reflection of the sun's rays on a person's fingernails; can accompany *palmistry*
OOSCOPY: Observing the pattern of eggs that have been burst in a fire
OPHIOMANCY: Observing the movement or pattern of snakes
ORNITHOMANCY: Observing the pattern of birds' flight
OVOMANCY: Divination in eggs
PESSOMANCY: Divination using beans
PHRENOLOGY: Reading the bumps on or shape of the skull; once considered a science in the Victorian era but is now considered obsolete
PHYLLORHODOMANCY: Divination by using rose petals and leaves; Greek in origin
PHYSIOGNOMY: Interpreting features of the face
PSYCHOMANCY: Conjuring departed spirits; similar to NECROMANCY
PYROMANCY: Gazing into fire
RHABDOMANCY: Divination with sticks or rods to discover hidden objects or caches of precious substances; also called *dowsing*
RHAPSODOMANCY: Opening a poet's work at random and interpreting meaning from the words; a form of *bibliomancy*
SANGOMANCY: Divination by way of blood
SIDEROMANCY: Throwing straws on a hot iron
SPHONDULOMANCY: Divination in spindles
STOLISOMANCY: Observing a person's manner of dress
TASSEOMANCY: Interpreting the shape of tea leaves remaining in a cup
TEPHROMANCY: Divination in ashes
TIROMANCY: Divination in cheese
XYLOMANCY: Observing the pattern of thrown sticks or staves

Chapter Three
The Astral Shadow

"The Horned God, so often associated with shamanism, not only illuminates Nature for us but also opens our eyes to the shamanic realms. Even Hades can be said to illuminate the world of the dead."

—Michael Alexandra Davida (Magdalena Merovingia)
from *Dominus Satánas, the Other Son of God: Rethinking the Bad Boy of the Cosmos*

ASTRAL TRAVEL & SOUL RETRIEVAL

The web of life is profoundly mysterious. Every intention, thought, prayer, and act of magick travels at will along this web. It connects every astral plane, physical location, thought, emotion, and, well, everything—period. It is nonphysical, of course, existing outside the boundaries of normal human perception. The appearance of separateness between people, objects, items, and thoughtforms is the veil of illusion, known in Buddhism as *maya*. The great web exists beyond this illusion. This astral web, both infinite and etheric, is the true shadow of the dimension in which we find ourselves incarnate.

In ritual, we enter a sacred space between the physical plane and the Otherworld. This Otherworld is very much connected with the ordinary waking realm, yet it remains separate in everyday life because of the separation of ego and the Higher Self. Though interconnectedness is so often veiled, spiritual paths rooted in shamanic practices, such as Neopagan paths, understand that no portion of life is isolated from the next. Think of a place and your energy is immediately transported there. Visualize someone and you've aligned with their energy pattern. The web interconnects "this" to "that," and it's through this web that astral travel is possible. Among Pagans, it's often accepted that the astral plane and physical plane were much closer together at one time, but grew farther apart as ignorance and intolerance began infecting the masses. Many of the realities seen in times past became buried and avoided as the vibration of fear overtook the common minds of subsequent generations.

Quantum physics recognizes the fact that all atoms making up physical reality are in a constant state of vibration. They are constantly moving—slow or fast—showing that nothing is truly solid; all matter is made of atoms condensed at different vibratory rates. It has been discovered that the entire atom, from the electrons to the nucleus, is constantly jumping in and out of reality. The particles exist, disappear, and return to the physical plane constantly. Where do they go?

Though I'm not an expert in quantum mechanics, my supposition is that the particles enter the astral plane—parallel with our reality, yet invisible to our physical eyes. If this is to be believed, an exact imprint of our physical reality exists on the astral, alongside exclusively astral matter. Many astral travelers note the visibility of the physical plane when seeing with "astral sight." The objects exist as real (or unreal) figures on the astral, just as they do on the physical. Because the astral is formed through thought and intention, these physical imprints are also mutable. The mind shapes the astral and determines the astral experience. The plane itself is a collection of thoughts and is constantly changing form. Physical laws don't necessarily apply to the subtle realms, and the traveler is unrestricted as with mortal existence. Both physics and metaphysics confirm the existence of additional dimensions, which adds to the validity of the astral plane, which, itself, may actually be a collection of planes and dimensions.

The astral is the plane on which emotion, imagination, and thought exist. The astral is the realm of pure unconsciousness. Dreaming exists on the astral as co-created by the mind. Visionary experiences and the effects of many drugs tap into the astral realm as well. The occult philosopher Éliphas Lévi theorized that all magickal energy is composed of "astral light," and this ethereal matter is the essence of the subtle realms. Writer and magician John

Michael Greer describes the astral realm as existing between the timespace-restricted physical/etheric planes and the timeless and spaceless mental/spiritual planes. This is one of the most concise descriptions I have found. It must still be kept in mind that many branches of occultism characterize the etheric, physical, mental, and spiritual planes as all interwoven, so the divisions between them may go only so far as one's own perception of them.

The astral plane has various levels and layers; some say the levels are infinite, which makes perfect sense considering the infinite nature of the mind and cosmos. With proper focus, planes that have been previously created may be accessed and new ones may be formed. Many magicians and Witches actually create personal "Lodges" in the astral plane, which they can later access to perform magick from that location; many have found it just as effective as performing magick on the physical plane. At the same time, however, when magick is performed on the physical plane it is identically performed on the astral. When energy is worked within ritual, its essence is drawn from the astral. This idea holds true for anyone who casts spells with actual intention, not simply going through the motions of blending herbs, stones, candles, and the like.

The astral plane is believed to house a variety of beings, including departed spirits, thoughtforms, larvæ, spirit guides, animal guides, astral "floaters," scavengers, faeries, elementals, dragons, shapeshifters, and a wide array of other ethereal residents, including creatures mythologized in many cultures. These beings may be contacted on the astral journey. Some are vibrationally restricted to a single form, though most can shapeshift at will. The form in which they choose to appear to the astral voyager is up to the being itself, which usually knows the best guise under which to approach the seeker.

Friends and magickal partners can meet in the astral plane if the appropriate time and place are secured. The two people must energetically link beforehand. They can talk on the phone or in person just before the projection to exchange vibrations, then reconnect moments later on the astral. If the two are very close, it will be easier to connect. If either is new to astral projection, the experience will take time and practice to become more real. When they project simultaneously, the two can shapeshift together, travel side by side, and journey to distant territories. If the two are also next to each other physically or on the phone, short sentences can be spoken if telepathy isn't a viable option, so long as brief speaking doesn't break the trance or bring one back to the body.

Various teas, spells, sigils, and focal exercises can help achieve astral projection for those to whom the ability doesn't come naturally. Experiment with various methods and find what works best you. The first plane you perceive is sure to be the mental plane, where thoughts run rampant. Though it's tough at first to distinguish between the thought plane and the astral, know that one builds on the next and that they're closer together than they may seem.

Before attempting astral projection, ensure that proper protection is in place. Evils exist just as much on the astral plane as they do on this one. The only difference is, instead of hurting you physically, they can sap your energy—and this can be just as devastating! Many people fear leaving the body. This unconscious fear is rooted in the fear of losing control of the physical body and even opening it up to harm if it is left behind. If astral projection is approached as similar to sleeping, it will be understood that the body is in no greater danger than it is every night. For detailed information on achieving astral projection, I highly recommend the following books (also listed in the bibliography):

- *Initiation into Hermetics* by Franz Bardon
- *Soul Flight: Astral Projection & the Magical Universe* by Donald Tyson
- *Mastering Astral Projection* by Robert Bruce & Brian Mercer

Ritual Meditation: Shamanic Soul Retrieval

The levels and layers beyond our immediate reality hold a special place for Witches and magicians, especially those of a darker flavor. Connecting to alternate levels of reality is a form of shadow magick. Those who use magick in their spiritual path regularly work with what is hidden from our usual view, that which is obscured in darkness.

As we know, the shadow manifests in a multitude of forms. The subtle planes lie beyond our usual sensory experience, yet they make up our very existence. We interact constantly with the subtle realms but may not recognize we're doing so. It can even be said that our minds and emotions exist on other layers of reality (mostly because they are nonphysical) and, in many ways, these are what make up the astral. Magick that deals directly with these layers and levels of reality is itself shadow magick. Its practitioners tend to concur that one manifestation of shadow-work is the act of journeying into the darkness, much as the shaman travels to the Underworld (or Lower world) to return with a pure diamond of light that manifests as knowledge and healing. Shamans across the globe have numerous similarities; such a role is found in virtually all tribal cultures. Unsurprisingly, their methodologies are often quite similar.

Shamanic soul retrieval is one of these common tribal practices. It is simply one of the duties of the shaman, a type of ritual community service that has been venerated for ages. In the following meditation, we can draw on this practice ourselves. Witches and magicians with tribal or shamanic inclinations can practice it, whether or not they fully identify as walking a shamanic path. In our eclectic culture, it only makes sense that we experience the rites and rituals of others. Not to mention that Witchcraft is heavily rooted in tribalism and shamanic practice, so rituals of this type can be easily blended with modern magick.

When we experience trauma, a portion of the soul (or "a soul" as it's often called) flees from our psyche with the fear that the self cannot continue to function properly if its presence remains. We thus become spiritually fractured…damaged. "Fight or flight" are two psychological responses to extreme experience, and the "flight" response is both the easiest and most comforting way to deal with a situation. However, avoiding something for an extended period of time can slowly and subtly cause harm, feeding on the vital energy of the "healthy" soul body, aching for some sort of acknowledgment or resolution.

When a piece of us is fractured, our perception is altered. We may feel a sense of emptiness or uncertainty about life in general. There seems to be a void…but we can't put our finger on it. We may be physically ill or at a loss mentally, but don't know why. We may feel that life is dull or that we are stuck in the pointless monotony of living with little chance of escape. We may be chronically depressed, fatigued, confused, or forgetful, or perhaps we have nightmares or inexplicable mood swings.

In some cases, the reasons may be at least partly clear, such as in cases of post-traumatic stress after events such as combat, abuse, or natural disasters. But often they are not so obvious. The painful and traumatic events in our past, perhaps in our childhood, become buried. Unconsciously, we long to return to them—to deal with and heal them. But our conscious minds instinctively strive to avoid pain and painful experience, which is why so many issues become buried. We isolate portions of our minds, freezing them in time.

Daring to experience ritualistic soul retrieval is one way we can come to terms with aspects of self that have been shattered and are now buried, suspended in time. Seriously setting time aside to practice this intense pathworking can assist a person in regaining a sense of wholeness and self-awareness. This meditation can be repeated multiple times if need be, but I recommend a maximum of twice a month. It can be difficult to encounter some of our fractured spirits, so please journey at your own rate; revisit the meditation if it's too painful initially. You may be shocked at what you discover; simply remember that these are portions of yourself and are nothing to fear. We all suppress aspects of ourselves for various reasons. Remember to trust your intuition, expand your senses, and be open to the experience. Wait until afterward to review it with a rational or analytical outlook.

1. 1. After constructing sacred space around you by casting a circle and calling the quarters as you normally do, sit comfortably to start the journey. Begin by clearing your mind. Take three deep breaths in through the nose and out through the mouth. Let the thoughts of the day drift away like moving clouds. This is not the time to focus on what happened today or what you need to do tomorrow…allow the common world to dissipate as you enter the sacred terrain of the mind. For several minutes, sense the oxygen entering your nostrils and exiting your lips. Bring absolute focus to your breath.

2. If you know your spirit animal(s) or spirit guide(s), call on them now to assist you on this journey. If you are unfamiliar with your guides, ask that they—whoever they are—be present and that they lend clarity, protection, and success to the endeavor.

3. After meditating some more and further expanding your consciousness, lie flat on your back to begin the descent. Imagine your astral or conscious soul body sinking deeper and deeper into the earth. Feel, with your psychic senses, the cold and comforting soil around you. Go deeper, feeling the stones, the bugs, the worms, and the life inside the earth. Continue descending, feeling the solid layers of stone, compressed and fossilized deep within the earth. Allow yourself plenty of time to journey into the earth. (If you have another, more familiar way of entering the Underworld, feel free to use it instead.) At this point, you should find yourself miles beneath the earth's crust. Stop there.

4. Sensing the deep, dark earth embracing you, open your mind's eye. You have entered the Underworld and must now find your way. Expand your psychic perception in all directions, intuitively feeling which direction is pulling you. You are sensing your soul.

5. Continue journeying in the direction you're pulled. You may descend further into the earth or travel elsewhere within. Allow plenty of time for the journey to continue. When you feel particularly close to your destination, you will begin to perceive a tunnel. Follow this tunnel: it is leading you to yourself.

6. Once at the end of the earthen tunnel, you will find yourself in a cave. Sense the cave: Is it damp or dry? Are there stalactites and stalagmites? Crystals and gems? Sense the environment.

7. As you walk further within, you begin to sense the location of your fractured soul. Continue until you discover this portion of yourself, and approach it with curiosity and compassion. What does it look like? How old are you in this vision? Does this fractured soul interact with you, or does it not notice your presence? Observe and sense this spirit. Why has it left your conscious mind? What trauma or incident caused this aspect of yourself to flee?

8. Spend some time getting to know this soul. With love and kindness, tell it that you would like to know it once again and ask it to merge with your present-day self. Hear any messages it has to give, and respectfully interact in return. Reassure the soul that you will continue to perform healing work with them. If the soul is willing to reintegrate, invite it to step into your astral body and become one with you again. If not, accept this for now, but plan to return in the future.

9. After this experience, monitor the area to see if any other souls—aspects of yourself—are present in the cavern. If so, communicate as you did with the first soul and see what results. When you are finished, bow to the cavern, thanking the astral space for its hospitality.

10. Turn around and depart, taking your time to travel out of the cave, out of the tunnel, and eventually out of the earth, back into your physical body. Once you have reached your physical body, move your fingers and toes, take deep breaths, and very slowly open your eyes. Take plenty of time to return to your physical frame.

11. When you have fully returned, meditate on the experience and write in your journal about your discoveries. How do you feel different? Did you experience the unexpected? Did you have an inkling that the soul(s) would be there? Do you need to return soon? Record your experience so you may continue to reflect on it. Finish by closing the circle and dismissing the quadrants as you normally would.

12. Following this exercise, if the fractured soul(s) told you their reason for leaving you at one point in time, devote yourself to working with the internal resolution of this energy for a long time thereafter. How has its fleeing damaged you in the present, and what can you do now to heal this aspect of yourself?

DARK ANIMAL GUIDES & ALLIES

The world of animals is enigmatic, fascinating, and enchanting. The beauty, the adaptable behavior, and the inherent wisdom of animals give us reason enough to admire them. Animals are everywhere around us, constantly adjusting to humans' invasions of the natural world. Their subtle presence is always felt but rarely acknowledged; they are the hidden seers of humanity. Our pets are our loyal companions. They are with us when no human seems to care, and their reliable presence is a gift from the gods.

The human species is, of course, part of the animal realm, but animal consciousness belongs to a vibration different from ours. Animals do have distinct personalities and character traits, though less defined than our own. They also have astral doubles, as humans do. Animal energies accompany us throughout the day, usually remaining unseen. Connecting to their energies connects us to Nature; animals are living and breathing emanations of Nature's beauty and must be wholly respected as such. Our respect solidifies the ties that bind humanity to the natural world and lead us to the mysteries of the earth.

Animals are telepathic, communicating on a vibratory level. This is natural and instinctive to all animal species, including humans, although most of us have forgotten about this inherent ability. As a species within their realm, we are connected to animals biologically and spiritually; we have numerous similar traits, hence our ability to connect with them psychically. Human fear and preoccupation with the material planes have damaged our telepathic links with animals. As we have turned from an earth-focused society to a monetary, industrial, and corporate society, we have grown more distant from the animal realm, even to the point of mercilessly destroying their natural habitats and painfully exploiting and horrifically mistreating them for monetary gain. Connecting to the medicine of our spirit animals and other astral helpers lets us rekindle the once-revered relationship between human and animal, reminding us that we are very much a part of their world.

In ritual, we can summon the energies of various animals and access their astral substance for good use. Many Witches and Pagans access and work with their animal guides regularly, especially in solitary ritualism. Not only does connecting with our animal helpers fine-tune our ability to perceive the astral, it adds to the energy of the animals' consciousness at the same time, so that human and nonhuman species are in a state of kinship and mutual development.

Some Pagans and earth-based practitioners use the term totem animal interchangeably with spirit, medicine, or power animal and sometimes equate the word "familiar" with them as well. This is only a matter of terminology, and the choice of words may vary by culture as well. But there is a difference between personal spirit guides, energetic embodiments, and projections of group consciousness. The terms below explain the interpretations I have discovered in my own journey.

The Spirit Animal

One's personal animal guide is called one's spirit animal or medicine animal. It is the embodiment of the collective animal consciousness of a particular species, the essence of an earthly animal, as opposed to a mythological beast or exclusively astral creature. It is typically an animal local to the place a person is born, for example, bison in North America, koalas in Australia, and dolphins in Jamaica. A spirit animal walks alongside someone from birth, though it may leave the person or drop into the background later in life.

Most people experience one to four animal guides in a lifetime. Some animals accompany a person throughout a whole lifetime, while others make themselves present only on occasion. Some people experience a plethora of animal guides, perhaps working regularly with many of them at any given time. The number of guides varies as a person's need for each animal helper changes. If a person changes little throughout life, multiple animals may not be necessary. Animals change as a person's energy dramatically shifts. In many Native cultures, multiple animals are ascribed to the cardinal directions as personal guardians and watchers: lenders of medicine. It is believed that each animal comes into our lives, physically or metaphysically, to teach us something about ourselves and reality. The animal simply comes to the practitioner rather than manifesting as a result of intention: that is reserved for the power animal, described below.

Animal guides are protectors, remaining invisible to mundane eyes but lending their energy in various situations. They can guard a house, ritual space, or property. They can also be ritualistically sent to other planes to gather and report information, assuming the request is meaningful and correct thanks are given. Spirit animals assist in meditation and dreaming. Many practitioners meet their spirit animals in dreams or meditative trances and align with their energy for astral travel and journeys to hidden planes. This draws on ancient shamanic associations of animals and humans; the idea of metaphysical animal helpers is not a recent revelation.

Everybody has at least one animal guide. Its presence may be felt when alone in a room or ritual setting, sometimes as though something unseen is watching. Members of a particular animal's species may insist on following a person for long periods of time—a sure sign that the animal's spirit has something to teach (even if it is not a primary spirit animal). A person may feel an inexplicable affinity for one species or another and wonder why. Conversely, someone may be appalled or repulsed by a particular animal or insect. This is a sure sign that the medicine of that animal has something grand to teach.

I can sometimes tell people's spirit animal simply by looking at face and body features. Both face and body often exhibit minor details pointing to the animal's presence in the person's energy field, as does a person's idiosyncratic behavior. This signifies the merging of the person's energy with the animal's and shows that the animal is being brought forth, almost always more than the person realizes.

Facial features aren't the only giveaway. For example, my longtime friend Erasmus asked me to figure out his spirit animal, but after many moons, I still couldn't tell by scrying his facial features. I researched the influence of animals who were potential candidates, but nothing seemed to fit. It was then that I and a few other people began to notice things about him that made his spirit animal quite apparent. When we were in ritual (nocturnal, obviously), Erasmus blended in with the darkness and people would forget he was in the circle—his presence wouldn't register! Not only that, he was energetically indistinguishable at a party or in a room full of people, ritualized or not. Erasmus preferred nighttime, had solitary tendencies, and the gift of acute psychic and energetic observation. He also tended to remain quiet and observant unless directly engaged in conversation. Finally, he exhibited some traits characteristic of a cat, such as "feminine" demeanor and cautiousness, though other feline medicine traits didn't fit him at all. When the realization finally tumbled into view, it was apparent that he had a fox spirit animal. As it turns out, Erasmus had even had a face-to-face encounter with a wild fox as a child—bingo! It's funny how we often tend to look for the hidden without first examining the obvious!

I see humans as creatures capable of embodying vibrations of the animal kingdom as a whole. The potential medicine of any creature, great or small, mustn't be dismissed—from eagle to dragonfly to anything in between. Reality itself is a living, vibrant pattern of immaculate synchronicity. Closely observing the signs, symbols, and omens around us helps us rend the veil between illusory reality (separation) and actual reality (Oneness). When animals and creatures make themselves known to our conscious mind, we can choose to pay attention to the Divinity expressed therein.

The Power Animal

While a spirit animal is more or less a "given" in a person's life, a power animal is conferred by another person, such as a tribal or Craft Elder, or invoked by practitioners themselves for their medicine. Like spirit animals, power animals are also astral helpers whose energy becomes attached to the person for one reason or another. Also like spirit animals, they are a piece of the fullness of the animal's group consciousness. By that, I mean that they are an embodiment of the specific animal's singular essence: a falcon is a splinter of the collective Great Falcon energy; the badger is an embodiment of the Great Badger energy and so forth. These are *oversouls*: the entirety of that animal's consciousness put into one body as an emanation thereof. These are the guides most often called forth in ritual when working with foreign animal medicine. The power animal, similarly, is a piece of the great oversoul.

Power animals are "gained" through intention. If the seeker honestly wants the help of a particular animal's medicine for a specific reason, that animal's essence can be petitioned for help by means of prayer, meditation, and appropriate offerings. Like the spirit animal, the power animal also goes by the name medicine animal, as it lends its sacred medicine from the astral plane to the human experience, including magickal workings. Certainly, the choice of animal summoned should depend on your circumstances. If you need grace and eloquence when speaking, perhaps Swan is the ideal invite. If you need more humor in your life, Hyena can help. For courage, Bear can lend a helping hand—er, paw.

Power animals have an infinite amount of energy to lend. With appropriate research and attention to detail, you can find a lifelong ethereal ally. Power animals and spirit animals are also friends in astral travel. During astral projection, the animal may meet and escort the seeker through a landscape. Riding the back of your animal helper through astral worlds can be fun and educational. Some who practice astral projection like to energetically shapeshift into the form of the animal helper before embarking on journeys or vision quests. This can allow for easier navigation and a deeper blending of the animal's energy with that of the seeker's.

The Totem Animal

Unlike the previous two, totem animals are often seen as guardians of a particular tribe, clan, family, or area of land. Land-based totem animals are called Land Spirits or *Genus Loci*. It is imperative for the magickal person to connect with the Land Spirits (and animals themselves) of the areas they reside in, visit, and move to. These spirits remain part of an area regardless of physical changes on a property. They will also influence magick the Witch performs, patterning the energy in part to their own vibrational essence.

Totem animals are projected manifestations of personal intention and in that sense are created, not unlike a gollum (golem) or thought-form elemental. They represent the collective consciousness of a group mind. Totem animals are often incorporated in a tribe's mythology and cosmology, and are ascribed specific traits. Several cultures do use amalgamated animal forms. For example, Persian and Scythian tribes created new mythological species that combine a number of animals; the gryphon is one of these.

Totem poles, used by First Nations of the Pacific Northwest Coast, sometimes serve as effigies of the unification of animal spirits between, for example, people of two families. Some Native tribal customs suggest that if someone of the Bear clan were to marry someone of the Eagle clan, the totem pole given to them would include both a bear and eagle in it, along with images of guardians and other associated animals significant to the tribe. Totem poles exhibit highly symbolic animal figures custom-made for the family or purpose they were carved for. In the Gelede sect of the Boni peoples of West Africa, people craft large masks to forge a connection with local forest spirits—a practice similar to making totem poles.

The word totem also sometimes refers to a physical representation of an animal helper, such as feathers, fur, claws, and bones, which are used as physical links to it. Such an item can be carried in a medicine bag, placed on an altar, or constructed into a *fetich* (or *fetish*). A fetich is simply a representation of a particular animal's medicine. It is a physical object linked to the animal's essence, like a sculpture, painting, or other effigy. It can act as a makeshift totem pole, serving the purpose of imbuing an area with specific animal energy. Each must be charged and dedicated appropriately.

The Familiar

Originating from the Latin *famulus* ("servant"), the term familiar gained currency with the European Witch hunts. Magick-workers have owned cats, dogs, birds, frogs, snakes, rats, toads, and other animals throughout the ages. But during the persecutions, Witch hunters deemed these pets devils and demons that supposedly carried out their owner's biddings—or they claimed that the pets were Witches who had shapeshifted into an alternate form. Sadly, these harmless house pets were brutally tortured and killed in horrific ways, alongside their owners in many cases.

A familiar is a physical animal connected to a Witch or magician, and typically has little to do with the spirit animal. For most Witches today, familiars are their pets who attend circles and meditations, helping in magickal endeavors by simply being present. They deliver spiritual signs through their behavior, acting as conduits of Divine energy. A familiar warns the Witch of strange shifts in energy, and the Witch in turn works magick for the animal's health and protection. The two are psychically linked and often communicate telepathically, at least in a broad sense.

A person's familiar need not be a pet. It may be a wild or feral animal that visits the home often, or an animal encountered in the past. Familiar energy can embody more than one individual animal: familiars may be wild animals whose presence is frequently noticed, perhaps several times a day. If your spirit animal is a squirrel or you have squirrel medicine, you may notice squirrels everywhere you go. If you find them nesting in your backyard tree, you understand that they were drawn there on an energetic level. Some Witches call their spirit animals their familiars, in a twist on the usual terminology. Others believe their spirit animal is incarnated in their pet, or that its spirit enters and leaves at will. This is possible (though less likely) even if the spirit animal and the pet have contrary natures.

A Darkly Bestiary

The animals listed in the following pages are a few of Nature's "darker" creations. By this I mean that they are naturally in sync with nocturnal and mysterious energies and particularly appeal to people attuned to darker vibes. Many shadow-workers have one of these as a spirit or power animal, though it would be folly to assume that all do.

I do believe it beneficial for dark Witches to call upon these animals' powers when needed, when a feeling suggests a mutual attraction between the practitioner's energy and the animal's. If you know your animal guide or wish to invite the essence of a certain creature into your life, it's beneficial to call its energy forth in personal rituals. Its presence will be amplified, and it will actively listen when you communicate with it directly. In this bestiary, I discuss the characteristics of each animal, physically and metaphysically. I review the many benefits of working with each animal's medicine, and also mention the possible dangers of using their energy when the work becomes consuming.

Not included here are mythological creatures such as dragons, phoenixes, werewolves, satyrs, and so on. This is not to say that these creatures don't exist—I've certainly had my fair share of astral encounters with some. But indeed, many of these beings are strictly mythological, existing only as archetypal astral thoughtforms.

A reminder: Always leave offerings to your animal guides. The ideal offering is a food that the animal enjoys on the physical plane.

It can be left inside on your altar or outside in a special place where physical animals will come and consume it. I also believe that natural incense, fresh fruit, and flowers make ideal offerings to any spiritual being. Whichever you choose, the guide consumes the food's essence; thanks are given and received.

Let us continue now to this darkly bestiary of sorts!

BAT

A symbol of intelligence, the bat journeys the night and sees things other creatures can't spot. In various cultures, bats represent anything from happiness, rebirth, and initiation to vampyrism and the death cycle. Seeing a bat signifies that you must lay to rest a certain part of yourself that you are holding on to, such as a bad habit or maladjusted mind frame. It signifies that you have been avoiding looking at unhealthy aspects of yourself—aspects you now must face and overcome. Bats also evoke an energy of awe and fear, pronouncing that deep-seated fears must first be understood in order to become healed. The bat is a teacher of transcendence, reaching to the darkest caverns of the mind to discover and heal the energies at hand. People with the medicine of these "miniature dragons" undoubtedly see the world through slightly different eyes and pay attention to details. They can see past the immediate and discover hidden things, like people's true intentions. For those with bat medicine, discernment is the key and intuition is the guide. They may also be able to discover pertinent information about an area based on its energy pattern alone. People with bat medicine naturally prefer a nocturnal schedule and mingle with mundane types only when necessary. The bat is the only mammal able to fly like a bird, so people with this medicine are therefore multitalented and unique themselves.

Because bats live in clusters, they symbolize unity among the like-minded. The bat will push its human companion to seek out like-minded types and join them in partnership. Some people may react to this with a tendency to self-isolate, which can be beneficial in appropriate doses, but detrimental if the person becomes over-sheltered. Bats also symbolize sexuality in some cultures and are said to evoke lust. People with bat medicine may be quite sexual or fascinated by acts of love and pleasure.

CAT

I must begin by saying that an archaic term for cat is *grimalkin* ("gri-MAL-kin")—I love using this word when speaking to kitty cats I encounter; it's just so wonderfully Witchy! But back to cats in general. All feline species symbolize grace, freedom, and luck, although we are most familiar with the housecats we keep as pets. Cats' eyes reflect the Full Moon's radiance, and those with feline guides are therefore attuned to the lunar cycles. Cats' eyes also represent psychic ability, so a person working with cat medicine will certainly develop in that area.

In many cultures' mythological systems, cats are emanations of the Divine. Early Egyptians kept domesticated cats as pets and held the species in high regard. The goddess Bast (Bastet), the daughter of Ra, was much revered in ancient Egypt. She assumes the shape of a cat, or a woman with a cat's head, and is the protector of felines as well as humans. In Hinduism, the childbirth goddess Shashthi is depicted riding a cat, and the all-encompassing Mother Durga has a lion or tiger as her vehicle, depending on her aspect. Greek mythological literature occasionally mentions the goddess Artemis/Diana shapeshifting into the form of a cat. The Teutonic goddess Freyja's chariot is drawn by two black cats.

The cat may very well be one of the most evolved animals on earth. Its pristine grace, along with its obvious ability to perceive spirits, faeries, and other etheric beings point to the fact that there's more going on than meets the eye. Likewise, people with cat medicine have both grace and a natural leaning toward clairvoyance. Just as cats have night vision, people with cat medicine can "see in the dark," perceiving what is unseen by others. They have natural visionary powers and an uncanny ability to astrally project and shift between planes: skills they can hone with rigorous practice and dedicated work with this astral guide.

Those with cat medicine are also observers who are aware of the happenings around them. They can be kind and compassionate but may just as easily be angry and defensive if they feel threatened. Paws up, claws out!

If you are pretty sure that you have a feline spirit guide, research the various species of cats, their behaviors, and their metaphysical associations, and try to specify which type is your own. Is it a housecat, cougar, lion, panther, lynx, bobcat, or something else?

CHAMELEON

These animals are known for changing their skin color at will. When chameleons are born in the wild, they do take on the colors of their natural environment. But, contrary to popular belief, their colors don't change drastically from moment to moment. If you place one on green, yellow, or polka-dotted fabric, it won't up and change to match the pattern. Their appearance doesn't actually shift with the look of their surroundings—though it would be wonderful to have pinstripe-patterned pets! Instead, temperature, light, and mood determine the change, which is achieved through the contraction and retraction of the animal's colored pigment cells. It is also interesting to note that true chameleons have a third "eye" on the back of the head, which is used to sense changes in light. Because of this, the chameleon's medicine is powerful in the realm of psychic awareness.

Just as the animal changes appearance based on a set of determining factors, people with chameleon medicine do the same. They have the unique ability to alter their appearance, be it immediate or long term. In an immediate social situation, they can identify with the topic being discussed and easily communicate their thoughts. In the greater scheme of things, they empathize with the interests of others and often determine much of their personality based on the people they surround themselves with regularly.

Magickally speaking, reality works in spirals and cycles, and those with chameleon medicine are able to "hop vibrations." They can be immersed in one thing and embrace the next right away. People with chameleon medicine have a tendency to change and adapt too frequently at times. What may seem interesting one day may not be the next, depending on the exposure to new things the person receives. Not to mention that emotions can be overly extreme if there is not a firm base in the self, as they have a natural empathic ability that can easily get damaged. It's up to people working with chameleon energy to understand what truly interests them as an individual instead of morphing too frequently. Because of constant shifting, the chameleon spirit must be worked with regularly to harness its power and unique ability. Most importantly, people with chameleon medicine can hop planes and access veiled layers of consciousness quicker than most; this skill is invaluable in spiritual and magickal practice.

CROW

Slightly smaller than its cousin the raven, the crow is associated with both light and darkness. It is diurnal (active during the day) rather than nocturnal, and its shiny black feathers remind us of the polarity of darkness in the light. The crow is a scavenger and aids in the end-of-life cycle of decomposition, speaking of the necessity of death to sustain life. After all, a flock of crows is called a *murder*! The Diné (Navajo) view this bird as the psychopomp, or transporter of dead souls. People with crow medicine have a greater perspective on the cycle of life and death, and have an innate ability to voyage the planes and communicate with departed souls.

Crows are avian watchdogs. They warn other animals of the intrusion of hunters and predatory animals. For this reason, they are associated with awareness and message-bringing, and their dark color reinforces this link with prophecy. They communicate with acute awareness, and each bird is closely tied to the others. I have noticed many a crow communicate telepathically (usually when I'm throwing them crackers) to call others to join them at the feast. Likewise, people with crow medicine are naturally connected to one another and can intelligently adapt to a given situation. Crows also keep a safe, protective, and neurotically clean nest. So those with crow medicine find themselves doing the same, putting much stock in the wellness of health and home.

Though the crow and raven are similar in many ways, they have different calls. Surprisingly, the crow is a member of the songbird family, though it is one of the few songbirds that doesn't have a steady song. Their caws can be likened to a summoning from the Divine: haunting and intense, permeating and constant, reminding us that Spirit is always present.

People with crow medicine may tend to be misunderstood, often finding themselves torn between extremes. They are naturally psychic to some degree but may have a difficult time coping with that fact. They are also master illusionists, able to skew and manipulate situations to their liking: a talent that can be used for both positive and negative ends.

FOX

This is another animal associated with mystery. The fox's ability to camouflage and remain hidden to even the sharpest eyes speaks of its powerful medicine: that of invisibility, analysis, and shapeshifting. Foxes are ideal to call on when one needs protection from outside influences and possible danger, including the need for immediate invisibility from creepy folk in public. Preferring nighttime, they use darkness as a shroud. The fox is elusive, and thus dawn and dusk are its prime times. Both times of day are associated with Otherworldliness: times when the veils shift from light to dark, dark to light. This is a reason the fox is associated with magick and the realm of the fae. Seeing a fox at random is said to be an omen that very soon the faerie realm will open before you.

Worldwide, mythologies speak of shapeshifting between foxes and humans. This came about from the fox's association with nighttime: the time of transformation and change. Most shapeshifting tales speak of the fox transforming into a woman or magician, and so the fox has gained associations with femininity and magick. As a member of the canine family, the fox has a masculine vibration. Still, it exhibits feline characteristics, which are associated with femininity. For this reason, the fox is a profound symbol of balance in both gender and energy.

In Japan, foxes have a great deal of mythology built around them. Japanese culture recognizes Inari, the Lord of Rice, who takes the form of a fox. He is praised in numerous forms with different attributes: spirit foxes are called *kitsune*, and those sworn to Inari's service are called *myōbu*. Inari is the healer, the guardian against illness, and the bringer of wealth. He is also a powerful shapeshifter and master of disguise.

A sly creature who hides in the woods, the fox is known as a covert watcher of others' lives. People working with fox medicine have the ability to see patterns in events unfolding around them and come to conclusions based on evidence at hand. They generally remain silent, but will come out into the open and speak when need be, usually not concerned with small talk. They have extrasensory powers in a multitude of ways and see things others neglect to notice.

Both actual foxes and people working with their medicine are solitary and monogamous in nature and are comfortable sticking to their own company more often than not. Foxes are associated with cunning; people working with their medicine have the ability to be sly or manipulative in order to get what they want, so these people must remember to keep their standards for behavior high.

OWL

Oh, the beautiful owls of this world…true keepers of mystery! Quite naturally, the owl has long been associated with Witchcraft. Its nocturnal nature points to its kinship with those attracted to the energy of nighttime. Owls can see in the dark, just as magickal folk have the ability to scry, seeing into the past, present, and future. Owl medicine helps the user develop psychic prowess and learn the mysteries of the moon. The word owl in Latin is *strix*; the same word from which the Italian *Strega* comes about, which is synonymous with the English word *Witch*.

Because of its all-seeing eyes and general body structure, the owl has been called the "cat with wings." Both the owl and cat are associated with nighttime, the moon, and nocturnal esoterica. One should pay strict attention to the silent flight and echoing hoot to decode omens the bird is trying to communicate. The owl is a channel of the Divine, and its presence can be perceived as good, bad, or anything in between. They are the silent seers of the nighttime, whose penetrating eyes tell the observer, "Wake up from the dream." The owl's moon-like eyes and seemingly expressionless face have earned the animal associations with both profound wisdom and fear.

The Native American Mescalero Nation has long believed that the hoot of an owl foretells death and that owls are inhabited by supernatural, usually evil, forces. The Ojibwa Nation has similar associations for the bird, but in the Pawnee and some other Native American traditions, the owl is seen as a protective being: an emanation of the Great Spirit. For many years, Christian belief held that the owl was a messenger of the Devil because of its ability to turn its head nearly 360 degrees around. (Reminds me of *The Exorcist*!) The "blink of an owl" was an old term for a Witch's curse. This paranoia, combined with some Native views of owls as prophets of death, gave the owl a bad rap and strengthened its association with Witchcraft and magick (which had already been maligned for years prior).

Owls are great astral guides for peering into past lives and getting to the root of present circumstance. People with owl medicine are watchers…observers of the world. They are also quite solitary by nature. Even owl pellets have their message. These are the regurgitated remains of rodents and other small animals the owl has consumed: bits of fur, bone, and any other substance not digestible by the bird. Owl pellets teach those working with owl medicine to reject that which is not beneficial to their path and to absorb only what provides spiritual sustenance—a lesson in spiritual discernment.

People who work with the owl can develop the ability to detect falsehood and discover hidden secrets, swiftly getting to the facts of the matter in a given situation. Divination comes naturally. Like the owls themselves, "owl people" notice sudden movements and thus can see when someone is lying and judge their character based on subtle cues in body language. This discernment feels invasive to some people who hide great portions of themselves from the rest of the world—even themselves. The owl is not fooled by the external and easily perceives the subtlety of things. A person working with owl medicine must consider when to speak and when to hold silent. A feeling of social alienation is a frequent reaction to having such psychic ability, and it's easy to think that no one else shares the gift. People with owl medicine must be aware of their powers, but not let those powers push them too far away from life.

RAVEN

A larger version of its crow cousin, the raven is known for its wide wingspan and haunting, guttural caw. The raven's caw is the dark voice of Spirit, calling and summoning others to hear the cries, reminding the world that the ancient mysteries are always present and should be sought out. Those with raven medicine do the same, which is reflected in their interests, speech, and behavior. Also, a flock of ravens is, interestingly, called an *unkindness* or a *conspiracy*…but I promise we're not all rudely scheming!

The raven is undoubtedly a most mysterious and enigmatic avian creature. It is the largest of the songbird family, and is akin to the crow but larger in nature. Similar traits apply for both ravens and crows. The raven has clear associations with rebirth and bringing the light from the darkness, as does the crow. The raven has long been seen as a messenger of the gods (primarily due to Norse mythology), and raven medicine can be used in magick to "send" a spell long distances through the night undetected, assuming the animal spirit is willing. The raven is also associated with shapeshifting, due to its dark and mysterious presence. In the darkness, all things can shapeshift and change. The raven is also associated with transformation and rebirth for this reason. Raven medicine is extremely helpful in magick dealing with change and adaptation. Ravens have long been associated with the occult, and are excellent allies in the Magickal Arts. They are the keepers of secrets and bringers of knowledge.

In the Christian tradition, the raven is a bird of ill-omen, foretelling plague, death, and warfare. These associations were given due to the bird's scavenger nature in feeding on animal corpses. The bird's black feathers speak of its dark nature, and we all know Christianity was anxious to turn anything black into "evil." The Bible actually forbids the eating of ravens due to their dark associations. (I don't think they'd be particularly tasty, anyway.) In Greek mythology, the raven was once white but was turned black as a punishment from the sun god Apollo. Similarly, in both Tlingit and Miwok Native American mythologies, the originally white raven was turned black from the sun. The Norse god Odin (Woden) is mythologized as having two ravens as his messengers; he could also shapeshift into raven form at will.

The Celtic goddess called the Morrigan was able to shapeshift into the form of a raven. She is the Queen of the dark fae and is the overseeing war goddess who swoops over the battleground to acknowledge death. The caw of a raven has been, since the superstitious Middle Ages, a foretelling of death and/or war.

One particular Buddhist community in a Himalayan region of the South Asian nation of Bhutan believes the raven to be a highly spiritual creature, each one being an emanation of the Bhutanese guardian deity Gonpo Jarodonchen. In fact, killing a raven is seen as a sin so serious that it is comparable to killing a hundred monks.

People with raven guides tend to be prophetic and observant. They have skills in divination and cyclical healing, and are experts at magick and spellcrafting (when practiced with precision). They may also be able to predict someone's physical death or know when the "death" of a negative pattern must occur in a person. They prefer simplicity and solve problems by looking for the easiest and most practical answers in given situations. People with raven medicine are also *excellent* writers. (Okay, so I made that one up.)

Like the crow, people with scavenger medicine have the potential to overly involve themselves in the affairs of others, sometimes unaware of boundaries. This translates as a nuisance to many people and, as with many bird spirits, their flighty or spacey nature can translate as naivety. Thus, the messages they are trying to convey can get convoluted or misunderstood, and those with raven medicine must always be aware of people's boundaries. Kept in check and given proper mindfulness, the raven's medicine is powerful and beneficial to work with.

SNAKE

Serpentine medicine is intense and powerful. Many Native American nations associate the snake with healing and endurance. Hermetic magicians associate it not only with healing but also with sexuality. The Greek messianic figure Hermes Trismegistus is depicted carrying a caduceus wand with two snakes spiraling around it, meeting at the top face-to-face. Still used as a healing symbol in Western medicine, the wand signifies the raising of consciousness in the form of *Kundalini*, as recognized in ancient schools of Yoga.

In ancient Egypt, a metal crown called the *uræus* was worn, usually by those in royalty. Showing a snake protruding from the center at the third eye chakra, the uræus was an initiatory symbol, signifying the wearer's entrance into realms of higher knowledge. The Egyptian Funerary Texts also discuss the snake as an ultimate creature of protection and defense.

The snake is an earthen creature that is associated with the Underworld. This association came about in ancient religions because of the snake's ability to travel stealthily through the grass, water, and sand, positioned lower and closer to the metaphorical Underworld than most other creatures. The cunning *nachash*, the Bible's mythical snake, carries Underworldly connotations from tempting Adam and Eve to disobey God in the Garden of Eden. Naughty, naughty!

In the tale of the Buddha Siddhartha Gautama, he is protected by Muchalinda, the King of the Nagas, preceding his enlightenment. Muchalinda takes the form of a cobra that coils around the Buddha, protecting him from rain and any possible attack. This story symbolizes snakes' protective qualities and their associations with intelligence. Those with the serpent's medicine can be fierce and predatory, vengeful and motivated. They can also be contemplative and dedicated, prophetic and wise. People working with snake medicine must monitor their actions and see where their energy is best placed. They must prioritize, knowing when to lend their encouragement to others and when to move on, when to attack and when to remain in the shadows.

Snakes have the ability to coil into a spiral: a sign of the everlasting and infinite cycles of life, reassuring us that nothing really ever begins or ends, only changes. The serpent also sheds its skin, a sign of growth and transformation. Anyone with snake medicine should work with it regularly to shed the old in order to embrace the new. When those with snake medicine neglect their spirit animal work, they often find themselves caught up in the tides of life and unable to move past a point in the natural cycle. When properly worked with, snake medicine is intense and highly spiritual.

SPIDER

Arachnids are interesting creatures that have long been maligned and misunderstood. A spider's venom is associated with death and poisoning. Spiders capture their victims and cocoon them in a suffocating death shroud before finally injecting them with venom. They are sneaky "creepy crawlies" who show up in the most unlikely of places. People with spider medicine must be very discerning, must be able to tell fiction from reality and know when an attack is justified, as they also have the inherent ability of psychic vampyrism, which can be used for both good or ill.

The nervous system is the "web" inside the human body. Information flows along the web of nerves to the brain and throughout every bit of the body. Spiders are shaped something like nerve cells. This parallel, and the web correlation, make this unique spirit animal attuned to the sending of information, magick, and energy, showing that the spider is a communicative and influential creature.

But as well as symbolizing death, the web-weaving spider is more appropriately a symbol of creation. The web is the symbol of life and the interconnectedness of all things, physical and Otherworldly. A web or orb is the crystallized spindle that shows its ability as a builder and artist of Nature. The spider is both the creator and taker of life. The bodies captured in the web are drained of life and fed upon to encourage the cycle of rebirth. The spider teaches these mysteries.

In many Native American traditions, the spider is the Great Grandmother, the weaver linking the past to the future, with all aligning in the present. She teaches that all behavior, activity, and thought in the present intricately forms the future. She reminds us that we are the creators of our own experience; that it is we who weave our own webs.

Spiders are teachers of balance, understanding that any extreme is unhealthy. Their many eyes teach the student to see all aspects of a situation on all levels and planes. They also teach the necessity of studying the past, including ancient and historical research and past-life regression, as well as other spacetime mysteries. If you come across a dead spider (do not kill one for this purpose), the shriveled body may be used in magick aimed at binding and capturing energy, even poisoning an aggressor. The body is also a channel of the energy of rebirth. If working with a spider corpse, call forth Grandmother Spider to invite her ageless wisdom.

People working with spider medicine are natural artists, musicians, and writers, bringing ideas in the mind to physical form. They are independent, creative, and natural daydreamers. With focus, they can develop acute self-awareness and knowledge of the workings of the Universe. They are excellent weavers of energy, projecting magick through multiple planes. Spider medicine is extremely powerful and must be approached with reverence and respect.

In any sort of relationship, people with spider medicine must remain conscious of how they feel about the other person, as they tend to become overly attached and consuming, much like the spider who captures its victim in the web. Although they might initially have difficulty forming an emotional attachment, once they do, a strong sense of trust is instilled that has the potential to last a lifetime. Some female spiders perform sexual cannibalism, killing and devouring the males after mating. This indicates the dangers one must consider when working with spider medicine, especially insofar as relationships are concerned. Let's not eat our partners.

VULTURE

Worldwide, vultures (also called buzzards) are aligned with death energy and the afterlife. Numerous creation myths incorporate the vulture, a member of the raptor family, as a supremely powerful animal. In addition to their deathly alignments, vultures have been associated with purification and transformation, and are widely seen as birds that are in touch with both the mundane realm and the spirit world. Vultures do not tend to be feared by societies who observe the animal regularly. Instead, they are seen as transcendent creatures whose role in the life cycle is worthy of veneration. Contrary to popular belief, vultures do *not* kill their own prey; they feast only on bodies whose lives have already been taken.

People with vulture medicine should pay particular attention to their actions, minding that others judge and view them by their deeds. Vultures have very keen eyesight. Those with vulture medicine likewise have the ability to hone astral sight and physically see things that others tend not to perceive, such as subtle energy patterns. Because of the bird's ability to fly effortlessly for miles upon miles, those who work with the vulture can similarly glide through life and gain an acute sense of their life's direction. Like people with other scavenging animals' medicine, those who work with the vulture should keep in mind that they have natural inclinations to "scavenge" and energetically feed on others. Any relationship can be dangerous if appropriate boundaries are not secured.

WOLF

The wolf is a very strong animal spirit to have in your life, whether momentarily or for as long as you live. Wolves are known as wild and free, and will invoke similar characteristics in those working with their medicine. Wild wolves have a strong family bond, especially to their children and social groups; those working with wolf medicine will undoubtedly seek their kin and remain close to them once found. They are protectors of themselves and their kind. They will metaphysically assist those who petition their help and are in need of protection or need to build strength. Wolves communicate in extensive body language as well as growls, whines, and whimpers, and also have highly sensitive sight, smell, and instinctual perceptions. Strongly bonded to one another in wild packs, they get along with each other for the most part and are generally more peaceful than is commonly believed. They are a disciplined species, having a very precise social structure wherein each member understands its place and responsibilities, each animal adding to the greater success of the pack.

In the Roman pantheon, the twins Romulus and Remus were the sons of the god Mars and Priestess Rhea Silvia. In the ancient story, they were abandoned and later found by a she-wolf who took care of them, suckling and nurturing them back to health. Later, a shepherd found the boys and adopted them as his own. In a fight over power, Remus was killed by his brother, who declared political dominance. Rome is said to have been named after Romulus. Even to this day, elements of the ancient Lupercalia festival, possibly an early St. Valentine's holiday, still live on in Rome. The word *Lupercalia* has the same Latin root as the words *lupus* and *lupine*, meaning "of or related to wolves." In the festival, Roman Priests called *Luperci* gathered at the cave where Romulus and Remus were allegedly suckled. After reenacting sympathetic magick to draw on the mythological event, the Priests ran through the town wearing only goatskin loincloths, striking townsfolk with ropes of goatskin, which was thought to make them fertile. This was also a purification rite: all who were touched by the ritually charged whips were cleansed, purified, and imbued with the venerated powers of wolf medicine.

The mouth is a prominent canine feature. In the wolf it represents death and the Underworldly Abyss. People with wolf guides can thus be outspoken, charismatic, and influential. They must remain aware of both the cycles they create and those they place their trust in. They naturally intensify any situation and always look out for their own best interests, as well as those of loved ones.

In the wild, wolves make the most of their environment, respecting territory and sticking close to their own. When hunting, they devour every bit of the hunted animal, signifying their influence on making the most of every situation, respectfully taking advantage of opportunity.

Those with wolf medicine can learn these characteristics when working with their guide. These people are also naturally quite determined. When a task is at hand, they will work on it until they are satisfied with every detail.

One problematic issue for people with wolf medicine is that they are predisposed to arguing for the sake of claiming "top dog" position. This is generally a subconscious instinct and occurs mostly between people of the same gender (remember that wild wolf packs have both an alpha male and an alpha female). There is also the "lone wolf" disposition: if someone with wolf medicine feels wronged, that person may end up angrily disassociating from the "pack" and becoming isolated, often for unhealthy periods of time. This usually occurs because the person has put such stock in the individuals or circumstances at hand that the separation seems all the more betraying and harmful. If it is a real betrayal, the disassociation may be rightful, but perhaps there are misunderstandings or misinterpretations. For this reason, discernment is the wolf's key to success.

The wolf is ferocious and bloodthirsty, yet at the same time compassionate and protective. These traits also apply to people working with their medicine. People with wolf guides have strong emotions and can be vicious as well as loyal. They have a very strong sense of kinship, be it to family, friends, or certain ideas and perceptions. If one idea makes sense, they are likely to latch onto it, hanging on to its energy for a long period of time. This is another reason why a person working with a wolf guide must carefully consider what is healthy and real, and what is idealistic or fantastic. Again, discernment is the key to utilizing this powerful animal's medicine for the greater good.

Ritual Meditation:
Discovering Your Spirit Animal

Do you know your spirit animal(s)? Not everyone does; no worries. Discovering these animals takes much time and reflection, and the answer may not come about as quickly as one would like. Sometimes the animal chooses to remain in the shadows and does not reveal itself until the appropriate time. But if the seeker has enough motivation and perseverance, these guides can be discovered and worked with for many years.

This meditation is useful in discovering one or more of your animal guides. If you already know your primary animal, or have an inkling as to what it may be, it's still beneficial to attempt this working as a form of reconnection and acknowledgment. It aids in discovering the spirit animal based on which elemental kingdom it belongs to. Keep in mind that just because an animal lives in a particular environment, that doesn't always mean you'll be drawn there in the meditation. For example, the lion may represent Fire to some people, though it lives on land and may thus be seen as Earthen. The jellyfish may also represent Fire, though it's a Water creature. For both of these examples, the seeker could be drawn to the Southern terrain of Fire just as easily as to the element of the animal's physical environment. Stay flexible; this meditation is not set in stone and the seeker should be open to accepting the unexpected!

When contact is made with the animal spirit, a metaphorical bridge is made between the individual human consciousness and the collective animal unconscious. The animal whose energy is most closely aligned to the seeker's own vibrations finds the seeker and makes its presence known. You must clear the mind of unnecessary thoughts first and foremost, going into the meditation without any preconceived notions about the animal.

There should also be no immediate judgment placed on any animal that presents itself. Believe it or not, even the hippopotamus, mosquito, and earthworm have essential things to teach any partner. Your animal guide may also give you a part of your magickal name during this meditation or introduce you to other spirit guides (who may or may not assume human form). These events come with time, as a person's astral senses are fine-tuned. Feel free to ask its name and it will reveal it to you if the time is right. Discovering the name is not necessary but will assist in calling the spirits forth in the future.

Again, keep in mind that a person's spirit animal (or spirit plant or tree, for that matter) tends to be present as a physical animal in the place where a person was born *or* where they currently reside. For example, having been born and raised in Montana, Raven is my personal "primary" spirit animal, and I know it will be with me for life. I've also been blessed, over the years, with the medicines of Cricket, Mule, and Moth, who have made appearances to teach lessons.

This meditation may be performed outside in a natural environment or at your altar. Cast a circle beforehand as you normally would; it's not good to risk the possibility of intruding energies that could throw you off guard or convey inaccurate information. I highly recommend burning sage in the area and around your body both before and after the meditation to ensure that all unneeded energies are neutralized. Finally, don't be disappointed if an animal doesn't make itself known to you the first time. Keep trying, and project your will to the Universe to manifest the attraction. It will happen when it is supposed to. And keep in mind that this meditation may spark visions of your animal in your waking life or in a dream, not necessarily within the meditation itself. The results vary for each person.

1. After constructing sacred space around you by casting a circle and calling the quarters as you normally would, sit comfortably to start the journey. Begin by clearing your mind. Take three deep breaths in through the nose and out through the mouth. Let the thoughts of the day drift away like moving clouds. This is not the time to focus on what happened today or what you need to do tomorrow…allow the common world to dissipate as you enter the sacred terrain of the mind. For several minutes, sense the oxygen entering your nostrils and exiting your lips. Bring absolute focus to your breath.

2. When you feel appropriately grounded and centered, it is time to begin the journey. Visualize yourself standing nude in your human form with only blackness around you. There is no gravity and your weight is supported; you are free to do as you please. Now that blackness surrounds you, it's time to feel your way around. You are naked before the Universe.

3. In your mind, call forth the elements associated with the cardinal directions. East and the essence of Air…South and the essence of Fire…West and the essence of Water…North and the essence of Earth. See the elements around your visualized body…Become aware of their presence and know that they are ready to assist you on your journey. See whites and soft yellows

in the area of Air. See orange and red in the area of Fire. See blues and deep greens in the area of Water. See browns and greens in the area of Earth. You are surrounded by their subtle energies and are aware that each element is a part of you.

4. You are floating in the middle of the four elemental energies. It matters not which direction you are facing, and you are free to move as you please. You are balanced and you are calm. This is a place of peace where nothing can cause harm. See a white cord connecting you to each direction, entering into the center of your body around the heart chakra. You have four soft, white cords of energy coming into the center of your body which extend to the elemental kingdoms around you. Look around your visualized body, seeing and sensing these cords.

5. Feel a magnetic connection between yourself and the elemental kingdoms; each one is of a different vibration and pulls you at a different rate. Allow plenty of time to feel out these connecting cords and perceive which one pulls you most strongly to its area. At this point, mentally call out to your spirit animal, asking it to present itself to you this evening. Pay attention to the signs, and see if any images flash before you. If you do get visions, determine which elemental kingdom they belong to. You are in the process of discovering which element your spirit animal belongs to.

6. Once you have determined which cord pulls you the strongest, begin to follow it into its territory. Brush off the other cords and journey to the kingdom that calls. Move closer and closer to that area, and feel surrounded by their inviting energies. So which one is it… Air, Fire, Water, or Earth?

AIR: If you feel yourself drawn to the element Air, enter into its kingdom by moving forward to its terrain. You are walking on air; white clouds are on either side of you. You now begin flying, slowly at first, moving faster. Your arms are outstretched like wings and you're welcome to travel anywhere you wish. You begin to notice a speck straight ahead, making its way toward you.

You feel relaxed and inquisitive in this weightless environment. The animal ahead may be large or small. You come to a stop and let it approach you. Now in front of you, the animal allows you to make out its shape. Take your time. Once experienced, bow to the animal and make your way back from whence you came.

Fire: If you feel yourself drawn to the element Fire, enter into its kingdom by moving forward to its terrain. You are walking on burning embers and flat volcanic rocks, yet feel no heat or pain. You are surrounded by unthreatening, flickering walls of flame. You feel happy and invigorated. You notice a spot ahead in the distance. Something is making its way toward you; you invite its presence. Now in front of you, the animal allows itself to be seen. You are permitted to perceive it as it wishes. Take your time. Once experienced, bow to the animal and make your way back from whence you came.

Water: If you feel yourself drawn to the element Water, enter into its kingdom by moving forward to its terrain. You are immersed in water but can breathe freely. Move forward by swimming. Clear blue water is around you on every side. You feel peaceful and at ease. You see soft movements in the distance and an oceanic figure making its way toward you. You are at peace while this animal begins to make itself known. Now in front of you, the animal allows you to make out its shape and get to know it. Take your time. Once experienced, bow to the animal and make your way back from whence you came.

Earth: If you feel yourself drawn to the element Earth, enter into its kingdom by moving forward to its terrain. You are now walking barefoot on soft, moist soil. Trees are on either side of you and the air smells of musk. You feel grounded and secure. Take a few steps forward and notice the movement ahead in the distance. You can see a shadow rustling ahead, making its way toward you. You feel a rush of pleasant excitement as this animal comes closer. Now in front of you, the animal allows you to notice the animal's characteristics. Begin to perceive the shape of its body and get to know it however it allows you to.

Take your time. Once experienced, bow to the animal and make your way back from whence you came.

7. After you have experienced an element, go back the way you entered and allow yourself to stand in the middle of the elemental kingdoms once again, all four white cords once again attached to your heart chakra. If, for some reason, you feel another kingdom pulling you in, follow that cord and enter that element. When you have experienced all that you were meant to, slowly begin to come back.

8. Allow the elemental kingdoms around you to spin deosil, faster and faster, until they merge into pure white light surrounding your astral body. Allow this sphere around you to grow larger and larger, spanning into infinity. Now in empty space, you wish to reenter your physical body.

9. Take deep breaths in through your nose and out through your mouth. Wiggle your fingers and toes, slowly beginning to sense your body. Make slight movements and very slowly open your eyes when the time is right. Remember where you are on the earth plane and allow awareness of the environment around you to come into vision. Ground and center yourself however you do best and take the rest of the day easy, knowing that you've just made connection with the elements, having come back with knowledge gained.

WHEN INVASIVE SPIRITS COME AROUND

A wide variety of people from virtually all cultural backgrounds believe that there is more to life than meets the eye. Civilizations from the dawn of humankind to the present day have long held onto beliefs in nonphysical entities of one variety or another. Still, others disbelieve in these forces altogether, feeling as though strict scientific evidence supersedes experiential data. (Which I personally find more sad than funny. *Le sigh.*) Mystics and magicians, however, understand the value of *experience* alongside scientific theory, and are more likely to consider alternate dimensions of existence if their own personal experience leads them to such conclusions. *Especially* if those experiences are intense and otherwise unexplainable.

Nonphysical beings each have their own personalities and motivations. Just like humans and animals, the personalities of astral beings can be greatly varied and often depend on the "type" of being they are. Many nonphysical entities are harmless and benign. Others most certainly are not.

Ancient Pagans and animists from a variety of cultures have long attributed physical and mental ailments to demonic spirits and astral invaders. While modern science brilliantly explains these ailments on a physiological level, mystics understand that the physical and nonphysical realms interact, and that the physical dimension is but one of many possibilities. This is not to say that all physical imbalances are caused by spiritual entities, but that it's worth consideration that the body works in conjunction with energetic planes. It is wise to be aware that the physical and nonphysical worlds are not always as separate as they may seem, and that the physical and metaphysical are not mutually exclusive.

Trust Your Instincts

Because the physical body itself is connected with various energetic planes, it's important to pay attention to our body's responses and reactions. When it comes to sensing spirits, or even sensing energy in general, it's valuable to first pay attention to our instincts. If we sense the presence of a spirit or foreign entity, which emotions or sensations are immediately experienced? As magickal folks, we tend to trust our instincts when interacting with fellow humans, so why would it be any different with the spirit world?

Whether or not we rationally understand or can accurately categorize the entities we encounter, it's of utmost importance to pay attention to our instincts and intuition. From there, we are more apt to make sense of an encounter, even if it's a momentary experience. I'm not gonna lie: it can be difficult to make sense of spiritual dimensions and astral dynamics. There are no solid answers because these realms are not solid structures. Metaphysicians of all varieties promote the belief that the mind, the intellect, and even the imagination are explicitly linked with unseen realms of existence. It is reasonable to assume that many of these worlds and realms are continually changing and being molded by human minds—and this may even hold true for the gods themselves. It's also worth mentioning that many nonphysical entities have the ability to change their appearance depending on who they are interacting with, serving to convolute things even further!

When you sense an external spiritual entity, pay attention to what your body and mind tell you. Do you get "good" or "bad" goosebumps? Do you feel a flight-or-fight sensation or heart palpitations, or do you feel at ease? Do you feel a shift in temperature? It's wise to pay attention to the instincts of the mind and body; after all, you don't want perform banishing exercises if you are receiving a friendly visitation from a spirit guide or a dearly departed loved one.

The Act of Discernment

As I mentioned, the intuitive and creative dimensions intermingle with unseen planes of existence, making it a challenge to understand where objective experience ends and mental projection begins. It's vitally important to question every experience with nonphysical entities, but is equally important to understand the validity of each experience, even if it's only on a symbolic level. For example, if I happen to randomly see a moose in my peripheral vision, it doesn't necessarily mean that it's a spirit animal, an animal oversoul, or even the ghost of a moose—but it could be any of these things. If nothing else, my subconscious mind is communicating "moose energy" to me for some reason, so either way it warrants some contemplation. If the moose were to repeatedly appear, the question could be investigated further: what is its origin and what is the purpose of the communication? Every experience with unseen forces has its own importance, whether it's actually otherworldly or is simply psychologically symbolic.

Allow me to be upfront here: I have interacted with countless people who have been in the midst of experiencing inconsolable "supernatural trauma." A spirit of some type is haunting them for one reason or another…the entity is unaffected by spellcraft, magick, prayer, and everything else…it's wreaking havoc in every aspect of the person's life, and so on. Rarely are these claims legitimate; in my experience, nearly all of these cases are occurrences of mental illness or delusions, not spiritual activity.

A person's psychological constitution, past experiences (such as those that cause PTSD), mental diagnoses, and coping patterns must be taken into consideration when approaching the concept of metaphysical intrusion. In many cases, medical assistance can be much more beneficial than metaphysical assistance. Therapy, psychiatry, and medical treatment are not signs of weakness, but signs of empowerment. We all deserve to take control of our mental and emotional constitutions, and by doing so we can more accurately examine issues such as invasive spirits and astral entities. As magickal and metaphysical practitioners, we have the responsibility to objectively determine the nature of our experiences to the best of our abilities. When it comes to invasive spirits, some apparent entities are nothing more than thoughtforms: projections of the unconscious mind. Others, however, quite obviously have their own distinct agendas and personalities.

A Strange Encounter

Back in 2008 I had an experience with a spirit that still sticks out quite heavily in my memory because of its insidious intensity. While I do sometimes sense earthbound disincarnates (ghosts) and other astral entities, I've never had one become attached to such an extent. This encounter began when I visited a city in Oregon as part of my book tour for the *original* version of this book, *Shadow Magick Compendium*. After doing book signings and Tarot readings at a local metaphysical store, my original plan was to explore the city with a tour guide. Unfortunately this tour guide had to cancel and I was on my own. It being a weeknight, there wasn't too much going on around town. I found myself wandering downtown and throughout quieter areas of the city. I recall feeling a particularly depressed or desperate sensation in one dark, empty street that I traversed on the way back to my motel. At the time I brushed off this feeling, but for some reason the sensation didn't really seem to leave, even weeks after returning home. This is not to say that I was especially depressed, but there was a subtle draining sensation that seemed to be increasing with time. Eerily, the sensation felt similarly to the feeling I experienced on that empty Oregon street. My instincts told me that something was off.

Over the next week, these sensations were palpably present on the upper right-hand side of my body—I didn't sense the presence anywhere else. During quiet moments of the day, it felt as if someone was standing next to me, watching every movement. It was an uncomfortable sensation that only seemed to increase in strength. Coupled with the fact that my general level of energy seemed lower than normal, I decided to meditate on the situation. It didn't take long to discover that a conscious being with an independent personality was clinging to my energetic body, and thusly also my physical body. In deep meditation, the spirit clearly felt like an adult woman. I could feel her astral hair and even feel her breath—slightly creepy! But it didn't stop there; I sensed myself empathetically affected by this spirit's desperate sorrow. I could feel her astral body attempting to draw closer and attach to my deeper levels of energy, such as through the chakra points. I even felt sexually aroused, which was a clear indication that she was attempting to merge with my body through sexual energy. (I don't tend to be attracted to women, which made it even more awkward.) It was clear that she attached to me on that dark and empty Oregon street; the feelings were just too uncannily similar to dismiss. This entity was most likely a ghost who, for all intents and purposes, became a parasitic and vampyric succubus.

By continually repeating protective exercises, such as those mentioned toward the end of this article, I was eventually able to shake her off my aura. The whole process took a couple of weeks and involved a lot of trial-and-error. Because the spirit was slowly and subtly feeding off my own emotional and sexual energy, I had to be extremely mindful and self-aware of both those realms. I had the responsibility of understanding which emotions and energies were my own, and which were "other"—luckily, as an empath, I had already grown familiar with the practice of emotional discernment. (For my fellow Witchy empaths, I urge you explore my book *Esoteric Empathy* for more information about the ins and outs of empath metaphysics.)

While all of the protective exercises and procedures I enacted were certainly helpful in relieving the situation, the most effective form of banishing was also the most difficult: I had to verbally *command* her, repeatedly and regularly, to go away. Because she had attached to my emotions and was attempting to merge with my energetic body, a feeling of rejection and sorrow would continually follow any statement of "go away and leave me alone." This, of course, was not my own sadness; it belonged to the spirit. Still, I felt like a cruel and heartless person for telling this stalker to disappear—and, in her attempts to stay attached, this is exactly how she wanted me to feel. Guilty. As difficult as it was, I built up the courage to forcibly evict the spirit and demand that she "go to the light." Eventually, it worked.

Ritual Meditation: Understanding an Encounter

If you are experiencing a strange spiritual encounter that you feel is invasive to yourself, your home, or another person, try analyzing the experience for yourself by following these steps. This meditation is but one suggestion of how to identify the being or beings you may be encountering. As always, use a healthy amount of discretion to understand what may be a mental projection and what is more likely to be an objective observation.

1. Situate yourself near the environment or person who has been experiencing a perceived spiritual invasion. If you are the person who is experiencing the invasive spirit, get comfortable in your own sacred space.

2. Close your eyes and use your subtle senses to locate the entity or energy in question. If fear arises, try to overcome it. If it feels attacking and *immediately* threatening, skip to the last step.

3. First, determine whether this is an energy or an entity; is it simply a body of energy or does it seem to have a distinct personality? If it feels like a negative body of energy, consider using some of the suggestions in the next section. If it feels like an individual conscious entity, move on to the next step.

4. Try to sense the general energy of the entity. Feel it out. Does it appear to be a kind or curious spirit, or does it legitimately intend harm? Could it have been sent by another person,

consciously or unconsciously, or is it simply a passerby? Does it wish to communicate with you? If you determine that the spirit "feels okay," try verbally and psychically communicating, noting the impressions you receive; the spirit might actually be there to help or might simply need a gentle "push" to move on. If you have discovered that the spirit or entity is peaceful, interact with it and see what impressions you get; you may also ask it to "go to the light," and then you can close the meditation. However, if you feel that the spirit is legitimately malicious, move on to the next step.

5. If you have determined that the entity you've encountering is in fact malicious and invasive, do your best to summon the courage to fight against it. *Demand* and *command* that it leave; explain that it is not welcome here and must depart. Claim your power and make your needs known without hesitation. Put your foot down! Tell it how it is! Next, proceed to follow some of the following suggestions and use your best judgment in dealing with the situation. You have a lot more influence and ability than you may think!

Spirit Cleansing

Regardless of its origins, if you feel the presence of a maliciously invasive spirit, these suggestions can help deflect their energy from your sphere. Experiment with different methods and see what works best for you personally.

- Burn sage around your body, using locally or Native American–sourced sage if possible.
- Asperge your aura with saltwater or water from a sacred location.
- Light matches: the sulfur/brimstone exorcises negative forces.
- Use a magick wand, athamé, or your pointer finger to draw a large Earth Banishing Pentagram (a star beginning in the lower left-hand corner) toward the direction of the entity. See this pentagram glowing in a bright blue flame.

- Perform protective rituals such as the Lesser Banishing Ritual of the Pentagram (LBRP).
- Wear high-energy stones such as selenite and citrine.
- Forcibly declare the Greek phrase *"Apo pantos kakodaimonos!"* This roughly translates as "Away, evil spirits!" The phrase is also incorporated in a basic ritual of Thelema called The Star Ruby.
- Hang protective herbs around the house such as bulbs of garlic, sliced onions, and cloves.
- Utilize symbols such as pentagrams, the eye of the dragon, *X*s, and anti-evil-eye symbols. These can be put onto items, clothing, candles, artwork, or charms, as well as drawn on the body.
- Call upon "Upper Level" beings such as gods, spirit guides, and angels; they are often believed to have the ability to intercede with "lower" affairs, such as hauntings, possessions, and unrested spirits.
- Make it a daily practice to visualize and reinforce your energetic shields.
- Recite prayers, affirmations, and inspirational readings of holy texts. Project positive and upbeat energy toward the entity or energy in order to help avert its influence.
- Most importantly, choose to remain as optimistically positive as possible throughout daily life; try to ignore it when it demands attention: your mood changes your energy, which in and of itself is profoundly protective.

Chapter Four
The Shadow of Nature

"Fully accepting our dark side might lead to nonconformity, however, it can also inspire sensitivity and creativity. The majority of those who understand these nuances of life consider themselves free. They understand that darkness is not simply the absence of light, but is an integral part of it; just as one side of the earth feels the sun's rays, so the other half dwells in shadow."

—Corvis Nocturnum
from *Embracing the Darkness: Understanding Dark Subcultures*

ROMANCING THE MOON

In the daytime, the sun reigns bright in the sky, showering the world with light and making visible the glorious world. But as the sun descends beneath the horizon, different energies begin to stir. A certain calm and stillness takes over, and the gathering sense of mystery invokes a curious shift in perception. The rustle of the former day begins to wane and another force begins to take shape. There is a unique comfort in the night. When the physical plane is shrouded with shadow, other planes become revealed. Deep night sets in and, at this time, the majority of the world is asleep, at least on one side of the globe. Energies are at a lull; everything moves a bit slower at nighttime and the world isn't quite so chaotic.

Nighttime is the subconscious or unconscious. Nature is a direct reflection of our inner landscapes—our internal reality—which is why Pagan spirituality is so sacred. Whereas daytime is aligned to our extroverted, conscious selves, nighttime reflects our deeper aspects. For the deep-thinking introvert, a love for the safe, unthreatening darkness of night is particularly holy. Because the night is the time of internal reality, it is the center of shamanic work. Because the essence of Witchcraft is based in shamanism, the nighttime can be considered the territory of the Witch. The night appeals to shadow magicians for obvious reasons. This is the best time to utilize magickal energies! Spells weave into the Universe with less interference, while the calm of night allows for reflection and contemplation. Magick is easier to send and project when the rest of the world is asleep. The invisible information superhighways—that is, the threads in the fabric of reality—are much more clear of mental traffic while the majority of the land is asleep and dreaming.

Many artists reserve their endeavors for nightfall, finding the energy more conducive to the creative process. Communication between the worlds also becomes stronger, the hidden areas more accessible. Ancestral and spirit contacts are strengthened while darkness enshrouds the land. Ancient Pagans of all types associated nighttime and the moon with hidden realms, often including the worlds of the ancestors and the fae. They saw these realms as far more accessible at nighttime when the veil is thinner. In the hue of night, the moon is queen.

Regenerative Introspection: The Dark Moon

As the moon rises, Witches are invited to dance in the splendor of night. In the Craft, the Great Goddess is represented by the moon. The moon stands for the feminine aspects of existence. Whether Full or New or in between, the limitless energy of the moon is there every night.

During the lunar cycle, the term Dark Moon refers to the three-day period when the moon is invisible: its illuminated half is facing the sun, and the dark half faces Earth. In some ancient cultures, this time was called the dead moon, in others, the mystic moon. The term New Moon refers to the middle of that three-day period: the day when, astronomically, the cycle is at its pivot point, poised between waning and waxing again. As with the Full Moon, the New Moon happens thirteen times a year. Because the common Gregorian calendar has only 12 months, there is always a month with a second Full Moon (a Blue Moon) and a month with a second New Moon (a Black Moon).

The shadow-shrouded moon represents the Crone aspect of the Goddess. In Celtic lore, the Crone is the wise elder woman who sees all and knows the mysteries of life. She is the most knowledgeable of all Goddess aspects and will lend a sliver of her wisdom before the moon rebirths and begins to wax in its youthful phase. Witchcraft also recognizes three nights for the Full Moon—the astrological apex date, the date before it, and the date after.

For those who work with the shadow, the Dark Moon is a time of great mystery, perfect for castings of growth and regeneration. Some Witches, however, choose not to perform any castings at this time, reserving the days for only personal reflection and meditation. This is understandable, as the darkened moon draws energy inward to be finally sorted with the waxing cycle.

The Dark Moon is the time of new beginnings. It is the time to plant the seed you wish to have permanently bloom in your life. It is the time of introspection and a healthy dose of withdrawal. The Dark Moon allows us time to analyze our lives, our security, and our happiness, and to plan for what's ahead. Dark Witches revel in this time because of the power of creation the moment holds. This is a great time to empower magickal tools and jewelry by drawing shadow energy into them, ushering metaphysical darkness (or "new-ness") into working tools. It's also perfect for divination, especially when looking at issues of a hidden nature. The deepest of questions and issues can begin to come to light if the Dark Moon's energy is utilized.

CELESTIAL SHADOWS: LUNAR & SOLAR ECLIPSES

One special and highly noticeable instance of natural shadow is the eclipse. Both solar and lunar eclipses have a certain "time out of time" feel to them, and their eerie presence speaks of something magickal afoot. For the metaphysically aware, eclipses can be harnessed for far-reaching personal transformation.

An eclipse takes place when the sun, moon, and earth are aligned. In a lunar eclipse, the earth passes directly between the sun and moon, shrouding the moon briefly in shadow. Sol and Luna appear in direct opposition to each other in the zodiac belt at this time; a lunar eclipse occurs only during a Full Moon. Conditions are right for a lunar eclipse about once every six months.

Solar eclipses are rarer. Here, the moon passes directly between the earth and the sun, which blocks our view of the sun, since both bodies appear to be about the same size in our sky. A solar eclipse occurs only at the New Moon, with the sun and the moon in the same sign. When this rare event takes place, we have a direct and accessible magickal doorway in the center of a planetary alignment. (Partial eclipses carry the same influences as full eclipses, but to a lesser degree. They are not as visually or energetically intense, but they have their own powers to be utilized.) Because of their surreal qualities, eclipses of both types were at one time associated with fear and dread, seen as bad omens or warnings from the gods. With the development of astronomy, eclipses came to be seen as natural, rather than supernatural, occurrences.

According to modern astrology, eclipses of any type represent extreme transformation. During an eclipse, energy is both totally vacant and immensely heightened at the same time. It is the ultimate paradox. The occurrence acts as a blank slate waiting to be carved, an empty canvas waiting to be painted upon.

This profound, enigmatic state should be used for magickal workings with deep personal balance in mind. Any magick performed during an eclipse should address great issues, not superficial concerns. For example, a spell to make someone fall in love with you could have extreme repercussions (this is always true, but especially during an eclipse), whereas a spell to improve health could have positive long-term benefits. Pathworking, meditation, and divination during an eclipse can also be very powerful and lucid.

Keep in mind that the moon represents the internal, covert landscape while the sun represents the external, the overt. Solar eclipses influence events on a more visible level and their effects are more noticeable. Because solar eclipses can only occur during a New Moon, they lend intense energies of rebirth and newness in an external sense. Lunar eclipses are more emotionally and intuitively based; they provide an immaculate setting for personal workings. Because they occur only during a Full Moon, they are ideal times to release old habits or cycles. Eclipses of both types present an extreme opportunity to realign with their illuminated zodiacal energies (see the following list).

When encountering an eclipse, call out to the gods, chant your spells, and take advantage of the tremendous boost of power this blink of time has to offer. All spells, rituals, meditations, sacred baths, and such should be determined and planned out beforehand, taking into consideration what is most beneficial for such a moment. The astrological signs that the moon and sun are in should be known previously, and the ceremony mapped out in accordance with its influence.

Many people believe that all eclipses have lasting influence over human affairs. Some astrologers say that the number of hours a *solar* eclipse lasts, from start to finish, translates into *years* of its enduring influence, and that the number of hours that a *lunar* eclipse lasts translates into *months* of influence. These views give significance to the astrological sign that the moon or sun is in at the time of the eclipse: that combination of signs will run its course for the period of time indicated. Other astrologers feel the influence of an eclipse lasts until the next one. Either way, the eclipse's power mustn't be brushed aside.

As noted earlier, lunar and solar eclipses amplify the energy of the sign they are in at the time. They reveal to us things that are hidden and open gates of consciousness in accordance with that astrological influence. This is the time to reevaluate everything in terms of the issues represented by the sign; it's time to make adjustments, come back into balance, and plan for the future. The sign that the moon or sun falls under during any given eclipse has much effect on the energies it exudes. In solar eclipses, the sun's sign is the most significant. In lunar eclipses, it's the moon's sign. Additionally, *all* eclipses, solar and lunar, take place during zodiacal polarities (opposites), when the moon and sun are in opposing signs. The zodiacal polarities are:

ARIES: Libra
TAURUS: Scorpio
GEMINI: Sagittarius
CANCER: Capricorn
LEO: Aquarius
VIRGO: Pisces

Connecting to the Eclipse: A Ritual Meditation

The following ritual, or a variation thereof, can be performed to connect with a solar or lunar eclipse. Included are calls to Sol (sun) and Luna (moon), depending on the type of eclipse, as well as a place for any desired self-crafted spellwork to be performed. Rituals like the one below can certainly be performed at times of partial eclipses, though, naturally, full eclipses are the most powerful. Similarly, visible eclipses contain the most potency for the practitioner, but eclipse magick can be performed even if it is nonvisible—that is, a solar eclipse on the other side of the globe, or a lunar eclipse during daylight hours, for example.

Humans cannot look safely at the sun with the naked eye, so don't try to do so during a solar eclipse. You can consider a viewing device or special sunglasses, or simply decide to observe the eclipse's effects on your surroundings.

When an eclipse is over, energies are born anew. This is the ideal time to create change in your life. I would compare the process of a lunar eclipse to the energy of an entire moon cycle compressed into a few hours, if that. The sun or moon appears full one moment, wanes to dark, and waxes back to full. *Theurgia potentissima!*

1. This ritual should take place outside, beneath the light of the eclipse. The working should begin about a half hour before its apex (the precise time of the eclipse's climax, as typically shown on an ephemeris or calendar). After constructing sacred space around you, sit comfortably to start the journey. Begin by clearing your mind. Take three deep breaths in through the nose and out through the mouth. Let the thoughts of the day drift away like moving clouds. This is not the time to focus on what happened today or what you need to do tomorrow…allow the common world to dissipate as you enter the sacred terrain of the mind. For several minutes, sense the oxygen entering your nostrils and exiting your lips. Bring absolute focus to your breath.

2. In the case of a solar eclipse, look at the sun only if you have special shades or a viewing box designed for observing the

eclipse. If you don't have a viewing device, observe the changing light's effects on the environment, wherever you are. Reflect on your wishes until the apex, noting the astronomical changes. In the case of a lunar eclipse, gaze at the moon until the apex arrives. Because of the lunar and thus psychic implications, this is a great time for divination with an oracular tool of your choice. Consider divining on issues pertaining to the sign in which the moon is eclipsing.

3. When the peak of the eclipse occurs, stand tall and breathe deep, filling yourself with the rare energy of the occurrence. Surrender to the energy in order to dance with the evolutionary influence the eclipse is gifting. Raise your arms to form a half-circle, inviting the energy into your person. You can also do the same with your hands, pretending to cradle the eclipse itself in the sky. Form an upward triangle with your hands by touching your thumbs and pointer fingers together, and continue to draw the energy from the celestial body into your own.

4. In the case of a solar eclipse, declare something like:

"Great Father Sun, He who rules all external reality, fill my spirit with your Divinity as I honor this spiritual transformation. Hear my prayers, mighty King; He who has been known as Sol, Helios, Ra, and a hundred thousand other names. Hail unto thee, Father Sun!"

5. In the case of a lunar eclipse, declare something like:

"Great Mother Moon; She who rules all internal reality, fill my spirit with your Divinity as I honor this spiritual transformation. Hear my prayers, mighty Queen; She who has been known as Luna, Seline, Diana, and a hundred thousand other names. Hail unto thee, Mother Moon!"

6. At this point, perform any and all spellwork having to do with the eclipse, be it lunar or solar, and considering the zodiacal signs present. There is no better time for weaving pointed

magick than now. Take as much time as needed. Meditate and soak up the energies.

7. When finished with any spellwork, say your own prayer of thanks to the celestial bodies, meditate for a while longer, and perform any other work your intuition guides you to do.

THE DARKNESS OF THE SOLAR YEAR

Naturally, the moon is the illuminator of the path of the shadow magician, especially those with Witchy tendencies. Keep in mind, however, that although we may prefer and feel more affinity with moonlight, we still honor the sun and acknowledge it as the central force of creation.

In common folklore, when the sun rises, the vampyre turns to dust: the light vanquishes the creature of the night. The ascending sun can be used in magick similarly, to shine off negative darkness, casting it away and back into the Abyss at sunrise. Why not utilize both and stay awake for both sundown and sunrise if time permits? Both times of day are very auspicious for magickal use.

In the sun's daily cycle, the shadow magician prefers dusk for obvious reasons. We revel in the beauty of the sunset, knowing that we are preparing to embrace the grand darkness to follow. Old Pagan beliefs say the souls of the dead who have passed that day descend to the afterlife with the sacred sun, escorted by a psychopomp, or transporter of the dead.

In accordance with this belief, you can cast away unwanted energies at the end of the day, asking the sun to let them die alongside the sun's descent. As the sun dips beyond the horizon, you can send your own wishes along with it. Thank the sun, the Divine representation of the God and the masculine current, for illuminating the day and for providing much-needed energy to all of the land.

Unlike the moon's monthly cycle, the cycle of the sun lasts the whole year round, determining the seasons and tides of Nature. The sun's influence is much more noticeable than the moon's, and the long solar cycle is marked by the Sabbats of the Witches' path. This is the Wheel of the Year, and these are the darker sides of the cycle of the sun.

Autumnal Glory

Autumn…truly the season of the Dark Witch! For those of us who work with the public, this is the busiest time of the year as far as community outreach, ritualism, and magickal workings are concerned. At this time in the sun's yearly cycle, the lush season of summer begins to die. The harvest is coming to a close and we are given time to reflect on the abundance of the year. Depending on where a person is located, the once-green may turn to yellow and orange, deep red to brown. Leaves fall and disintegrate, smelling of earthen decay. The world truly looks aflame, and anyone whose spirit is attuned to the glory of Nature is naturally taken aback and overwhelmed by the splendor of the dying year.

The dying season has a special place in the heart of the shadow magician, particularly those who walk an earth-based spiritual path. Seasonal shifts alter emotions and affect the mind. For many, the autumnal tide is just as depressing as it is enchanting. Seasonal Affective Disorder (SAD) is a very real thing. Scientists describe SAD as a mental disorder occurring in some people during the dark months of the year, when the days are shorter and light is limited.

With this shift in light, a person's circadian rhythm changes, affecting their mood. Levels of serotonin in the brain decrease with less exposure to sunlight. This neurochemical balance modulates emotions, mood, and sleep, and lower serotonin levels can easily make a person depressed and lethargic. For people who experience SAD, going to bed and snuggling up in the blankets for days may feel like a better option than going about the daily routine… autumn and winter lethargy is just part of our biological structure! Our ancestors understood the seasonal shift; they slowed their metabolisms and body processes in autumn and winter to function more efficiently and expend less energy. Even if modern indoor heating provides comfort from the cold, our bodies still respond to the season in ancient ways. Witches understand that science and magick are interlinked and that the scientific explanation of SAD is certainly valid. One modern treatment is spectrum light therapy, whereby the person sits under a light box to absorb the mock "sunlight" it generates. Many portable commercial lamps are also available on the market.

Highly sensitive people also empathize with the death energy of the season. The archetypal Oak King—the force of growth and light—begins to metaphorically die at Midsummer and isn't fully laid to rest until Lughnasadh. Death energy is all around, reflected externally in Nature and internally through shifts in mood. For Witches, the dying tide of Nature is metaphorically enacted in ritual with the Oak and Holly Kings. These two brother amalgam-gods exchange the throne at the two major seasonal shifts, summer and winter, and each is an archetype for its seasonal polarity. (Of course, these seasons refer to the Northern Hemisphere; the Sabbats and seasonal observations are reversed for those in Australia and other places in the Southern Hemisphere.)

The Holly King is the embodiment of winter and the cold months, reigning from Midsummer to Midwinter. Santa Claus, the bearded sage reminding us of winter's joy, is a modern embodiment of the Holly King. His brother the Oak King represents the sun and the warm months. He reigns from Midwinter to Midsummer, bathing the earth with the light needed for sustenance. The Oak King's descent is metaphorically reenacted in traditional Wiccan ritual that is designed not only to honor Nature, but also to hone the magick of the seasonal shift within ourselves. When the Oak King dies, something dies within each and every one of us. If enough mind is given to this change, we can appropriately banish that which is unwanted and unneeded in our lives through ritual.

Corn dollies can be burned as they were in old Europe (and elsewhere), honoring the dying Sun or Horned One making way into a place of slumber beneath the earth's crust. Memoirs, written petitions, and other effigies can also be set aflame alongside the dolls to aid in the banishing magick. Create your own spell or ritual for the Fall Equinox or Samhain that draws on your own observations of the season.

In autumn, Pagans can take advantage of the changing greenery. If a tree's leaf catches your attention, use it in your autumnal magick. I've found it extremely powerful to pick a tree's leaf (with the Dryad's permission, of course) that's half green and half yellow, red, or orange. This catches the leaf in suspended transformation and is ideal to use in a spell aimed at personal change in attunement with the autumnal tide. And if you see a single leaf fall from a tree, make a wish! It's a nod from the Universe.

Halloween: Honoring the Other Side

Hail be Halloween! Samhain (meaning "summer's end") begins at nightfall on October 31: the verge of November 1, and thus directly opposite Beltane (May 1) in the solar year. The energies of Samhain balance those of Beltane, as each Sabbat would not exist without the other acting as a polarity. November 1 marks the beginning of the Celtic year. Therefore, sorrows of the past can be left behind on Samhain, and the turning of the day to November represents a sacred shift from the yearly cycle of the past to that of the future.

Just as Beltane celebrates the experience of life, Samhain celebrates the inevitability of death as a necessary and beautiful part of the infinite cycle. It is the peak of the dark season and helps connect us to the depths of our spiritual experience on Mother Earth. According to Wiccan tradition, the seasonal Goddess is in her Crone aspect at this time. She is the elder sorceress and bestower of the wisdom of the ages. To some, she is the Bone Woman or Lady of Truth. By her side is the Lord of Death: the empowered Reaper or Holly King in his dying aspect. The greenery of the earth is now laid to rest; thus begins the slumber of the year to rejuvenate for spring's rebirth.

The early Christian church didn't approve of honoring all dead souls at this time, only those who were hallowed, or "blessed by God." Thus, Samhain became known Hallowmas or All Hallows' Day, and later All Saints' or All Souls' Day.

In European pre-industrial times, livestock were often gathered at this holiday to be either ushered into the barn for safekeeping or slaughtered and salted to preserve their meat for sustenance through the cold months. This is another reason the Sabbat is associated with death. In those times, people also left plentiful offerings of food and alcohol for spirits passing by. It was believed that if these offerings were not given, the spirits would be left unsatisfied and play malicious pranks and practical jokes on the household. This, along with the tradition of dressing up to blend in with the spirit world, is the origin of today's trick-or-treating.

Old Celtic customs and activities associated with Halloween are still practiced by the masses, albeit now diluted. Jack-o'-lanterns used to serve as devices to scare away evil spirits. Apple bobbing was a form of divination, and costumes were worn both to frighten away malicious spirits and to blend in with them. Many ancient Hallows' traditions are carried over to our own time, and many non-Pagans adore this holiday, spending countless hours decorating, planning, getting made up, and preparing for the trick-or-treatin' kiddos! On an unconscious level, they are resurrecting ancient folk customs in order to integrate the energy of earth- and ancestor-based spirituality with modern life, even if for just one day in the year.

Ancient Celts saw Samhain as a day out of the boundaries of time, the one day of the year when norms fell and chaos ran rampant. The astral and the terrestrial planes intersected, time periods overlapped, spirits came forth, and lucid reality became much more unstable than any other time of the year. The dead were believed to come back and walk the earth on the first of November. The fae, too, came out and danced, capturing mortals and bringing them into the realm of the fae.

Witches always say that "the veil between the worlds is at its thinnest on Halloween." This veil is not only the dimensional separation between the living and the dead, it also separates ourselves and our ancestors, the conscious and the unconscious, the physical and unseen planes, the idealized and the actualized. This veil separates polar aspects of our existence during Samhain, letting us access the formerly hidden portions of our minds that need contemplation and healing. At this time, mourning and its rituals are common because the season acknowledges those who have crossed the veil into the world of the dead. Pains of the past tend to surface, and learning to accept our circumstances becomes our guiding light. Experienced astral travelers journey to the Otherworld to guide souls to the light, and modern necromancers work magick to release earthbound disincarnates (ghosts).

Samhain is traditionally the final day to collect plants, herbs, vegetables, and fruits of the earth before winter. It's not only a time of mourning, but one of celebration. The celebratory aspects of this High Holiday are to welcome forthcoming change and cultivate an understanding of the tides of life. Fires are often lit to remind practitioners of the light within the darkness. All Hallows' Eve is considered the darkest holiday due to its associations with death. But technically, Midwinter (the Sabbat after Samhain) is the darkest day of the year, with the shortest period of sunlight. The Solstice solidifies the energies raised at Hallows' and welcomes the beginning of the tide of rebirth.

As we cast away and banish certain things at Samhain, the "dark eighth" of the year allows for reflection into the mysteries of life. What I term the "dark eighth" is the 1/8 turn of the Wheel between Samhain and Midwinter (Yule; the Winter Solstice). Upon the arrival of Midwinter, the sun finally begins to wax again and increase in strength, helping manifest new wishes in place of those banished at Samhain. This is, of course, reflected in the rebirth of the Holy Child Sun God throughout his many archetypal forms.

THE DAY OF THE DEAD

Native Mexicans traditionally celebrate the Day of the Dead (*Día de los Muertos*) on November 2, and many additionally celebrate the day before it as well, which is also the official date of Samhain. (Although the astrological date of Samhain falls around the seventh of November every year, when precisely looking at the Wheel of the Year in astrological degrees.)

Oh what a beautiful, enchanting festival this is…Sugar skulls! Chocolate coffins! Shrines to the dead! Corpselike face paint! Parades of death! Picnics on graves! Deathly masks and floral bouquets! Colorful ribbons, streamers, paintings, sketches, and artwork…of death! Spells, prayers, and charms to the deceased! Grinning, fiddle-playing, sombrero-wearing, bride-and-groom skeletons! All these things and much, much more characterize Día de los Muertos.

Indeed, our beloved Halowe'en has come and gone at this time. We continue to both mourn and celebrate our ancestors and beloved kin who have crossed the veil. Though Samhain is a Gaelic Celtic (and also Wiccan) holiday, numerous cultures across the globe have long celebrated their ancestors around the same time of year, logically because of the "harvest death" occurring in the natural world. For Mexicans, the Day of the Dead marks the pinnacle of ancestral celebration. Quite naturally, the *vast* majority of Hispanic and Latinx individuals who observe this festival invite the rest of the world to *also* celebrate this most sacred of days, as long as one approaches with cultural reverence and wisdom rather than appropriation.

The traditional merrymaking on this day is not a glorification of death and dying, but is an optimistic view of the inevitable. To get stuck on the depressive and morose aspects of dying is to wallow in stagnation. Our dearly departed don't demand tears; instead, they're quite pleased to be celebrated and held on high! By looking death in the face, the spiritual bridge between this world and the Otherworld is made stronger.

Día de los Muertos originally lasted the duration of an Aztec calendar month, which fell approximately around our modern August. Historically, upon Mexican Christianization, this summertime holiday was moved to align with the Celtic All Saints' Day, thus also giving it modern alignments to the Celtic Samhain. Now, the Day of the Dead is recognized as November 2, though some families celebrate the holiday for a number of subsequent days. Additionally, the holiday is celebrated in many areas of the globe and is frequently blended with local ancestral celebrations.

A number of activities mark this festival. Because death is the theme of this fiesta, and optimism is its vibration, all activities rotate around both death and joy. Many participants construct intricate, death-themed art projects designed to praise those who have gone before us. Many participate in huge celebratory parades where people dance, sing, joke, perform, and dress in all varieties of deathly costumery. Death-themed cakes and sweets are made as a traditional practice, and children are also celebrated during Day of the Dead festivities. This is a recognition of the continuity of life: the new in place of the old.

Many participants adorn their homes with decor representing death, and many construct shrines and altars dedicated to their personal ancestors. These shrines also tend to include depictions of saints, spirits, or deities, depending on the person or family's religious path. Families, both in Mexico and elsewhere, carry on the tradition of gathering around these shrines, leaving offerings to their ancestors, and telling stories and anecdotes about the dearly departed. Because celebrations of death are focused on love and communion, familial bonding is a necessity. Because Día de los Muertos is celebratory and joyous in nature, it's a great time of year to put both family struggles and personal struggles to the wayside, and bring your focus to the joys this world has to offer. If nothing else, this celebration reminds us of our own mortality, which can positively encourage us to enjoy the little time we have on this plane!

To take part in this holiday, you can perform some of these activities and create your own. Paint, sketch, or papier-mâché death-centric artwork! Offer marigolds (a flower of the dead), liquor (especially tequila), and death-themed food to spirits of dead! Construct a shrine to honor those who have passed, both in your family and otherwise! Tell your children about life and death! Cook a traditional Mexican feast and invite the dead to partake! Visit your favorite cemetery and stay for a spell (or two)! Gamble and drink if it's your thing, being sure to reserve a cocktail and hand of cards for the "visiting spirits!" Meditate on the spiritual implications of death, dying, and the unseen world! Dress like a corpse and light a candle for the Otherworld!

You may also wish to do some deeper research into the celebration, both historical and modern, and find a group of Día de los Muertos celebrants in your own town or city. There is literally an endless number of activities you can personally perform to mark this most beautiful and ancient holiday.

HERBCRAFT & WORTCUNNING: A DARKLY HERBAL

In Latin, the word for Witch is *venefica*—a word associated with the ability to heal magickally and medicinally, suggesting knowledge of the poisonous properties of herbs and how to use them. The earliest word for Witch in Western literature is *pharmakis*, meaning one who has knowledge of healing and the use of natural remedies, and we can see this root in our words pharmacy and pharmacist.

The Old English word for herb was *wort*. *Wortcunning* means herbal wisdom. Witches work with herbs magickally and medicinally. All herbs and plants have both physical and metaphysical properties, and these are the very essences that Witches and natural magicians utilize in spellcraft. Witches make use of the earth's medicinal and magickal gifts, knowing that every natural substance can be utilized both physiologically and esoterically.

Witches have a special connection with Nature. We hear Gaia's voice regularly, and we pay attention to messages being delivered from Spirit by way of reality itself. The earth has created a cure for everything, on every level. It's just a matter of knowing how to use the gifts surrounding us, including those that sprout from the land. Each herb (and plant, tree, animal, mineral, and so on) has its own spirit, its own individual vibration. Each carries its own associations with metaphysical properties such as healing, love, luck, protection, peace, binding, cursing, and so forth. Herbs can be cultivated according to particular lunar and solar phases to further imbue them with specific properties. Those who don't have garden access can hop on down to a reputable local herb or Witchy store to secure their supplies.

When an herb is used in spellcraft, the practitioner must connect with its energy to bring out its magickal properties. It must be analyzed and meditated upon. The practitioner can focus intent into the herb through the projecting hand until it feels "full" of the intention, as matched with the vibrational properties of the herb. From there, the herb can be used in a spell or magickal working. Beforehand, it's best to meditate with the herb—while picking it live or while grinding it with a mortar and pestle—to get to know its spirit, gaining a direct rapport with the spiritual helper.

The magick-worker should also take some time to visualize the herbs radiating with specific energies attuned to the spell. When the enchantment is complete, the herbs will seem to "glow" with an ethereal vibration tailored to the working. There are a number of things one can do to acutely awaken the metaphysical properties in plants, minerals, and other substances.

Keep in mind that even a small piece of an herb can be used just as effectively as an enormous amount. For example, say you wish to add a boost of luck to a spell and are drawn to Lucky Hand Root for this purpose. If you find in your herb cabinet that you only have a bit of dust from the root remaining, use it in the spell just the same. As long as what you add carries the genetic imprint of the plant (or stone, feather, shell, or whatever), it still constitutes a speckle of the substance, and its energy is added. At the same time, with such a small amount of a spell component, I advise taking more time to "awaken" that specific property in the working.

The longer an herb dries, the less available its magick becomes. Still, magick can be brought out of the herb at any time regardless of its age. It just takes a little more work to fully charge and enchant older herbs than it does fresh ones. Herbs can be sprinkled in the ritual space, added to incense, boiled in a cauldron or on a stovetop for potions, placed in a medicine bag, and so forth. If the spell or working is designed to banish forces, the spell's remains, including the herbs, are generally cast to moving waters or winds. If the spell is to manifest, the herbs can be buried or sprinkled about the property, or kept nearby in a sachet or bottle to continue weaving their magick. Only herbs documented to have positive health benefits are taken internally in the form of teas, tinctures, and gel caps (or vegicaps).

Through the ages, various herbs have become known for their dark qualities. Most magickal books don't speak fondly of them, if they mention them at all, so some of the most common—and useful—are listed here. The herbs I present in this list are for magickal use rather than internal medicinal use.

Throughout centuries, it has been understood that herbs with toxic properties can be used in moderation for physical healing or psychedelic journeying. The same concept holds true in metaphysics: these dark herbs can be used for spiritual ends but mustn't be approached nonchalantly. The outcome of a spell could be quite different than intended if the practitioner doesn't give careful attention to the plant's correspondences, which, in many cases, are indeed sinister.

Many of these infernal plants are part of the Solanaceae family, whose broad range of flowering species includes the everyday tomato, potato, eggplant, and petunia. The dark side of the Solanaceae family is its group of toxic plants, often called the *nightshades*. These include belladonna, henbane, datura, mandrake, and tobacco—herbs long used in medicine and magick, but ones that aren't exactly comparable to your ordinary chamomile or peppermint tea. Because of their poisonous properties, these dark herbs became known as Witches' herbs in the Middle Ages because, obviously, Witches were doers of evil.

Two of the items in this Darkly Herbal are known as signature plants. Signature plants are those whose medicinal traits can be seen symbolically in their own anatomy. For example, creases in certain types of beans resemble the vulva, and beans can be used medicinally for vaginal problems. Surprisingly, in some Indigenous cultures, people refrain from eating beans entirely, and in others beans are eaten only for purposes of fertility and reproductive health. Even Pythagoras and his followers refused to eat beans, seeing them as germinal souls. Along the same lines, the small Amazonian plant called *eh-ru-ku-ku* that grows in the shape of a snake can be used to withdraw venom from a snakebite wound. Mandrake roots are shaped like little humans, and the root has been used to aid in childbirth through the ages. One can also apply this in a magickal context: the mandrake root has also long been used for working any sort of magick having to do with a person, be it yourself or someone else.

Beyond any literal resemblances, signature plants can also hint at their metaphysical uses, predominantly through personal identification, as herbs and plants can represent different things for different people. Perhaps you associate certain bell-shaped flowers with music, and would thus choose to use them in magick aimed at honing your musical or artistic skills. Perhaps you associate weeds of any type with mental poisons or negative external influences, and thus choose to make weeding your garden a psycho-magickal act, or to use weeds in banishing spells. There are many ways to utilize and personalize items drawn from the natural world in the Magickal Arts. Magick is driven by intention, and intention can be channeled in limitless forms.

This wee Herbal also includes a few roots that have been used in Hoodoo (rootworking), Vodou, Witchcraft, and other magickal traditions for centuries. The root of a plant sustains its life-force and therefore contains the most powerful essence of the plant itself. It is for this reason that only a tiny amount of a root is needed in magickal work. Roots can also be seen as a plant's darker half. Most roots are entirely immersed in soil, never seeing sunlight until they are pulled. Therefore, they are connected to darkness. I would imagine that magicians of old recognized this, perhaps seeing roots as linked to the chthonic (Underworld) realms. This seems likely, considering the ancient belief that the dead were connected to the Underworld when buried.

Some Cautions & Recommendations

Please don't use any of these herbs internally, and handle them carefully (wash your hands after touching them, k?!). Most are toxic and can kill you deader than a doornail if used improperly. Witches who use these herbs are careful to attune each plant with its intended magickal purpose when using it in spellcraft. Due to the laws of metaphysics, the properties of herbs can be brought forth when used both internally and externally. Please don't brew these herbs as teas; their effects won't be pleasant! And please don't burn these herbs unless it is outdoors and no smoke is inhaled; these herbs are poisonous even in a combusted form. (Exception: it's okay to burn dragon's blood resin, as it is nontoxic.)

Ideal ways to utilize these so-called "dark herbs" are to incorporate them in medicine bags or sachets, put them at the base of candles, bury small bits on the outside of a property, or bubble 'em in an outdoor cauldron to release their properties. (After boiling, discard the mixture in the trash or bury it deep in the earth, depending on your intention.) One can also engage in a meditative journey wherein the practitioner's consciousness voyages into that of a plant. Keep the plant nearby during the meditation, and it will communicate its essence or spirit to you, helping you form a closer relationship with both the herb and the earth.

Another warning: If you use any of these herbs in spellcraft, please balance them with the use of "lighter" herbs, so that any dark energy raised will not overwhelm the spell or ritual. Balance is essential; all of these herbs should be used alongside others that will not restrict the workings at hand. This goes especially for any type of cursing or crossing.

And now, a tour of some of these darkly herbs.

ACONITE (*ACONITUM NAPELLUS*)

GENDER: Feminine
PLANETARY RULERSHIP: Saturn
ELEMENTAL RULERSHIP: Water

Aconite is also known as wolfbane or monkshood. Believed to be sacred to the goddess Hekate, it was actually known as *hecateis* at one time. True aconite is probably the deadliest plant associated with Witchcraft. The name wolfbane or "wolf's bane" comes from the ancient Greek practice of dipping arrows in the poisonous extract of aconite for the purpose of hunting wolves.

Aconite and its botanical relatives are used in shapeshifting magick and for connecting with the animal realm. It's also used for astral flight, invisibility ("cloaking") magicks, and general protection. Infusions of aconite have been used in the past to cleanse and consecrate magickal blades such as the blade of an athamé, sword, or boline. Aconite is an ideal herb to use in spells for voyaging the Underworld or communicating with chthonic deities.

A great substitute I have found for aconite is the nontoxic herb arnica, which, like aconite, has been known to some traditions as wolfbane. In magick, arnica can be used for the same purposes as aconite. It is relatively inexpensive, and its flowers are usually sold in herbal shops due to its plentiful medicinal uses.

BELLADONNA (*ATROPA BELLADONNA*)

GENDER: Feminine
PLANETARY RULERSHIP: Saturn
ELEMENTAL RULERSHIP: Water

The word belladonna means "beautiful lady" and is associated with improving one's beauty and self-image . Some say the plant's name is derived from the Roman death-bringing goddess of war Bellona. Some Renaissance-era women used extracts of the herb's poison to dilate their pupils for a more "innocent" look, which is apparently more sensually alluring (I haven't noticed, myself). Belladonna is a strain of nightshade; it's called "deadly nightshade" for a reason. Its alkaloids are extremely toxic, and many people have skin reactions from merely touching the plant. Its black berries are the most poisonous parts of the plant and have long been called "Devil's apples."

Belladonna is a strong feminine herb and can be associated with the sphere Binah on the Qabalistic Tree of Life. It can be used to access the Divine Feminine, the Goddess Mysteries, especially that which is aligned to the energy of the Crone. It is also associated with astral projection and vision seeking. Though the latter most likely came about due to its physical toxicity, belladonna does not have to be used internally for one to access its potency. It is best used in medicine bags or in potions or brews that are not to be used internally. Any part of the plant can be utilized. Belladonna is associated with darkness and illusion. It appears very beautiful but is deadly in reality. Thus, the herb can be used in magick to uncover disturbing secrets about a situation—something very pertinent to shadow magick. Belladonna can best be utilized when working with any dark, painful occurrences that the mind is holding on to. Its energy brings the Witch to face their darkest fears, even if emotional pain may result.

BLOODROOT (*SANGUINARIA CANADENSIS*)

GENDER: Masculine
PLANETARY RULERSHIP: Mars
ELEMENTAL RULERSHIP: Fire

Bloodroot can be used for any issues regarding the blood or that which is represented by blood: from physical blood (including familial or DNA magick) to love in general and other workings of the heart. Members of some Native American nations would decorate themselves ceremonially with the root's red extract, and also smeared it on their hand before shaking the hand of the person they wished to marry, in a sort of spiritual effort to win favor. This shows its longtime metaphysical associations and it's believed that the darker the root, the greater the potency.

Bloodroot can be substituted for iron (associated with blood) in a magickal working and is best associated with the protection of a household. It may also be worn in a medicine bag to avert harmful vibrations sent by others. In my own practices, I like to incorporate bloodroot, bloodstone, and a couple of drops of my own blood when performing magick aimed at the "heart" of any personal issue or dilemma.

CLOVE (*CARYOPHYLLUS AROMATICUS*, ETC.)

GENDER: Masculine
PLANETARY RULERSHIP: Jupiter
ELEMENTAL RULERSHIP: Fire

Cloves have long been used in Witchcraft for various purposes. Whole cloves are often substituted for nails in cursing spells to "drive" a lesson home and in protection charms such as a Witches' bottle or sachet. Their sweet smoke is highly protective and clears a space of harmful vibrations, also aiding in memory. It's also reputed to stop gossip and attract money and lovers. Perhaps, for those readers who are into dark subculture, clove cigarettes do have benefits at Goth nightclubs!

Though clove cigarettes are a nice treat (especially the black ones), use the herb with caution! In this form, "clove" is actually tobacco with bits of ground clove. Usually imported from Indonesia, the tobacco is typically of a finer grade than in typical American cigarettes, but the clove actually makes it unhealthier than most. Ironically, clove cigarettes were originally invented for medicinal purposes in the 1800s by Haji Jamahri of Java. An asthmatic, Jamahri used to rub clove oil on his chest to ease difficult breathing. He also rolled ground cloves into cigarettes and smoked them for what he erroneously thought were health benefits. Later they became popular for recreational smoking.

DATURA (*DATURA SPP.*)

GENDER: Feminine
PLANETARY RULERSHIP: Saturn & Venus
ELEMENTAL RULERSHIP: Water

Datura, also known as thornapple, Jimson's weed, or Angel's Trumpet, contains tropane alkaloids and is a close relative of belladonna. When thrill-seekers attempt to get high off datura root or belladonna foliage, more often than not, they report horrifically terrifying experiences both mentally and physically. The internal effects of tropane alkaloid-containing plants are nothing to fool around with. Even the tiniest of doses can lead to permanent injury or death. When used purely energetically, it works similarly to its cousin belladonna: it helps us handle the mind's darkest places. If there is an experience you wish to come to terms with or a dark aspect of yourself you wish to understand, datura can assist. The herb also carries associations with astral projection, dream magick (such as dreamwalking, encouraging prophetic dreams, and remembering one's dreams), and protection from harmful vibrations.

It's also used for breaking hexes another person may have sent your way and can be used for hexing and cursing itself, if the need is dire. Bits of datura can be used for banishing; it seems to be one of the best herbs available for this. I've found that it makes an excellent addition to a sealed sachet or medicine bag designed for the aforementioned purposes, particularly protection and magick dealing with darker emotional realms.

DRAGON'S BLOOD (*DAEMONOROPS DRACO*)

GENDER: Masculine
PLANETARY RULERSHIP: Mars & Pluto
ELEMENTAL RULERSHIP: Fire

Dragon's blood is a deep-red resin which, in liquid form, looks as if could have been drawn straight from draconian veins. The resin actually gets its name from the tree whose fruit it's extracted from: a palmlike Indonesian tree covered in dragon-like scales. Dragon's blood has long been used as an astringent; that is, it restricts the flow of blood from a wound by constricting body tissues. This is an example of a signature plant, one that mirrors physically its effects medicinally. In this case, the bloody appearance speaks of its ability to help in ailments of the blood. Like bloodroot, dragon's blood can also be a sympathetic link for actual blood in a magickal working, and also targets issues of the heart. It is associated with love and lust because of its color, and has long been used in spells of that sort.

For use in ritual, dragon's blood resin is awesome. It is used to strengthen any spell; just add a pinch of it in your concoction to amplify its power. The resin is incredibly aromatic and enchanting, adding an "air" of mystic ambience to any magickal working. It's also used for cleansing an area of negative vibrations in rites of purification and exorcism. Not only does it drive away unwanted forces, but it also invites strong energetic protection to any area where it's burned. The smell is *incredible* and the resin is nontoxic, so burn away!

FOXGLOVE (*DIGITALIS SPP.*)

GENDER: Feminine
PLANETARY RULERSHIP: Venus & Pluto
ELEMENTAL RULERSHIP: Water

This gorgeous but deadly plant has long been associated with Witchery. Of foxglove's alternate names, the terms "Witches' bells" and "faerie thimbles" point not only to the structure of the flower but to the plant's mystical associations.

Though foxglove is used in spells of protection; its most potent use is that of communication with the Otherworlds, particularly the realm of the fae and the realm of the dead. Like most of the herbs listed here, foxglove is aligned to the Underworld because of its poisonous associations and can be used in necromantic rites. (The modern use of the broad term necromancy can include anything from summoning the dead to simply meditating and speaking aloud to the dearly departed; please see the final chapter of this book.) Foxglove is one of the plants most associated with the faerie realm. It has been said that faeries favor the thimbles (flowers), whose variety of vibrant colors (varying with the species) give them associations with the world of fae. The plant can be carried, planted, or left as an offering when performing any sort of communal work with the faerie realm. It is said that such work should be pure of heart and never deceptive, lest ye shall become an enemy of the wee folk!

Appropriate to the name, and to its faerie alignments, foxglove has associations with invisibility. While physical invisibility may not be an option, carrying the herb when you wish to remain incognito or in the background of a scene can serve to deflect attention, rendering you invisible in a sense. Additionally, when performing "covert" magick—that is, any type of spell wherein you wish to cloak or mask your energy pattern—use a bit of foxglove in the working.

The medication Digoxin or Digitek, also known as *Digitalis* (the Latin genus name), is a *digitalin*: a medicine containing foxglove extract. These drugs are used to treat a variety of heart conditions. Magickally speaking, then, foxglove could be applied to magick dealing with metaphysical issues of the heart. Obviously, it should not be taken internally. Foxglove can be dried for use in sachets and the like, or can be planted and grown in an area undisturbed by animals (as with most of these herbs, it is toxic to them as well).

HEMLOCK (*CONIUM MACULATUM*)

GENDER: Feminine
PLANETARY RULERSHIP: Saturn
ELEMENTAL RULERSHIP: Water

Hemlock has a pretty bad reputation in Witchcraft. It is said to have been used to cause quarrels between lovers, destroy sexual drive, summon evil spirits, and leave both crops and animals barren. Jeez! Whether or not this was a Christian fabrication to further persecute supposed heretical magick-workers, hemlock is in fact a dark herb that can be used for both beneficial and harmful purposes.

Hemlock is actually a member of the carrot family. It's a sedative when used in small quantities and a poison in larger doses, if taken internally. In ancient Greece, an extract of hemlock was used to put convicted criminals to death. The philosopher Socrates killed himself by drinking an extract of hemlock. For this reason, the plant is associated with death and the depths of sorrow. Thus, the herb's energy aids a person in coming to terms with the shadow self, inducing sadness to be faced and recognized. Curiously, some ancients believed it could counter insanity and give balance to a person. It's good to use in magick for this purpose: bringing balance to the off-centered, especially if the imbalance came as a result of emotional pain. Beware if looking for wild yarrow: hemlock looks very similar! Hemlock tea will have quite the opposite effects of yarrow tea, so don't ingest anything unless you're absolutely certain of what it is.

HENBANE (*HYOSCYAMUS NIGER*)

GENDER: Feminine
PLANETARY RULERSHIP: Saturn
ELEMENTAL RULERSHIP: Water

A member of the nightshade family, henbane is also known as black nightshade. The ancient Greeks associated it with the sun god Apollo and with divination. In Greek mythology, the dead receive a crown of henbane leaves upon entering the Underworld. Magickally, the herb allows the caster to summon demons and dark forces, and to evoke and perceive spirits, especially through burning. Though only a handful of Witches actually practice this style of magick, it does have its time and place. The herb is also associated with barren wastelands and is said to have the power to render an area of land (or a person) infertile.

On a lighter note, henbane is said to aid in matters of psychic perception and in the concoction of love spells. It can also help induce prophetic dreams if kept in a sachet close to the bed. Henbane's greatest magickal property is in helping a magician see through the veil to perform great acts of divination, astral projection, and spirit communication.

MANDRAKE (*MANDRAGORA OFFICINARUM*)

GENDER: Masculine
PLANETARY RULERSHIP: Mercury, Uranus & Pluto
ELEMENTAL RULERSHIP: Fire

Mandrake is one of the most popular roots used in Witchcraft, and is certainly the most widely used root in shadow magick. In ancient Germany, it was called *Hexenkraut* ("Witches' plant"). Ancient Greeks referred to it as Circe's plant because of the mythological Witch's use of the root in her potions. It has been used since ancient times to induce states of trance. Be extremely careful if ingesting it; numerous people have overdosed and there is a good chance it could kill an inexperienced user, as has been documented. Some herbal and magick shops have actually stopped carrying the plant because of teenage misuse. Many shops carry American mandrake (mayapple), a plant unrelated to true mandrake but sold under the same name because of its nearly identical magickal associations and visible similarities.

Mandrake is also called sorcerer's root because of its vast magickal powers and its metaphysical effectiveness. The root is a signature plant, growing in a roughly human shape with a head, arms, and legs. Because of this, it can be used for magickal workings concerning oneself or another person. If a person's energy pattern is locked into an effigy of the root, it is said to have power over that person: a belief that has long been used for everything from healing to cursing. A whole root does not have to be used, as a simple pinch contains its imprint. Mandrake is much more widely available than most (semi)toxic herbs and is a perfect substitute for any of the nightshades. It has aphrodisiac qualities and is ideal in spells for spiritual love and communion. It's also said to ward off disease and misfortune, and may be hung in the home to invite protection. Mandrake is also associated with spells of binding, health, money, love, and fertility. It is ideal to use in spells requiring banishment of harmful people, ideas, or energies. Its energy vibration is intense and should only be used in the most meaningful of workings. Maybe the old folktale of mandrake roots shrieking and screaming when pulled from the earth is indicative of their esoteric power! I've always felt that mandrake is one of the most powerful plants in the book, and its accessibility (even if it's mayapple) makes it tempting to use in any deep magickal working.

POPPY (*PAPAVER SPP.*)

GENDER: Feminine
PLANETARY RULERSHIP: Saturn, Moon & Neptune
ELEMENTAL RULERSHIP: Water

Are you a friend of Dorothy? Who can forget the infamous scene in *The Wizard of Oz* wherein Dorothy, Toto, and the Cowardly Lion fall under the lulling spell of the poppy field? Indeed, the flowers were the creation of the Wicked Witch of the West in the film, a spell cast to divert the group from their destination, the Emerald City. Though it is theorized that the film was making a deliberate reference to the influence of opium in the nineteenth century, I find it more interesting that poppies are associated with Witchcraft. In a sense, it speaks of their power.

Others have written extensively on opium's historical influence on trade, politics, government, and economics, but I'm more interested in its magickal use—or more accurately, the magickal use of the flower from which it is extracted. Opium is the resinous extract of the ripening poppy pod. It is from this resin that we get morphine, which can be processed into heroin. Opium also contains the opiate alkaloid codeine, which, for medical use, is either isolated chemically or synthesized from morphine. It has also long been used for the relief of pain, as well as to inspire restful sleep, and it was used as an aphrodisiac for centuries in

China. This factor, in addition to the romantic appeal of the flower, make the plant one associated with love and lust. Because of its associations with both dreaming and the numbing of pain, poppy is also linked with death: the release of the physical body.

Poppies, even the varieties that contain no opiate qualities, have been used in folk magick for a variety of purposes. It has been said that carrying the seeds can attract vibrations of wealth and financial luck. Poppy, like foxglove, is also reputed to render a magician "invisible," and can be used similarly to foxglove in that regard. In magickal terms, the energy of all the properties of opium can be accessed by simply planting or placing the flower or dried pods in the home. To inspire creativity, any variety of living or dried poppy can be placed in an area where one creates art. To intensify sensuality and sexuality, or to combat insomnia, poppies can be placed by at the bedside. If making a sachet to aid in physical healing and pain relief, either for oneself or another, why not add some poppy seeds to the mix?

PSILOCYBIN (*PSILOCYBE SPP.*)

GENDER: Feminine
PLANETARY RULERSHIP: Neptune
ELEMENTAL RULERSHIP: Earth & Water

Oh how I love you, psilocybin: a guide and wisdom-keeper to the mysteries of existence. Also known as magick mushrooms, and not to be confused with the semi-poisonous red-and-white-capped *Amanita muscaria* (fly agaric or "Alice in Wonderland") mushroom, psilocybin—which is scientifically recognized as virtually *nontoxic*—has long been ingested for shamanic and ritualistic purposes in various cultures. Perhaps most notable are the Mazatec Indians of southern Mexico, who ingest psilocybin for purposes of vision quests, shamanic healing, and experiencing community and kinship. The Aztecs referred to mushrooms as *teonanácatl*: "the flesh of the gods."

In addition to cannabis, psilocybin is considered a holy sacrament by many Witches, Pagans, shamans, magicians, mystics, and psychonauts. Psilocybin is an *entheogen*: a mind-altering substance taken for ritualistic and spiritual purposes. Worldwide, shamanic traditions include entheogens in ritualistic practices aimed at healing, spirit communication, ancestral magick, divination, and communal experience. Mushrooms in particular are said to be connected with the energies of death and rebirth, and many users report experiences of this nature.

Above all, mushrooms are linked with vision quests and visionary experiences, which comes about from the perceived rending of the "veil of reality" between this world and others. I personally know magicians who gained visions of their life's destiny whilst dancing with the psychedelic spirits, others who have accurately perceived the faerie realm and Otherworlds, and others still who have reported life-changing psychological, emotional, and spiritual rebirths. Of course, such rebirths are only possible by facing our inner demons and past darkness, coming to terms with them, and releasing them.

Because many of us are heavily haunted by past experiences and their imprints, it can be difficult to undertake a mushroom trip in a purely social setting, rather than a more deliberate, spiritual one. The equal-opposite paradoxes of extreme sorrow and extreme joy can become blurred (and even experienced simultaneously) when the veil of reality is lifted. If the mushrooms are ingested in the wrong setting, or in the wrong frame of mind, a "bad trip" can ensue. The results of any drug are relatively unpredictable and depend largely on the surroundings, including other people, as well as the user's mental, physical, and emotional health. Mushrooms can also force-release much of the ego and catapult seekers into deeper, and yes, "shadowed," aspects of the mind. So users should be balanced and comfortable with themselves before navigating the planes. Psychedelics and psychological imbalance (or even a history thereof) are rarely a good combination.

The effects are wide-ranging. Experienced 'shroomers report a direct connection to the spirit of Gaia, a perception of the fabric of reality, a realization of synchronicity and the immaculate construction of the Universe, a profound dimensional shifting, intense psychic development, spirit guide contact, astral travel, the honing of healing and magickal abilities, past-life regression, bilocation, and mystical connections to Oneness or God(dess). Some Witches and Pagans enjoy "taking a trip" once or twice a year to reconnect to their spiritual path and gain visions for the year. Psilocybic medicine is closely linked with the vibrations of the faerie realm (both benevolent and cunning), as well as to spiritual purity/innocence, the astral planes, euphoria, and spiritual joy, usually in the form of belly laughter, exaggerated humor, lots of yawning, spacing-out, and creating trippy art. Of course, I know none of this from personal experience...

RUE (*RUTA GRAVEOLENS*)

GENDER: Masculine
PLANETARY RULERSHIP: Mars
ELEMENTAL RULERSHIP: Fire

Rue has long been used for its hex-breaking and counter-magickal properties, and is said to be particularly effective when added to bathwater. Its use is prevalent in African diaspora religions such as Vodou, Ifa, and Santeria (Lucumi), as well as in Hoodoo. Its energetic feel is simultaneously light and dark, honest and vengeful. It can be used for many purposes, especially those of deep spiritual transformation or much-needed protection. Its most widely recognized and utilized property is exorcism and the banishment of harmful forces. Rue is a great herb for protection and has been used as such since Etruscan times. It has also long been associated with purification (the smoke or a watered infusion of rue can purify an area) and protection against malicious sorcery. It can enhance psychic or clairvoyant powers, expose the truth about a situation, help unlock hidden realms, and clarify chaotic thoughts, bringing balance to those who use it.

The herb is associated with depression and sorrow, and can help one emerge from these mental states. It's also linked with death and necromancy, and is used in ancestral communication: in ancient Greece, necromancers used a rue ointment for communication with departed souls. In Italian Witchcraft, it is called the "bitter essence of the God" and is associated with the Lord of the Harvest. The plant's name comes from the Greek *reuo*, meaning "to set free."

SOLOMON'S SEAL (*POLYGONATUM OFFICINALE*, ETC.)

GENDER: Feminine
PLANETARY RULERSHIP: Saturn
ELEMENTAL RULERSHIP: Water

This herb's root is associated with high magick, and its mysteries are both accessible and limitless. Pieces of the Solomon's seal root can be tailored into talismanic amulets or inscribed with sigils to use in a spell. It is said that all the herb touches becomes enchanted. The root lends protection and security to any environment. Its feel is very dense and powerful. It stores a profound wallop of energy just waiting to be tapped! It is also said to be useful in rituals involving disciplined or intense forms of magick, such as exorcism or the controlling of spirits. Its other uses include increasing wisdom, gaining luck, guidance, success, personal growth, and sustenance. It's best used as an incense for this purpose. Sealing a spell with an emphatic "So Mote It Be" or "Abracadabra" whilst using a bit of Solomon's seal can close a working like none other!

King Solomon, the (debatably fictional) last king of Israel and son of King David, as according to the Qur'an, was said to be a practicing magician. He wore a ring known as Solomon's Seal, which was said to bless him with the ability to accomplish any task and, through a stone set in the ring, to scry thoroughly on any situation, no matter how fantastical. When the plant named for Solomon's ring dies in autumn, hexagram-shaped markings are left on the root. Folklore says that Solomon left his mark on the plant to point toward its magickal potency.

Regardless of origin, the hexagram images on the root signify the herb's magickal potential. In early Hermeticism, the hexagram represented the alchemical combination of the four elements and seven recognized planets, so Solomon's seal root carries similar properties. The herb is rare but can be found through some occult supply shops.

TOBACCO (*NICOTIANA SPP.*)

Gender: Masculine
Planetary rulership: Mars
Elemental rulership: Fire

The tobacco plant is associated with wisdom. In the Native American Yokuts Nation's creation myth, the hawk spirit chewed tobacco to become wise before creating the mountains. The Apsáalooke believe that tobacco is a star that descended to earth, implying that the plant may be extraterrestrial. The Kickapoo and the Cahuilla both say that the Creator took tobacco from his own heart and gave it to the peoples of the earth. In some Native cosmology, it is believed that the gods themselves smoke sacred tobacco. Many Native peoples perceive tobacco as a female energy, though some nations, such as the Cherokee, see it as a masculine force and refer to it as Father or Grandfather, believing the plant to be an incarnation of celestial bodies.

In general, the tobacco plant is seen as an intermediary between the physical world and the astral world. It is smoked, often in a shared ceremonial pipe, to send prayers to spirits, the directions, the ancestors, and the gods: the smoke carries intention and can be blown to the winds to project prayers. The leaf is also smoked to induce mental calm and expanded awareness. A shaman or healer can blow pure tobacco smoke on a patient to strengthen the healing process, to spiritually see the cause of the ailment, and to chase off harm. Tobacco is also one of the best offerings one can give to the spirits, and has been widely used by Native Americans and other Indigenous cultures for this reason.

According to some Native traditions, tobacco is protected by ethereal beings—beings who seem to be similar to the gnomes in most Pagan and Wiccan traditions. Following this belief further, every herb may have its own set of personal guardians, just as trees have their Dryads. Because tobacco smoke is an intermediary between the worlds, it is plausible that the addictive act of tobacco smoking is a person's unconscious attempt to reconnect with the spiritual world. It is for this reason that spiritual "voids" may be temporarily filled by the act of smoking, much as with other drugs.

People who use the herb very sparingly don't tend to develop nicotine addiction, but still can be prone to it if they don't monitor their use properly. Many people like to use tobacco in combination with alcohol in social settings, but at no other time. Some Pagans restrict the use of tobacco to ritual circumstances only.

If one chooses to smoke tobacco, the kind that is not "chemically enhanced" is preferable from a health point of view. There are only a handful of cigarettes on the market, for example, that do not contain chemical additives. I must say, if one enjoys smoking, a briarwood tobacco pipe matched with a natural mellow blend can be a classy alternative. Certainly, not inhaling smoke at all is the healthiest choice.

VALERIAN (*VALERIANA OFFICINALIS*)

GENDER: Feminine
PLANETARY RULERSHIP: Venus & Jupiter
ELEMENTAL RULERSHIP: Water

The only root that officially smells like dirty socks, valerian has a long history of both medicinal and magickal use. Valerian is first and foremost associated with protection because its strong smell creates an "astral bug repellent." The cut, ground, and sifted root can be sprinkled around a property to help form a protective barrier, and hanging valerian root in the house ensures that harmful energies will be kept at bay.

Valerian is also said to bring peace and harmony to a situation and is useful for soothing quarrels between lovers. It is also used for magick working to physically manifest what one desires, such as money or even a sex partner. Physically and metaphysically, valerian root is used to promote deep, sound sleep. (This is, of course, also the case when it comes to the medicinal use of valerian tea and capsules to promote sleep.) It can also help manifest self-acceptance and ease the mind of sorrow. The root may also be used in some manner whilst doing magick to contact one's spirit animal. Like catnip, it also drives most cats bonkers. Give some to your kitties!

On a darker level, valerian is associated with the energies of the Underworld. African-based tribal practices such as Hoodoo, Vodou, and Santeria include the use of "graveyard dirt" or "graveyard dust." Valerian, alongside mullein and sage, is said to be a substitute for this spooky ingredient. Because of its power as a pungent root, its vibrations are inherently connected to the lower astral levels. For this reason, the herb can be used in death magick, cursing, and necromancy as well.

VENUS FLYTRAP (*DIONAEA MUSCIPULA*)

GENDER: Feminine
PLANETARY RULERSHIP: Venus, Mars & Saturn
ELEMENTAL RULERSHIP: Fire

Few plants are as mysterious as the carnivorous varieties. These plants grow in areas low in nitrate ions, the form of nitrogen easiest for plants to assimilate. As a result, they are forced to capture their own meals as a living supplement.

Ruled in part by the planet Venus, the flytrap (and its cousins) is a very curious plant indeed. The double leaves of this insectivore are hinged like a clamshell, each half with a row of soft but spike-shaped "teeth" on the outer edge. When a bug walks on the inner surface of the leaves, small hairs are triggered and the trap closes shut. Soon thereafter, the leaf releases acidic fluids to dissolve and absorb the insect's body in a slow and agonizing process of digestion.

The association with Venus, the Roman goddess of love, came about because of the double leaves' resemblance to the vulva, the "mouth" of the vagina. Therefore, its metaphysical uses include alignments with both love magick and lust magick, as well as any sort of capturing, especially capturing a lover. But ethical issues accompany any sort of manipulative love or lust magick, especially if it's performed on a specific person; I don't recommend it whatsoever. (The plant's acidic digesting fluids suggest just how "consuming" and destructive the possibilities are.) In keeping with its double-edged properties, the flytrap is also said to be able to both enhance and destroy feminine sex drives. The results of sexually centered magick with this plant could be quite adverse.

The flytrap can also represent confinement and isolation. Thus, it may be used in workings centering on this energy, as well as in binding magick. If performing binding magick of any type, be sure to intend it for the goodwill of all involved and add a hefty dose of "light" for balance and potential progression for the other party (poor thing).

Since so many animals eat plants for sustenance, it's only proper that some retaliate and eat animals in return. A few carnivorous plants are actually capable of devouring small rodents and lizards, though most are simply insectivores. Sorry, no real-life *Little Shop of Horrors*! Some varieties of pitcher plants (one of the flytrap's cousins) undeniably resemble snakes and fangs in their physical appearance, telltale signs of their lethal prowess. At a glance, it would almost seem that insectivores represent a merging of the plant and animal kingdoms. This and countless other wonders of these kingdoms are, for me, undeniable evidence of a metaphysically interconnected world.

WORMWOOD (*ARTEMISIA ABSINTHIUM*)

GENDER: Masculine
PLANETARY RULERSHIP: Mars & Chiron
ELEMENTAL RULERSHIP: Fire

Wormwood was held sacred by the Greeks, most notably in Greco-Roman Egypt, and was said to be an herb venerated by the gods. In some ancient spells, it was also called the "blood of Hephaistos," Greek god of smith crafts and son of Hera.

Wormwood is a member of the Artemisia family. Its Old English root word, *wermod*, means "spirit mother." Its Greek name, *apsinthios*, means "absent of sweetness," as it's a very bitter herb. It is poisonous in large doses and its green oil extract is particularly toxic in large quantities. Wormwood is the primary ingredient in the legendary liquor absinthe (the name derived from the Greek). Both absinthe and wormwood were and still are associated with artistic creativity, love, and lust. In antiquity, wormwood was also used for summoning spirits in necromantic rites, and it can still be used for those purposes in shadow magick.

Because absinthe that includes wormwood is addictive, the herb can be used in magick for breaking addictions. Wormwood is externally used for sleeping and dream magick. It can also be used to target issues of anger and ego, and is said to have the power to remove curses as well as create them, which makes sense considering its Mars energy. Like its cousin mugwort (which it's often mistaken for in the wild), wormwood is excellent to use in divination. I like to keep a small bag of mugwort and wormwood with my Tarot decks and seal bits of it to candles specifically designed for divination.

Appropriate to artist types, wormwood is associated with improving creative ability. It's not a bad idea to keep a bottled or bagged herbal charm in an area where artistic endeavors are undertaken. It's also a good herb to use as an incense in meditation, especially for reflecting on a loss of any type. It helps one come to terms with the reality of losses that accompany life changes.

Ye Olde Flying Ointment

I simply can't forego mentioning the Witches' flying ointment, also called "Faeries' Oyntment," "Witches' salve," and *sabbati unguenti* in days long past. Everyone knows the image of Witches flying across the moon on their broomsticks (called *transvection*), sweeping the stars and cackling through the night. This seems like a far-fetched fantasy, but in truth, it's not entirely fictional. A mix of fact, fiction, and metaphor may say it best.

The Witch's flying ointment is but one "historical" example of drug use for magickal means. I place the word "historical" in quotation marks because, well, scholars are still on the fence about its reality versus fabrications by early Witch hunters. In pre-industrial times, many peoples enacted rituals to foster the fertility of the land. European Pagans ran through their crop fields, jumping up and down to encourage their productivity: magick for survival's sake. Women did indeed straddle broomsticks, while men typically did the same with pitchforks or shovels. In addition to this suggestive magick, a homemade hallucinogenic herbal concoction, now known as a flying ointment, is said to have been smeared on the practitioners' nude bodies to induce astral projection and amplify the magick; it would allegedly be rubbed on the areas that would quickly absorb it, such as the neck, wrists, underarms, genitals, and feet. These ointments may have sometimes been used along with the aforesaid broomstick fertility rites, but they were generally reserved for astral projection rituals, as is commonly thought.

The broom-jumping activity, along with a heavy dose of herbal drugs, could well have produced the illusion of flight. Reportedly, the person fell into a nearly comatose slumber for anywhere between four hours and four days and, during that "trip" (especially the early part of it), the person shapeshifted astrally into animals and mimicked those animals whilst under the trance. Upon awakening, the person reported fantastical experiences and information about the planes they had visited. Modern scholars have considered this herbal drug magick akin to hallucinogenic shamanic practices outside of Europe, noting such similarities in virtually all forms of ancient entheogenic use. Narcotic potions have been used in varied forms by Witches, shamans, and religious peoples of many cultures worldwide, each culture using locally available ingredients. But some Craft scholars debate whether "flying ointments" were really used by early Pagans. Was the practice a modern-day fabrication to explain the origins of the broomstick flight myth? I agree that it is questionable, and that fiction may have been blended with fact (with such *known* rites as jumping through the fields to encourage crop growth). This need not negate the flying ointment's validity, but it's good to question all the "facts" of allegedly ancient Witchcraft, regardless of the source.

Witch hunters knew of the Pagans' belief in the Otherworlds (astral planes) and translated associated activities like hallucinogenic "flying" into myths of actual flight by means of sorcery with the Devil—see the next chapter for more information on this horrific Christian history. It is up for question whether these practitioners believed they were physically flying or not, as the advent of common science (and common sense) hadn't occurred until the Renaissance, when it was disproven that they were actually flying. Science accompanied religion during the period of the 1400s to 1600s, and the Church's concept of Heaven, Earth, and Hell being the whole of reality excluded shamanic-based understandings of the multi-faceted layers of existence.

The oldest documented mention of flying ointment in one of its forms seems to be a classical text dated 1458, translated around 1900 by modern occultist Samuel Liddell MacGregor Mathers. In *The Book of the Sacred Magic of Abramelin the Mage*, book 1, chapter 6, an Austrian Witch presents Abraham with a hallucinogenic unguent that induces the experience of astral projection for hours on end. While this account isn't concrete evidence, it presents the idea that flying ointments were known and most likely utilized to some degree in the fifteenth century.

Many of the ingredients in the varied forms of ointments are either obscure or illegal in this day and age. Today, some magickal practitioners use "modern flying ointments" made of less harmful blends, often only legal herbs. Rather than having major psychoactive effects, the herbal ingredients are used magickally to help with trance meditation, psychic awareness, visionary powers, and astral projection.

Included here strictly for historical interest—not for use at home—is a flying ointment recipe said to be a traditional English one from a Gardnerian grimoire; the resulting mix was blended with oil or lard. A number of these plant species belong to the family Solanaceae and contain atropine, as well as other hallucinogenic alkaloids such as hyoscyamine and scopolamine. Just finding all the ingredients and researching their risks for a blend could take at least a life or two! (Get it?) Not to mention, if the brew was not administered safely by someone well-versed in the effects of rare and toxic herbs, the result could be lethal. In other words, *don't don't don't* try this at home, for gods' sake! Besides, most modern Witches do not require herbal blends and potions to induce astral projection (although nontoxic ones can be helpful), as they have learned to draw upon inherent abilities for such endeavors.

TRADITIONAL RECIPE—*FOR HISTORICAL INTEREST ONLY!*

- 250 grams Indian hemp (a white-flowering plant related to the poisonous herb dogbane—not actually cannabis)
- 50 grams extract of opium (poppy resin)
- 30 grams betel (a Southeast Asian climbing plant)
- 15 grams belladonna (deadly nightshade)
- 15 grams hemlock (water parsnip)
- 15 grams henbane (black nightshade)
- 6 grams cinquefoil (a powerful herb bearing the properties of the pentagram, whose yellow flowers have five petals

and whose leaves grow in sets of five; also called five-finger grass in Hoodoo)
- 5 grams cantharidin (a chemical compound from the bright green European medicine beetle cantharis)
- 3 grams annamthol (possibly referring to anethol, a substance derived from parts of anise, fennel, and other herbs)

Other ingredients used in flying unguents around the world include these herbs: aconite (monkshood, wolfbane), mandragora (mandrake), foxglove (*Digitalis* spp.), climbing nightshade, sweet flag (calamus), datura (thornapple), smallage (wild celery), saffron, poplar, marijuana/hashish, tobacco, hellebore, briony, mugwort, thistle, skullcap, gum tragacanth (astragalus), asarabacca (hazelwort), toadflax, benzoin, vervain, sandalwood, morning glory, sunflower, and basil.

THE WEIRD SISTERS OF MACBETH

The magickal uses of herbs are famously chanted in William Shakespeare's *Macbeth* (Act IV, Scene I). In this scene, three Witches have gathered 'round a cauldron during a thunderstorm to create a brew of mischief and mayhem. Before crafting the spell, the sisters make mention of their animal familiars, who were referenced in Act I. They include Graymalkin (a cat), Paddock (a hedgehog), and Harpier (an owl). Upon Harpier's cries ("'Tis time, 'tis time"), the Witches begin:

> *Double, double toil and trouble;*
> *Fire burn, and cauldron bubble.*
> *Fillet of a fenny snake*
> *In the cauldron boil and bake.*
> *Eye of newt and toe of frog,*
> *Wool of bat and tongue of dog,*
> *Adder's fork and blindworm's sting,*
> *Lizard's leg and howlet's wing,*
> *For a charm of powerful trouble,*
> *Like a hell-broth boil and bubble...*

The spell continues, ending with an encounter with the goddess Hekate, their patron deity and overseer of their deeds. The Witches then go on to empower their brew in Hekate's presence. Upon her departure, the second Witch seals the spell with blood: "By the pricking of my thumbs, something wicked this way comes!" (Some believe that Hekate's scenes were added at a later date by another playwright, while others believe that the part originated entirely with Shakespeare, while others believe that "Shakespeare" was actually the philosopher Francis Bacon!)

So what does this scene have to do with wortcunning? Most of the ingredients used in this spell are actually the folk names of various herbs and plants. Others, like "liver of a blaspheming Jew" and "baboon's blood," which are used in the second portion of the spell, may have been either associated with other natural ingredients or added for theatrical value. Some obvious herbs were also included in the mix, like hemlock and rue.

In premodern times, many herbs were named for their physical characteristics. This simple form of classification allowed for easy identification of local plants. In a literary sense, mentions of obscure and bizarre ingredients maintained the mystique of Witches as being extra-special, having access to all sorts of unfathomable goodies. We still see the practice of naming herbs after body parts carried over today with some common flora having names like cat's claw (a bark) and dragon's blood (a resin).

I suspect Shakespeare had a fair amount of information about early European Pagan practices, or at least common charmery, making the task of devising this spell that much easier. Some theorists believe he gathered information, realistic and fantastical, from the numerous people he interacted with, later incorporating portions into his plays. In his life, Shakespeare interacted with a wide array of individuals with radical and blasphemous ideologies for the time, many of which most certainly influenced his writing.

The Witches of *Macbeth* are called the Weird Sisters. The word *weird* is rooted in the word *wyrd*, meaning "fate" or "destiny." The ancient Greeks personified fate and the cycles of life in the form of three sister goddesses called the Fates or the *Moirai*, who were daughters of Zeus. In the mythology, the Fates oversee and control the lives of both gods and mortals, weaving their destinies moment to moment. Clotho spins the threads of the web of life, beginning its course; Lachesis weaves the threads, deciding the duration of life; finally, Atropos cuts the threads, ending life.

In Ásatrú and Norse heathenry, three sisters are also recognized in a nearly identical tale. Called the "Sisters of Wyrd" or the "Sisters of Fate," they are the presumed basis of Shakespeare's tale. The first sister is named Wyrd (or Urd), the second is Verdandi, and the third is Skuld. They have virtually the same life-directing roles as the Greek Fates and are seen as the guardians of *Yggdrasil*, the ancient Norse Tree of Life. They represent the past, present, and future, as well as the stages of existence.

Modern Wicca also recognizes the triple goddess: the Maiden, Mother, and Crone. Each represents a phase of life and is further associated with the stages of the lunar and solar cycle, probably having direct links with the Greek idea of the three sisters.

Back to Shakespeare: I invite readers to similarly experiment with herbal name associations for personal use. Giving alternate names to plants used in magick can both fancify a spell and codify the ingredients (such as in a Book of Shadows). It can also be a fun way to add theatrics to a public ritual, which can in fact lend power to a working through an added air of mystery. (When we *feel* spooky, we can get mysterious and Witchy.) Of the folkloric herbal associations made in *Macbeth*, a number have been either identified or speculated about, as shown here.

> FILLET OF A FENNY SNAKE: Probably chickweed, though some believe it to be bistort.
>
> EYE OF NEWT: Refers to the "eye" or central part of flowers, probably either of daisy or horehound. Others believe it to be a form of yellow mustard seed resembling a small eye, formerly used in medicinal blends.
>
> TOE OF FROG: Bulbous buttercup.
>
> WOOL OF BAT: Holly leaves or moss.

Tongue of dog: Hound's-tongue (a European leafy, toxic plant also called gypsy flower).

Adder's fork: Dog's tooth (a type of violet) or plantain.

Blind worm's sting: Possibly wormwood, poppy, or a twisty twig.

Lizard's leg: Lizard's tail, a swamp-dwelling plant characterized by its long, drooping flower clusters. Some believe "lizard's leg" to actually refer to a sort of common creeping plant instead.

Howlet's wing: Holly leaves or a similar leaf.

Chapter Five
The Shadow of Society

"The shadow and its projections not only affect us individually, but also collectively. Every society—every nation—has an identity of its own to which we relate. This group mentality creates its own shadow whereby people identify with an ideology or leader that gives expression to their fears and inferiorities as a whole, giving rise to religious or racial persecution, Witch hunting, scapegoating, and genocide. The collective shadow is the root of social, racial, and national bias and discrimination; every minority and dissenting group carries the shadow projections of the majority."

—John J. Coughlin
from *Out of the Shadows: An Exploration of Dark Paganism & Magick*

A SAD & BEAUTIFUL WORLD

Throughout human history, violence, iniquity, and social injustice have been widespread and constant. Today, our problems are myriad: severe poverty, bombings, torture, deceptive governments, overpopulation, pollution, rapid global warming, political and religious violence, manipulation, genocide, animal abuse, climate change, and the rape of Mother Earth for her resources—these are but drops in the bucket of the world's suffering, and all filter into the everyday lives of everyone on this planet. If these issues keep escalating as they are now, our species is doomed. Massive changes in the earth's atmosphere and global consciousness are inevitably and irreversibly upon us as a species, but the degree and intensity of the impacts are yet to be determined.

In many ways, the tainted quality of the world is more visible now than it ever has been. Along with this fact comes the necessity of self-responsibility. Are we doing our part to positively change the world, or are we enabling its decay? How do we really treat other people? What corporations, products, and industries do we support or boycott? How do we individually make use of what we are given, including natural resources, human-made materials, and our own emotions and bodies? To what extent are we functioning as cogs in the human machine, and in what ways are we reclaiming our freedom and lessening the suffering of others? Do we really, truly care where the world is going, or do we apathetically and conveniently ignore our own impact? Do we care about global consciousness or just our own? Do we honestly help other people, including those who live far from us, or do we just think about doing it, focusing instead solely on our own survival? Do we just send energies of love and light to beings who are suffering, or do we actually act on those energies in the physical world as well? These are key questions to ask as we examine society and our place in it.

Our society is a strange beast, yet this animal can and must be tamed, one person at a time. As magickal, spiritual individuals, we must do all we can to attune ourselves to the welfare of the earth and its beings. We must change our ways accordingly and dare to conquer apathy with action. We are here for many reasons, not least to help the planet; now more than ever, it is imperative that we awaken to our ways and attune our lifestyles to the beauty and peace we wish to see overtake this plane. At this moment in human development, we must turn our focus away from the trivial and toward the world at large.

Ritual Meditation: Scrying the Small Screen

This meditation offers insight into how the media, television in particular, shapes our culture and our own psyches. It's vital to look in depth at how our Western society operates, where we stand within it, and how our contributions affect the greater whole. Initially, the thought of performing a meditation in front of the TV might seem a bit odd. Well, it is. But there's good reason for it! Along with the Internet, television is the most highly influential medium in the world. Any idea, suggestion, or social issue can be conveyed and amplified on the screen. There are programs and channels devoted to almost everything under the sun. By analyzing and deconstructing this magickal tool of communication, we can get a better sense of the society in which we live, and the dread shadow that dwells beneath the plastic masks.

Like any other medium, TV can convey supremely spiritual messages, destructive messages, and anything in between. For this exercise, I invite readers to sit in front of their television set (or someone else's if you have chosen against owning one—a wise choice indeed) and look at this catalyst of our culture in a different light.

If, like me, you don't own a television, this can also be accomplished by browsing YouTube videos at random and forwarding the videos to different spots. Get divinative-creative!

1. Begin by sitting in front of a turned-off cable television. That's right, just sit there with the remote control in hand. Today it will serve as a makeshift anti-brainwashing magick wand (hence the sacred "mute" and "off" buttons, which shall luckily be utilized). Get comfortable and begin by clearing your mind. Take three deep breaths in through the nose and out through the mouth. Let the thoughts of the day drift away like moving clouds. This is not the time to focus on what happened today or what you need to do tomorrow…allow the common world to dissipate as you enter the sacred terrain of the mind. For several minutes, sense the oxygen entering your nostrils and exiting your lips. Bring absolute focus to your breath.

2. Having entered a slightly altered state of consciousness, declare your intent, saying something like:

"Great Spirit of Truth and Wisdom, I ask you now to part the veil of illusion, illuminating for me both the sacred and the profane of the society in which I find myself. As I sit now before this Pandora's Box of pixels and satellite signals, I ask that my mind become expanded rather than numbed. I ask that I may clearly see reality through this machine of illusion."

3. Close your eyes and envision an indigo-colored tentacle of energy between your *Ajna* chakra—your third eye—and the center of the TV screen. Then see this tentacle breaking

off from the TV and retracting about halfway toward you. Envision the tentacle growing an eye; it is now becoming an extension of your third eye.

4. Now that your perception is somewhat separated from the influence of the television, take a deep breath and click it on with the remote, opening your eyes. Visualize the third eye tentacle watching the screen as your physical eyes do the same.

5. The TV is now tuned to a commercial, an infomercial, a sitcom, a drama, a movie, the news, a documentary, or something else. If it's static, click to the nearest channel. Turn off the closed captioning (unless you use it for accessibility reasons) and set the volume low. Regardless of the program, view it for a couple minutes: not "watching TV," but rather "monitoring the programming." Do not laugh at the jokes, wince at the violence, or absorb any of the conveyed emotions: remain neutral and expressionless. See beyond the facade presented. Note how your psyche becomes transfixed and even hypnotized by the screen. Observe the actors: to what extent are they acting, and what might they really be thinking? What messages are the writers, producers, and directors of programming trying to convey? Get inside their heads. Are they trying to charm you into buying a product (and if so, why do they personally want your money)? Does the program emphasize sexuality or certain body types (and if so, for what purpose)? Are they simply trying to entertain the audience (and if so, might there be something deeper...a hidden agenda)? Ask yourself questions upon questions. See "behind the scenes" and psychoanalyze the image in front of you. Try to be as realistic as possible; that is, not overly paranoid nor overly trusting.

6. Now hit the "mute" button and analyze the programming in that manner for two more minutes. Again, visualize the tentacle not linking you to the TV set, but remaining independent. This time, pay particular attention to people's expressions,

the images shown, the colors used. How calculated are these details? Why are they displayed in these manners, sequences, speeds, and patterns?

7. Close your eyes and reflect on what you just witnessed. What energy, emotion, or influence is being conveyed to the viewer? What do the programmers want you to think? What social norms, ideas, taboos, expectations, fears, or glorifications does the programming seem to reinforce? What details do you observe that might usually go unnoticed or unseen? Deconstruct what you just viewed; "deprogram" the programming. Contemplate how many people might be under the spell of the programming at this very moment. Reflect on how this may influence our society.

8. Unmute the TV and continue the exercise for another 30 to 40 minutes, moving to a number of other channels. Use your intuition to decide where to stop channel surfing, or, if you are familiar with the stations, flip to one that might be of particular interest for this exercise, such as an infomercial, a fundamentalist preacher, or a youth culture program. Cover a wide variety of material but, for purposes of this exercise, shy away from intelligent programming.

9. Click the "off" button. Close your eyes and ground your energy. Visualize the tentacle receding into your third eye, blessing you with psychic sight and discernment.

10. Take time to write down your observations and insights, and keep this list for comparison when you do the exercise again in the future. (What are the similarities between the lists, and what does this suggest about our greater society?)

11. When finished, thank the Spirit of Truth and Wisdom in your own words. Give homage to the energies summoned forth, stating that you are gaining more knowledge regarding the "programming" of society, and that you will actively strive to align your behavior to spiritual ideals over social falsity.

Fantasy Magick:
A Shadow Side of the Occult Scene

In a chapter focused on the shadow of society, I cannot fail to discuss a "shadowed" aspect of the modern magickal scene that far too often goes overlooked, yet poses a serious problem to the legitimacy and balance of our chosen lifestyle. I term this syndrome "fantasy magick." Many of this book's readers have probably encountered this all-too-common form of manipulation in Pagan and magick communities. Fantasy magick takes hold when a person's mental line between fantasy and reality blurs or is or erased altogether, thus intermingling those worlds to an unhealthy degree in the person's life. This dishonest negation of the perimeters of reality is often displayed by a person's vehement proclamations of supernatural powers, superhuman abilities, and nonhuman status. Personally, I have encountered self-proclaimed kings and queens of the faerie realms, descendants of the Nephilim and the Anunnaki, interdimensional warriors and voyageurs, time travelers, and people with "98 percent faerie blood" or "40 percent dragon DNA." I have also met a number of "incarnate" deities, archangels, and role-playing game characters, and at least a good handful of Crowleys, Merlins, and Cleopatras. Still, some practitioners wonder why Pagan spirituality isn't always taken seriously.

Sadly, it is begging to be said: it is highly unlikely that we are reincarnations of ancient gurus, gods, or gremlins. We are not fallen angels, archangels, demons, dragons, faeries, elves, mermaids, sirens, griffins, sídhe, unicorns, Wookies, Gelflings, or Ewoks. We are human. We are all human. As magicians, it is our responsibility not only to seek to recognize when we are being lied to, but to assist others who may, themselves, be victim to any sort of magickal manipulation. Often, a fixation on fantasy magick is rooted in escapism. When a person feels dissatisfied with life, and is also aware of magick and the existence of other planes of reality, an easy-seeming remedy for the emotional pain is to over-embrace, exaggerate, and otherwise go overboard with one's participation in these magickal spheres. Blending reality with fantasy can make life seem less dull. Merging the worlds of fantasy and mythology into ordinary existence can make everything seem more attractive. If our magickal lives really were like they are in *Charmed*, *The Craft*, *Practical Magic*, *Sabrina*, and role-playing games, it would make things more exciting and dramatic—most definitely! However, the worlds of fantasy and mythology should be recognized and enjoyed for what they are; they only lose their artistic value if they are fancied as "alive" beyond a mythical or psychologically archetypal sense.

Escapism often grows out of a desperate need for a sense of self-worth. Believing oneself to be a creature of fantasy, for example, can add to one's sense of importance and also justify feelings of loneliness and isolation. An ego-inflated person who presents this illusion to others can psychologically trick themselves into actually believing the fantasy, beginning a downward spiral of lies, manipulation, and possible psychosis. More often than not, these beliefs are formed as a result of others' attempts at manipulation. When a person is awakening to the magickal world and is coming to realize that reality is much more intricate than it seems, new doors of perception are opening. It is while a person is in this state that manipulation from others can be most effective. A metaphysical teacher or initiator is likely to realize this spot of vulnerability, which is why the student has the responsibility to question and analyze everything that is taught, regardless of the source, and step back to consider the direction in which they are being taken.

To comment specifically on nonhuman identification, I will say that though our physical bodies are very much human, our astral bodies can vary from that form. This is where the difference lies: a part of us may vibrate and resonate with these nonhuman things on a spiritual level. For example, I "am" a raven and I "am" a creature of the Water element. I have friends who "are" faeries or elves in the sense that they feel a kinship with the archetypes of these forces. We may feel a strong, and perhaps past-life, connection to Avalon or Egypt, but that does not mean that we "were" Morgan le Fey, King Arthur, Isis, or Tutankhamen.

It is also worth saying that our spirits may not necessarily be "from here." Many discerning, reality-based members of Otherkin and Starseed communities recognize that their bodies are 100 percent human, even if their souls feel predominantly nonhuman. There are plenty of people who feel as though their spirits hail from elsewhere, and this is certainly a valid perception. Is it possible that some people's spirits are

Pleiadian or Andromedian? Or that they existed in Atlantis or ancient Greece? Who knows? These things cannot be proven; they can only be felt or experienced. Personally, I feel that beliefs such as these should not be instantly accepted when the idea arises, but should be explored with honesty, skepticism, and objectivity. Otherwise, it is too easy to blur the line between actual experience and mere flights of fancy.

Imagine a young man who frequently practices astral-body shapeshifting into the form of a wolf (which is also likely a spirit guide), performs magick and meditation using wolf medicine, and identifies as a werewolf for these reasons. If he describes that to a person who doesn't understand the concept of astral shapeshifting, the person may assume that this guy thinks he actually grows wolflike fur, claws, and fangs when the moon is full. This is, of course, just as silly as thinking that New Age lightworkers can ascend the physical plane at will, or that those who practice Goetic evocation have half-animal/half-demon fetches or familiars. Then again, I'm sure that there are still people out there who claim these things of themselves.

Some people don't intentionally twist facts and inject fiction into any given situation; they may simply have been misinformed. If a person has been told that dragons, demons, archons, specters, wraiths, wendigos, and hellhounds lurk behind every corner just waiting to be vanquished or ghostbusted, or has been taught to believe that a particular person is a supernatural being, that's manipulation. The person must *unlearn* these things to come to a greater understanding of these astral planes and mythologies. Reality is profound and mysterious enough as is; why must true magick be diluted with fiction?

When a person presents known fantasy as if it were actual reality, it can give genuine practitioners a bad name. A few examples: For a person who really does work with Enochian or angelic forces, it is demeaning to be considered alongside others who claim they can grow wings and feathers if they focus hard enough (or who have been manipulated into believing such things). For a real Druid Revivalist, it is insulting to be considered alongside those who boast of tracing an unbroken, thousand-some-year-old lineage to the original Druids (of whom we historically know next to nothing about in the first place). For someone who was raised in traditional Wicca, it's degrading to be considered alongside those who claim to have a Book of Shadows from their great-great-great-great-great grandmother, or to belong to a secret underground "ancient family tradition" of Witchcraft (more on this in the next section of this chapter). Such tales are spread regularly in modern occult circles. When a person's introduction to the Magickal Arts comes in the form of some other person's fantasies, that person is being misinformed, and may come to think that all Witches, Pagans, and occultists have such beliefs; it's a matter of guilt by association. Such pseudo-magickal spirituality also undoubtedly turns off potential practitioners who could have otherwise benefited from esoteric study. It's a bloody vicious cycle!

Fiction is metaphor; fiction is mythology. It is beautiful and powerful, but most of it is simply representational. Discerning this from our experience of reality is key in our search to know ourselves, and it is that very key that helps fuel our spiritual evolution and builds the strength of our community.

DECONSTRUCTING THE BURNING TIMES

In this book we are analyzing the shadow. While we have primarily examined philosophical spirituality and practical magick, an overview of the "dark times" of the Witchcraft persecutions will ground that understanding in history. It's time to shift gears for a section and enter the realm of academic history.

As we review the European Witch hunt era, you will encounter more academic detail (straightforward and scholarly, but hopefully not dry) than in previous chapters. You have been forewarned! I pursued this research both for the benefit of readers and for my own benefit. I wanted to convey an accurate history, and I enjoy academic work as a balance to heavy metaphysics. My career at the University of Montana helped tremendously in encouraging these studies. Not to mention that the chaos magician in me wishes to ensure a balance of lighthearted and intellectual material within this book, just to keep myself and others on our toes. Additionally, huge thanks to John Michael Greer for his valuable edits and suggestions with the following material.

The European Witch Hunts

Long before the European Witch hunts (or "Witchcraze"), and most certainly to this day, what can be termed "black magick" has been viewed as a very real and powerful source of agony and human suffering. Whether this perception of magick-at-large stems from ideas of evil spirits, demons, Satan, earthbound disincarnate ghosts, sorcerers, or Witches, the concept of evil as a
spiritually opposing force is a strong cultural archetype. It has been and will continue to be a major player in religious and cultural developments across the globe. It seems as though people psychologically require an archetypal adversary to justify their own pursuits.

When Americans are asked to think about the Witchcraft persecutions, they tend to think of the Salem Witch Trial of 1692, in which twenty people were tried, convicted, and executed by hanging as a result of an eruption of hysteria in Salem Village (now Danvers), Massachusetts Bay Colony. Hundreds of townsfolk were imprisoned, at least five of whom perished in confinement.

Though the trial in Salem is significant, and is well documented, it is the tip of the iceberg that is Witchcraft's persecution. Or, more accurately, the persecution of that which is deemed Witchery. Because the Salem incident is relatively insignificant in the scope of the persecutions, as well as because it occurred in North America instead of Europe, it won't be discussed in detail herein.

Magick was originally used to describe the Arts of the Magi in classical antiquity, encompassing astrology, divination, ritual, and curative magick. The period of time now commonly known as classical antiquity began after the Bronze Age with the founding of Rome in 753 BCE and ended when the last Roman emperor, Romulus Augustus, was forced to relinquish his throne in 476 CE.

Early Christian writers were quick to point out that the Pagan gods were in fact demons, demonstrating that they viewed Greco-Roman thaumaturgy as devilry. Not until the thirteenth century did writers begin to differentiate between natural and demonic magick, the latter often termed *maleficia* or sorcery.

The image of the evil Witch began to form in classical antiquity and can be seen in numerous liturgical representations of the time.

Because women were viewed as inferior to men, a view held popular in ancient Judaism that was certainly perpetuated and expanded with the rise of Christianity, Witches were originally portrayed as women. Certainly, male sorcerers existed in the ancient worldview, and men were frequently condemned. The belief in individuals being capable of having malefic magickal abilities was on the rise, and represented the gradual humanization of the demonic in common worldviews.

In the Greco-Roman world, a division between magick and religion gained prominence, with "magick" being seen as malicious and not associated with the "natural" world, and thus became part of the sphere of Witches. Originally the Pagans dominated religious thought and practice, often deeming early Christians as magicians, a view due especially to the control of demons they exhibited in exorcism rites, as well as their use of secret magickal names. Because the view was that magick relied on the help of the gods (Pagan or Christian), Greco-Roman Pagans opposed magick and its antisocial, maleficent implications. As Christian thought grew, Christian writers spoke out against magick as a demonic activity and even turned the table on the Pagans, deeming their religion both inauthentic and inherently bound to magickal practice. These views of magick were strong in antiquity and saw a revival of sorts in the thirteenth century.

THE ETYMOLOGY OF WITCHCRAFT

It is in Old English that the word *Witch* has its roots. Originally spelled *wicce* in the feminine and *wicca* in the masculine, the word referred to a diviner or fortuneteller. Many modern Witches, a large number of whom follow the twentieth-century, syncretistic, earth-based religion Wicca, mistakenly believe that the word originally meant "wise," thereby earning the modern Witch the title of "wise one" and their Arts the "Craft of the Wise."

This etymological misconception was pushed in the 1950s by Wicca's founder, Gerald Gardner, whose intent was to promote his new syncretistic religion as a positive and life-affirming path. Linguistically, the Old English term for "wise one" is actually the root of the modern word Wizard. Wicca and wicce, however, come from a verb meaning "to bend or twist." This meaning has also been interpreted in a positive light by many practitioners of modern Witchcraft, who view it as implying a magick-worker's ability to bend, twist, and shape reality to their will. However, if we examine the Old English usage of the term, we find that "twist" was the antithesis of "straight" (meaning "proper"), revealing that the term was used to refer to someone who was twisted, crooked, or otherwise morally unacceptable.

Modern practitioners of Witchcraft belong to both schools of thought: those who believe "Witch" to have been derogatory from the start, and those who believe the word was maligned only as a result of the Witch hunts. Neither uses the word to self-marginalize. Instead, Witches in general seek to reclaim a once-maligned term and alter the public perception of it, much as we see with terms such as "queer" in current times.

Additionally, despite common misconceptions, the word *warlock* was not originally gendered. Rooted in the Old English *wærloga*, the word means "oathbreaker" and was an Anglo-Saxon insult that was eventually used against those who practiced magick. It's likely that "warlock" as a term implying masculine sorcery was an eighteenth-century notion; at that time the words warlock and Witch were both being used as slanderous terms. Though the term warlock was rarely used, Witch was recognized in antiquity and was referenced in literature at the time. The image of the malicious sorcerer gained momentum in the Late Middle Ages when Witchcraft was aligned with the gravest of all crimes: heresy.

Magick in the Middle Ages

The era in Western European history now commonly known as the Middle Ages, or the medieval period, began with the fragmentation of the Roman Empire's political power in the fifth century CE and lasted until the sixteenth century, spanning from the Migration Period to the Protestant Reformation. The Early Middle Ages are generally seen as the fifth to eleventh centuries, the High Middle Ages as the twelfth and thirteenth, and the Late Middle Ages as the fourteenth and fifteenth centuries.

For nearly the entire expanse of the Middle Ages, Christian tradition and Hermetic tradition (including its accompanying magickal and alchemical practices) coexisted in Europe without issue. Many Christians also practiced magick, divination, and astrology. It was only near the end of the Middle Ages that a strict division between the scientific and magickal spheres was distinctly drawn. Before then, it was simply assumed, correctly, that an astronomer was an astrologer. It was likely that the classical notion of the philosopher-magician persisted to some degree at this time, though people practicing in these two fields were often separate, distinguishable by class and social status. Medieval European intellectuals recognized two forms of magick: the natural and the demonic. Natural magick concerned hidden powers within Nature and was originally seen as a branch of science, including astrology and herbalism, for example. Demonic magick was seen, instead, as a perversion of religion that turned away from God.

THE HUNT BEGINS

In the Early Middle Ages, the Church was not overtly concerned with issues of Witchcraft, although it had laws forbidding the very belief in the existence of Witches. In the High Middle Ages, especially in the 1200s with the rise of the Papal Inquisition, the Roman Catholic church sought to discover and punish heresy. Beliefs about Witchcraft were varied at this time. As many people began to view Witchcraft as less fictional and more legitimate, Witchcraft allegations started to rise, as people equated Witchery with heresy.

The Witch hunts began in what is now western Switzerland and the bordering areas of France. The "new heresy" of Witchcraft as a growing public threat was officially introduced to the Church around 1375, only twenty-four years after the end of the bubonic plague pandemic. It was also only fifty-one years after the final eradication of the Knights Templar, a step that had proved that the Church was capable of wiping out entire groups of perceived heretics. And after the fact, it was easy to identify Witchcraft as a possible cause of the great bubonic plague—the Black Death—which had killed one-third of the population of Europe. According to this perceived threat, Witchcraft practitioners were working directly with the Devil himself, selling their souls and creating pacts to gain worldly wealth and self-serving magickal powers. Over time, the mythology of the Witches' Sabbath evolved to include fantastical accounts of demonic evocation, flight on broomsticks and pitchforks, human and animal sacrifice, cannibalistic infanticide, the use of black magick and cursing, demonic butthole-licking, and all styles of fornication.

From modern-day Switzerland, Witch hunting and the resulting trials made their way up the Rhine River to areas of modern Germany and elsewhere. (For reasons unknown, the interest in hunting Witchcraft declined heavily for the first half of the sixteenth century.)

The Revival of Roman Law

In the 1200s, Church scholars and civil governments revived ancient Roman legal doctrines. According to these laws, certain types of magick were deemed acceptable, such as those dealing with agricultural growth or medicinal healing. Any sort of magick aimed at empowering a person like a god, and thus having sway over the material world, was viewed as immoral and, according to the Church, heretical. Magickal scholar and practitioner John Michael Greer characterizes the revival's effects this way: "Roman law also brought a major change in the way criminal charges were handled. Most of Europe before the revival of Roman law followed a traditional "accusatorial" process—that is, charges had to be brought by a person who had been harmed by the alleged crime, and if the charges proved false, the person bringing them faced severe penalties. Roman law, by contrast, made use of an "inquisitorial" process—that is, charges were brought by a public official, who was exempt from penalties in the case of false accusations. The study of Roman law in the universities led to the adoption of inquisitorial procedure over much of Europe. All these changes made heretics and magicians much easier to charge and convict."

The revival of Roman law also influenced the legal use of torture, making it an acceptable method of extracting confessions. This methodology was on the rise and saw its greatest use as the early modern times began.

What we call the early modern period began around the sixteenth century with the European Renaissance and spanned the Protestant Reformation, the Age of Discovery, the rise of the modern European state in the 1600s, and the beginning of the Age of Enlightenment. The Industrial Revolution of the late 1700s and early 1800s marks the beginning of late modernity. By this time, the social and religious mainstream concerned itself very little with seemingly obsolete notions of Witchery. In the late modern period, the question of the Christian Church's position on Witchcraft had essentially lost its importance.

The Height of the Witch Hunts

Contrary to the common perception that the medieval period saw the height of Europe's Witchcraft persecutions, they actually began on a large scale only in the mid-1400s, the cusp of early modern times. From then until the late 1700s—virtually the whole of the early modern period—Witches were sought out, accused, tortured, and executed. This occurred all across Europe, with no area left untouched. Some areas had less activity (for example, fewer than 1 percent of all Witchcraft-related executions took place in all of England, believe it or not!), but nobody escaped the fear and paranoia that gripped all Europeans socially and psychologically.

The belief in Witches was widespread and constantly reinforced socially. Even the most socially upstanding upper-class people were not exempt from the ideology and, in many cases, from its resulting persecutions. Virtually everyone believed, or feigned to believe, that Witches existed and that in fact anyone could be a Witch and could strike at any time. Anything that went wrong could be blamed on demons or the Devil, with whom Witches were obviously in league. During the craze, if something went wrong in the natural cycle, such as a poor harvest yield, ill health of farm animals, or unfortunate weather patterns, Witches were the prime suspect. Similarly, imbalances in a person's health, luck, mental state, or sexual performance was evidence enough to accuse Witches for the misfortunes.

It didn't help that churchmen, upon realizing that Witchcraft and heresy were closely tied, frequently excommunicated or otherwise punished secular authorities who refused to confer the death penalty on the convicted.

The Witches' Sabbath

Some scholars have argued that the infamous but imaginary concept of the Witches' Sabbath has its origins in the canon *Episcopi*, a ninth-century Catholic text written in what is now France. The mistaken belief that this canon dated from the Council of Ancyra in 314 CE was perpetuated at the time, and it was incorporated in a number of authoritative medieval canonical texts.

The canon *Episcopi* helped perpetuate the image of Witches flying through the night and gathering at designated locations at certain times of year. It originally cited Diana, the "goddess of the Pagans," as the Divine sorceress in charge of executing these rites, placing the roots of Witchcraft in classical mythology. As European folkloric beliefs about Witches and their activities became solidified, the Church solidified its own view of Paganism during the High Middle Ages, essentially dismissing it as nonsense. The concept of the Witches' Sabbath may represent a malignment of ancient European Pagan fertility festivals which, because they honored deities other than Christian, were increasingly seen as inaccurate and spiritually invalid.

Some scholars argue that the Witches' Sabbath stereotype may come from the claims of the *benadanti*, an agrarian cult in the Friuli district of northern Italy. The group's regular fertility rites had caught the eye of church inquisitors, who based their concern on material in the canon *Episcopi*. In 1570, cult members told inquisitors about their activities during the Ember Days, days of fasting and prayer: they would often fall into a trance, astrally project from their bodies in a shapeshifted animal form (or in the form of the soul-body riding an animal), and engage in an ethereal battle with Witches who sought to destroy their crops. The inquisitors had sought out the benadanti with the goal of gaining a confession of sorcery, one that was justified by the cult with the explanation that they were "born with cauls," this implying that their prowess was beyond their control and assumedly God-given. Over time, the cult's relatively simple descriptions of their rites morphed into very colorful depictions—essentially, the Witches' Sabbath in all its sinful glory. It is likely that, to protect their own safety, the benadanti "spun" the rites in a way that made them appear victimized by demonic forces.

In the sixteenth century, fear heightened exponentially, and the Witchcraze climaxed between 1560 and 1660. Mass Witch trials and executions were occurring in Switzerland and Belgium in the 1580s, and in France and Scotland a decade later. German Witch hunters, who fancied mass genocides, were burning people alive by the hundreds in some areas as early as the 1600s, including France, Germany, and Switzerland, and later in Sweden. It was popular to enforce a "catch-all" tactic of discovering, accusing, and punishing all people who even potentially had ties to Witchcraft.

The hunts continued during the 1600s across Europe. In England, they were ended in 1682. Over the next century, Scotland, France, and Germany followed by putting an end to legal Witchcraft executions, and Switzerland stopped a century after England, in 1782.

Thou Shalt Not Suffer a What to Live?

During the early modern religious reformations, a strict and literal reading of certain of selected biblical passages was encouraged, namely Exodus 22:18, which was translated as "Thou shalt not suffer a Witch to live," even though neither the original Hebrew text nor the Greek *Septuagint* (the ancient Greek translation of the Jewish scriptures) used the term Witch. The word Witch was used in the King James Version of the Bible, first printed in 1611. As accusations of Witchcraft grew, King James himself actually intervened on more than one occasion (even as early as 1616, just five years after the first printing), worried that innocent people were being convicted of things they had not done. King James did not translate the Bible himself, but had sanctioned the legality of translations by dropping formerly enforced penalties for doing so. Douglas Linder, in his *Brief History of Witchcraft Persecutions before Salem*, notes that, "the word Witch in Exodus is a translation of the Hebrew word *kashaph*, which comes from the root meaning 'to whisper.' The word as used in Exodus probably thus meant 'one who whispers a spell.' In context, the Exodus passage probably was intended to urge Jews to adhere to their own religious practices and not those of surrounding tribes."

Various other editions of the Bible translate the term as "sorceress," which does, in this case, imply evil magick performed by a woman, and is undoubtedly the most accurate translation in modern English. It makes sense historically, as early Judaic cultures generally held unfavorable views of women.

At the time Exodus was written (around 600 BCE), the word kashaph was meant to demonize more than just the Hebrews' surrounding tribes. It probably also referred to early Jewish mystical traditionalists such as the Ma'aseh Merkabah mystics and Kabbalists (who we do know were somewhat persecuted), Coptic Christians and other early Christians who used spells, charms, *voces magicæ* (Words of Power), and sympathetic or "imitative" magick—and, in particular, female practitioners. One could go as far as to say that early modern Witch hunters who backed their case with this Exodus passage were themselves unknowingly using charms and enchantments that would presently be considered Witchcraft: the very thing they believed the passage itself forbade. Oh, the irony!

The Malleus Maleficarum or The Hammer of Witches

Secular courts and private groups—not the institution of the Catholic Church—were the source of the majority of Witch trials and executions. However, one publication helped not only to fuel the Witch hunts but also to link them more closely to the Church in readers' minds. Written by Heinrich Kramer and Jacob Sprenger, the vomit-inducing *Malleus Maleficarum* was first printed in Germany in 1487. The cover of a 1520 Cologne seventh edition of the manual reads *Malleus Maleficarum: Maleficas, & earum hæresim, ut phramea potentissima conterens*, translating as *The Hammer of Witches: Smashing the Witches and their heresies with a mighty spear.*

In 1484, Pope Innocent VIII (note: "innocent" my fuckin' ass) had issued the papal bull *Summis desiderantes*, which spoke against Witchcraft and sorcery in Germany and encouraged the extermination of Witches by any means necessary. This charter was included as the introductory portion of the *Malleus*, which gave readers the illusion that Rome fully backed the manual. The manual described pacts with the Devil (as a result of feminine lust), Witches' activities and evil abilities, how to discover a Witch, and how to properly prosecute and execute. The text assumed that Satan was quickening in strength, exceeding even God's influence on the earthly plane and its peoples. To back his publication, Sprenger promoted the idea that objecting to the manual, even questioning it, was an act of heresy in and of itself. This branding of any sort of skepticism as heretical helped broaden the definition of what could be considered heresy.

The manual has strongly contributed to the perception of Witch hunting as woman-hunting, as it singled out women as Witches, never men. Women, according to the *Malleus*, were more inclined to devilry and heresy because of their inherently insatiable carnal desires. Similarly, the Devil was usually thought of as being male, so women were his obvious lusty disciples, an idea that is graphically described in the manual. Still, the *Malleus* was not used by Witch hunters as widely as is often believed. The manual was viewed unfavorably by most secular courts and inquisitors, who saw it as paranoid and inaccurate at best. Its influence is actually still unclear. The few court cases that referenced the manual in their notes make it clear that its influence was relatively small in the larger scheme of things. Still, the ideas perpetuated by it likely fueled the hunts to some degree.

The Catholic Church officially condemned the manual in 1490, just three years after its printing, and actually encouraged people to disbelieve in the existence of Witchcraft as anything more than superstition. A number of Witch hunters and judges unrelated to the Church continued to use the *Malleus* for their own hunts over the time of its multiple reprintings, and the manual influenced subsequent demonological literature.

Torture & Witch Testing

The rise of Roman law in Europe aided in justifying torture as a legitimate method of discovering heresy. Demons, it was perceived, both possess people and fear pain, making torture and horrific violence against the accused entirely permissible. These were practiced both in the Middle Ages and the early modern times. The extent of torture inflicted on accused individuals is, to any sane person, virtually impossible to wrap one's mind around.

In France, for example, records have been discovered attesting to drawn-out treatments, such as imprisoning the accused in dungeons or tiny stone cells. The immured were given only bread and water and in many areas, such as in Spain, were brutally lashed every day to aid in the exorcism of demons. Many died of terror, confined to darkness, in their own excrement and sometimes the bodily remains of others. A great number were also publicly humiliated, tormented, and jeered.

A number of sadistically brutal torture methods swept Europe. These included the limb-stretching rack; the strappado, or pulley; thumbscrews and toescrews; red-hot irons; the submersion of hands and feet in boiling oil, water, or baths of scalding slaked lime (calcium oxide); leg vices; whipping stocks containing iron spikes; starvation; extreme beatings; and other indescribably gruesome procedures. If the accused did not confess to the charges, they were usually seen as being assisted by the Devil, and were clearly just as guilty *as if they had confessed.*

Methods of "Witch testing," the practice of discovering if a person was in league with Satan, included swimming, weighing, and pricking: all agonizing and often resulting in death before conviction. Swimming, or dunking, was the practice of submerging the accused in water: the person who floated was a Witch, while the person who sank was innocent (and usually drowned). Weighing was the practice of placing the accused on one side of a scale and a Bible on the other; a person who weighed more than the Bible was guilty. (Who the hell weighs less than a book?!) Pricking, by pins and needles, was used to discover a Devil's mark on the body of the accused; this was an area on the skin that seemed to be insensitive to pain. In most cases, the individuals were stripped naked and had all of their body's hair shaved. Even a small mole, wart, or birthmark could suffice as enough evidence of guilt. Inquisitors would also look for a "Witch's mark," any sort of unusual protuberance on the body that could possibly be considered a teat from which demons would suckle in the guise of familiars or pets.

It should be noted that in many countries, torture was not used as a confession device. And in those where torture was used, it was not the exclusive domain of Witch hunters, but was a general method of "discovering" heresy by forcing victims to confess to anything, true or not. Under agonizing torture, the accused would admit to virtually any theory or rumor the inquisitor or inquisitors proposed, and would accuse other people (often either projecting their own accusations onto another person or creating a new heretical story altogether) just to escape the pain. Of course, in most cases, the number of people blamed for maleficia increased with each session of torture. Harsher methods of torture were justified with each new conviction, and the torture resulted in a multitude of additional accusations. The question of whether the accused had actually performed the proposed acts of Witchcraft was almost never asked; the question was when, how, and with whose assistance were those acts done.

The definition of magick and its resulting persecutions changed with each generation, changed with the hype of the era (and area), and changed with the constantly altering view of moral versus immoral, sacred versus profane. The history of Christianity, however, will be forever tainted by the blood of innocents.

The Spanish Inquisition

Although the Catholic Church's Spanish Inquisition is often associated with Witchcraft persecutions, the secular courts were actually far less lenient about these cases and far more responsible for the hysteria of the times. Self-styled *independent* Witch hunters, or groups thereof, were the prime movers, perfectly capable of sadistic methods of confessional torture. Among these was the infamous bloodlusting asshole extraordinaire Matthew Hopkins, "Witchfinder General," who killed 230 accused Witches in England: more than half the total executed in England during the entire span of the Witch hunts.

Instead, the Spanish Inquisition focused on heretics of other types, as it had for centuries. This body was one of the Church's four commonly recognized inquisitorial systems, and it hardly played a role in the European Witch hunts at all. The Spanish inquisitors were highly organized, seeking out heretics, trying them, and punishing them in vicious ways. These included Jews, Muslims, and those deemed sorcerers (although they were much less frequently condemned). The organization was also skilled at discovering whether individuals feigned their conversions to Catholicism or were actually practicing.

When one particular Spanish Witchcraft panic broke out in the early 1600s as a result of the French Witch hunts, a Madrid-based inquisitor was sent to investigate the claims. Upon his return, he explained that his exhaustive research had found no evidence of any sort of anti-Christian organization involved in devilry, and further pursuit of the issue would be a waste of time.

Given the Inquisition's determination and its many prosecutions of heretics through the centuries, it's easy to see why it's often assumed that it administered parts of the Witch hunts as well. In reality, the inquisitors were extremely skeptical about allegations of Witchcraft and sorcery. In 1526, the Suprema, the body's main council, made it known to its officials that bad weather or even the wrath of God were more likely culprits for crop failures than were Witches. The Inquisition was much more concerned with solid evidence, often viewing the

Witch hunts with an eye of cynicism. Beyond a case in 1610 where a few accused Witches were burned at the stake in Logroño, Spain, and another comparatively small incident in the early 1500s, the Spanish Inquisition was little concerned with the realm of Witchcraft.

THE BURNING TIMES

The phrase "The Burning Times" is used in Neopagan circles to refer to the European Witch hunts. It was actually coined by Gerald Gardner, who was of course the founder of the modern Wiccan religion, in the 1950s. In scholarly terms, the phrase itself can be misleading. In England, accused Witches were hanged rather than burned. (Lynching was definitely faster than burning, and it preserved resources. It was also a far easier method of killing a number of people in a relatively short period of time.) Although accused Witches were not burned alive in England, they were burned at the stake in other areas, most notably Spain and Germany. In reality, the methods of torture, execution, and the levels of mass hysteria involving Witchery varied from region to region across Europe.

One of the most misconstrued points about the Witchcraft persecutions in Europe is the actual number of people put to death. One widely cited but erroneous figure is *nine million* people (or "women"), which nearly matches the number of people murdered in the Holocaust. According to the historical studies of Brian Levack, the most accurate estimate of the Witch hunts' death toll is 60,000, itself a very high estimate in the scholarly sphere, but it does include an approximation of unreported trials and trials for which logs are now lacking for whatever reason. The difference between these figures should be noted: nine million is *150 times* the more historically based estimate of 60,000. (Many current sources give estimates of only 40,000 to 50,000 victims executed on account of Witchcraft specifically.) It seems that the figure of nine million was never a well-founded scholarly assertion.

This high figure was first proposed by an eighteenth-century historian and was a miscalculation unrecognized at the time. Still, it was spread through publication, and Gerald Gardner used the figure in his work in the 1950s. It continued to be cited by feminists, notably in the 1970s, and again in the 1990 PBS documentary *The*

Burning Times (part of a three-part series on Witchcraft), which put the statistic in the public eye. A number of modern Witchcraft traditions with ties to radical feminism also perpetuated erroneous ideas about the persecutions, including estimates of nine million and upwards in their accounts of *her*story. Not only do countless books mention such a figure, but a couple of Pagan folk songs and a number of Craft teachers (who were themselves simply taught the misinformation) also cite the slaughter of nine million Goddess-worshippers in the Burning Times. When they realize their error, many of them take no issue with correcting themselves, but others hold strong to the incorrect figures for reasons likely to do with pride or emotional attachment.

But even at the more realistic 60,000, the number of people tried and put to death for Witchery in Europe was both unprecedented and horrific. At the same time, the brutality is no surprise in the scope of history. According to historian Jeffrey Burton Russell, "This mania, this eagerness to torture and kill human beings, persisted for centuries. Perhaps we put the wrong question when we ask 'how this could be.' The past half-century has witnessed the Holocaust, the Gulag Archipelago, the Cambodian genocide, and secret tortures and executions beyond number. The real question is why periods of relative *sanity*, such as those from 700 to 1000 and from 1700 to 1900, occur."

The Accused:
Midwives, Herbalists & Goddess-Worshippers?

In her book *The Witch in History: Early Modern and Twentieth-Century Representations*, author Diane Purkiss notes that the Burning Times era "is often linked with another lapsarian myth, the myth of an originary matriarchy, through themes of mother-daughter learning and of matriarchal religions as sources of Witchcraft."

Contrary to the belief of many in current Neopagan circles, absolutely no evidence exists to suggest that the Witch hunts were an attempt to annihilate a surviving organized or underground Pagan religion, much less an ancient Age of the Goddess that was driven underground by misogynistic men, nor that the people accused actually followed a religion of this sort. In fact, by 1100 CE, there were essentially no Pagan fertility cults remaining in Europe.

The idea that most Europeans were still Pagan in the Middle Ages and early modern times is a notion that now seems to have been fabricated by author Margaret Murray, or perhaps was an exaggeration based on others' previous assumptions. For example, her 1921 publication *The Witch-Cult in Western Europe* included an array of theses, partial case studies, and assumptions that are frequently perpetuated even to this day by some modern esoteric groups. Murray's hypotheses were, for the most part, accepted as factual history in scholarly circles through the 1960s. It was only upon renewed studies of Murray's source material that much of it was revealed as inaccurate. Simultaneously, and paradoxically, many of these assumptions helped influence a great number of people to find their place in modern Wicca.

Additionally, no evidence exists to suggest that most accused village Witches were herbal healers or midwives. Herbal healing, midwifery, and other "feminine" activities of the domestic sphere were not specifically targeted for persecution with the rise of modern Western medicine, though this idea was proposed in the 1970s. However, many of the accused, as has been recorded in numerous sources, were in fact elderly widows or people with unique personalities who could seem threatening, including those who were particularly eccentric or had mental disabilities. It was not the use of herbs or charms that perpetuated Witchcraft accusations, but people's perceptions of their neighbors; particularly those at whom fingers could easily be pointed in blame for local misfortunes of any sort.

Many of the accused did practice herbalism or midwifery, but this was not the actual cause of the accusation. Common things such as herbs, charms, amulets, and potions could easily be construed as devices for heretical magick, which may be the area from which some of these misunderstandings arise.

Undoubtedly, folk remedies and healing techniques, both medicinal and magickal, were widely used in early modern Europe; these activities were not the exclusive domain of Witches or specialized healers and were not forbidden or otherwise controversial activities for anyone. Many midwives and herbalists are actually documented as assisting Witch hunters. Not all twentieth- and twenty-first-century political challenges in the West are the remnants of antiquated European political extremism. What is fringe or taboo now was not necessarily then, and vice versa.

The Oppression of Women

When considering the European Witch hunt era, many have viewed it as a form of female oppression resulting from patriarchal misogyny. This is an argument that has endured to a great extent in modern circles. In actuality, most accusations of Witchcraft at that time were from female, rather than male, "witnesses," whose hysterics were neither gendered nor an exclusive result of a patriarchal age. European society, for the most part, was just as oppressive of women before and after the period spanning 1400 to 1700; there was not a notable increase in misogyny during this time.

It's easy for modern Witches to see these persecutions as a feminine holocaust or even a *gyno*cide, and to fantasize about the nature of a glorious pre-Christian, Pagan age of matriarchy, magick, and Goddess worship. It simply did not exist. Personally, I identify as a man who is pro-feminist—one who strives for balance between all genders. The best I can do in this field (which, admittedly, is not my expertise) is to present the most accurate information I've discovered upon thorough academic research.

Some strains of radical feminism make claims that are based on only partially examined history. Because of increasing awareness of feminism and its implications in modern Witchcraft and Neopaganism, a number of emotionally loaded, exaggerated, and altogether erroneous notions have woven themselves into modern thought. Luckily, these notions seem to be losing power with time. Still, the fact remains that women sadly were, and continue to be, more societally demeaned than men, on a global scale! It would be folly to think that gender played no role in the Witch hunts: it most certainly did. Though most of the accused were women—about three-quarters of them—plenty of men, children, and countless animals were also murdered across Europe, a great number of whom were cats, especially our beloved black cats. Yes, animals were actually *put to trial as defendants* in the eighteenth century, showing the enormous amount of insecurity and paranoia still present in the populace. And yes, the animals, who were alleged to be shapeshifting demons or familiars, were often represented by lawyers. God help us all.

The view of the Witch hunts as a specifically female genocide took hold in the feminist movement at around the time that its members were shifting their focus from public issues (such as social and political rights) to private issues. At this time, many proponents of radical feminism linked issues such as sexual abuse and domestic violence directly to the influence of a patriarchal society, which is perfectly understandable. Naturally, the image of the renowned evil female Witch came to be seen as an archetype of the victimized and helpless woman made inferior by male political domination.

Presently, it is sorrowing and likewise empowering for a modern Witch or feminist to contemplate the possibility of an enormous persecution of innocent herbal healers, midwives, benign spellcasters, and others who are free-spirited and altogether naturalistic. Such activities are viewed as belonging to the domestic sphere, which is, more often than not, paralleled with privacy, femininity, and secrecy: things that both modern Witches and feminists are familiar with.

European history's horrific events, including minority persecutions of all types, trigger highly emotional reactions in people like us, who are proudly different from the norm and are anything but "ordinary." While this is quite understandable, especially for those whose biological or spiritual predecessors were oppressed, history mustn't be only partially examined. The validity of any claim, however emotionally charged, must be researched. This is not to downplay the seriousness of the European Witch hunts and their horrifying brutality, but only to say that discernment is crucial when seeking to understand the facts of any violent minority oppression (or any extreme issue for that matter), especially if the claims seem curiously grandiose. This is not to say that emotions must be nullified or done away with, but only that attachments to subjective viewpoints can easily skew or exaggerate events. This can actually weaken the legitimacy and credibility of one's viewpoints, which can in turn influence future events where a persecuted or once-persecuted group is concerned.

Over time, accusations against European women, men, children, and animals for being Witches and devils faded into history. New scientific and psychological advancements served to make this ephemeral hysteria obsolete. When the last Witchcraft Act was repealed in England in 1951, only a glimmer of the fear present in the Witchcraft persecutions remained. Because many people seem to require a spiritual arch-nemesis to operate, it's doubtful that fears of Witchcraft or other forms of magick will disappear in the West. Indeed, it's apparent that these fears haven't dissipated in South Asia, Southeast Asia, areas of Africa, and many other parts of the world, which makes a total disappearance questionable. However, we can at least hope that history has revealed itself to a large enough degree of comprehension and accuracy to, like the charm of an old Witch, ward against its repetition.

Chapter Six

The Shadow of Death

"The gap between death and rebirth is one of life's greatest mysteries. It holds everything we fear, and everything we wish for. For example, when trees and wildlife die in a forest, they decompose and become fertilizer for the earth in which new life grows. Without this death, new life couldn't exist. This illustrates that while darkness and death mark an ending, they also contain the next beginning."

—Kate Freuler
from *Of Blood & Bones: Working with Shadow Magick & the Dark Moon*

DEATH MAGICK

I believe it's safe to say that Pagans are aware of death's processes occurring constantly on various levels, including cellular, agricultural, and otherwise. Dark Witches identify the reality of death as a beautiful and natural transition. While some may believe that we glorify or are obsessed with death itself, this misconception comes about from the fact that we choose not to fear death, but embrace it as a sacred part of reality. We think about it more often and allow ourselves more time to contemplate its essence. When fires sweep the land, luscious greenery springs up from the destruction: the death and rebirth process at its finest. Destruction spawns creation, and when life has run its course, it then serves as a sacrifice for the (re)birth of others. The cycle continues and flows ever onward.

In modern Western culture, corpses are embalmed and preserved, poisoning Mother Earth, breaking the natural cycle. Mortuaries and funeral homes charge families a high price to "properly" put the beloved to rest. The dying process is pushed aside, away from the eyes of the masses. It is crammed away in nursing homes, generally apart from the rest of society. People have become unexposed to the reality of this transition, and therefore pay it little mind. Aging goes unacknowledged and death itself is denied. As perhaps one consequence, violence is in turn glorified in movies and television. Death is portrayed as romantic and the concept both idealized and de-emotionalized.

In actuality, another individual's death is a horribly difficult process. Losing someone we love, whether human or animal, can be nearly impossible to come to grips with. A part of ourselves dies along with a loved one's passing, and simply being unable to answer the questions "why?" and "what's next?" is often reason enough to be tormented for years.

In the ancient Western world, death was given attention constantly, and the dead were honored accordingly, in part thanks to the belief that the dead still had strong sway over the living. Cemeteries were called *Necropolises*, or "cities of the dead." They were sacred lands where the restless dead would wander and which the Great Ones oversaw. It's curious to note that even atheists still carry the tradition of bringing offerings of flowers to their deceased loved ones. This shows not only that death expands ordinary thought by pulling on emotional strings, but that longtime spiritual practices have inherent validity, even in the most unreligious of folks.

Death is considered to be the greatest of all mysteries and is, according to Oscar Wilde, only second to the mystery of love. What happens after we die? Is there a soul and does it continue on when the physical body ceases? Because natural science only studies the concrete, it would have us assume that once the physical body ends, there is no more to be had. This *linear* view of life is actually relatively new in the mind of humanity.

While we are still incarnated on the earth plane, the afterlife can only be left to speculation. At the same time, though rare, some people do have vivid memories of the transition between life and death, which tends to come from either an intuitive knowledge or personal near-death experiences. A countless number of individuals who actually endure near-death experiences that include physical death and revival report various occurrences. These include astral projection, a "reviewing" of the present life, the "light at the end of the tunnel," meeting ancestors and Divine beings, and having deeply moving mystical experiences, amongst other things. While these may be hints as to what's next, there's no saying what is to come. Even experienced necromancers often have trouble getting a logistical answer from the departed spirits they communicate with because the spirit appears in a form the human ego can identify.

It would be silly to think that death is the end…to think that once the physical vessel ceases to function, consciousness also dies. This is an easy cop-out assumption about death: that there is no continuance, and that consciousness comes to a complete stop. However, if we look at the process of Nature and the cosmos, we see that everything works in a cyclical nature; nothing is linear, nothing ever really ceases to be. Everything recycles, regenerates, and takes different forms. Greenery grows from the land; it dies in autumn and is reborn in spring. Our cells are constantly dying and regenerating; life is beginning again. There are no voids in reality; everything has its own essence. Though a very Taoist notion, balance is always the central point and is what all of reality comes back to. If something like human consciousness departs the earth, a corresponding energy must fill the gap. This is regeneration and is the reality of rebirth. This is not to say that our souls remain attached to our human desires and preferences; these are mundane aspects of life and the soul continues as an energetic pattern disassociated from present experience. It is often theorized that the soul, when reincarnated, exhibits similar patterns of behavior as in previous lifetimes and is born into a number of similar life circumstances.

Upon death, I would imagine we transcend the normal parameters of human experience and, if we don't trap ourselves as ghosts, eventually ascend to a connection with Oneness, the whole of the Universe. Time and space are then nonexistent. We become only energy, waiting to be recycled into the system. Perhaps energy is sorted onto various planes when the human ego is shed. If this were to happen, the "self" that was once known would be left behind. Our lower mental selves, or personal identities, are determined by our energetic pattern when we incarnate in human form. From there, the energy—which is really just a fractal manifestation of the infinite in the form of a person—follows its vibratory pattern by forming opinions and discovering interests aligned with the pattern of the spirit.

Through the whole of our lives, we develop an identity and personality, and that is what I believe is shed at death. If death is not accepted and the human "ego" experience is held onto, the person becomes an earthbound disincarnate or ghost. Otherwise, what can be called the True Self is realigned with Oneness and returns to the vastness of infinity before being once again sorted via reincarnation. Reincarnation is believed to follow similar patterns to one's previous lives, such as being reborn in the same planet, region, culture, or even family as the previous life. But then again, we have no way of truly knowing what happens when life ends, and these are only speculations.

A strong spiritual message accompanies the raw reality of death. The fact of impermanence and change is directly experienced. Nothing is forever. We can only assume that all things happen for a reason. Death is the equal-opposite of birth and is just as beautiful a change.

The Requiem

Burial rites have been performed since the times of the Neanderthal (130,000 to 30,000 years ago) and are, of course, currently practiced with much elaboration and care. These rites vary in every culture. Many Indigenous and traditional cultures use drumming to attune to the energy of the departed soul and send it on its way. In drumming, life is celebrated and transition is recognized. The physical beating of the drum is attuned to the element Earth (into which the body decomposes if buried) and the music it creates is attuned to the element Air (which is appropriate for cremation). The drum's rhythm can bring the listener into an altered state of consciousness. Naturally, drumming is thought to echo into the Otherworlds, being heard on many planes simultaneously. In death ceremonies, the hollow resonance symbolizes the finality of death and the beating of the drum is aligned to the beating of the heart and the rhythm of life. Drumming also serves to push the spirit of the departed from its liminal habitat to the afterlife.

The South American Amazonian Yanomamö tribe is one of the few tribal cultures whose ancient ways have been almost entirely preserved. Surprisingly, they are virtually the only tribe that actually does not use drumming in their ceremonies. Instead, they rely almost entirely on dance and chanting as ritualistic instrumentation. The Yanomamö also practice endocannibalism. When a member of the tribe dies, the body is decorated and finally burned with all of their belongings. The next year, the remaining bones from the cremation are finely ground and stirred into a porridge or juice that the entire community consumes. This keeps the energy of the person circulating in the tribe while their spirit is released to the Otherworld. This way, no sign of their body or physical existence remains present, cutting the ties between physicality and ascension.

The Berawan tribe in Borneo (Southeast Asia) creates rhythm and percussion during their loud, elaborate funeral ceremonies using instruments like gongs, xylophones, rattles, and sticks in addition to constant drumming. Participants dance and chant; the whole ordeal can be heard for miles in the forest. Noisy ceremonies such as this are not exclusive to death, but take place in any Rite of Passage such as birth, tribal initiation, and fertility festivals similar to Pagan Sabbats. For the Berawan (and other tribal cultures), the grieving process is shown very little in funerary rites. Rather, death is come to terms with through celebration and ritualism, and is accepted as a cultural and spiritual reality.

Some members within the Dayak peoples of Borneo neglect to cut or style their hair or care for their body after a loved one dies. They will neglect bodily care altogether: no bathing, washing, changing clothes, or anything else. Harvard anthropology professor Peter Metcalf noted in his ethnography that this practice is in place so the deceased's loved ones can resemble the corpse. As the deceased can no longer care for their body, the family members imitate it. They believe this will prevent the corpse from becoming jealous of the living and deter them from taking the living to the grave alongside them, as it would appear to the spirit that their loved ones are also deceased. The family also leaves offerings of food, drink, cigarettes, and other materials to bountifully send their loved ones into the afterlife and persuade them to overlook the living and not take them along to the gates of death.

Personally, I strongly devote to is Hinduism's Lord Shiva (Siva). Having numerous aspects, including the primordial Rudra, Shiva is well-known for overseeing death and rebirth, much as his counterpart Kali Maa (who mythically transforms into Goddess Parvati and gives birth to the loving Ganesha). A number of Tantric Hindus who follow primordial Shaivism and Shaktism do not shy away from covering themselves in human ashes, utilizing human skulls and bones, and separating themselves from the world as *saddhus*: wandering ascetics. Although *extremely* fringe in the vast expanse of Hinduism and Vedic religions, the *Aghori* are the most visible among these devotees; in fact, one of my own living gurus, Sshivani Durga, is a respected Aghori, Tantric, Witch, and teacher to many.

Many cultures use the color black in their death rites. Black symbolizes the mystery of life, the darkness of the earth, and the loss of consciousness—the entrance into the Otherworld. Other cultures use white in their ceremonies to signify the paleness of the skin and whiteness of the bones associated with the physical body's decay.

In addition to black and white, the third most common color used in death rites is red. Red symbolizes blood and the connection between the self and the earth. Red may also be associated with death in that sunsets often cast various shades of red upon the sky; Greco-Romans even believed that departed souls leave the earth when the sun "dies" every day. Red is the color of menstruation, a monthly "death cycle" for women, and represents the fullness of the blood mysteries of the Great Goddess.

The traditional Wiccan passage-into-death ritual is called *Crossing the Bridge*. The soul of a person is seen as crossing a bridge from the physical plane to the afterlife. *The Legend of the Descent of the Goddess* is often read at this time as well; some even reenact this Pagan tale as a theatrical play to better display the cycle of death as a holy process.

When a Pagan is in their last stages of life, their spiritual family gathers around them to perform various rites in order to guide the dying person into the afterlife and come to a place of acceptance themselves. Pagan death rites are performed both as a person is dying and at the burial service or wake in commemoration. Pagans have no strict code of conduct for performing death rituals and will tailor the ceremonies to the dying person's tradition and personal beliefs.

Often, a Priest or Priestess is invited to oversee and help conduct these Rites of Passage. Instead of performing rituals that only comfort the living, participants' personal discomforts are set aside as much as possible so that the dying or deceased individual can be focused on during their transition. The Priest, Priestess, or overseer might read passages from a variety of books including The Tibetan Book of the Dead, The Egyptian Book of the Dead, and even Starhawk's fantastic *The Pagan Book of Living and Dying*, to name a few. The family may play instruments, chant, ritualize, and meditate with the dying person to make the last days pleasant and to peacefully usher the passing soul to the Great Beyond.

The Afterworld

All religions have their own viewpoints on what happens to the soul upon death. Every tradition in history has its own afterlife theories and mythos. An afterlife abode mentioned in Pagan circles is the Underworld. The Underworld is the realm of chthonic spirits and gods recognized in ancient Mediterranean religions as the place where souls voyaged after leaving the body. In classical times, it was called the dark earth, or the land of darkness beneath the rest of the world.

In Greco-Roman mythology, the Underworld serves as the place souls enter upon physical death and is recognized as a liminal territory where the soul exists before being appropriately sorted. This is often called Hades, which is also the name of the Underworld's ruler god. Hades the god is Persephone's consort, as well as the brother of Zeus and Poseidon.

One of the Underworld's many realms, which is comparable to the biblical Heaven, is the paradise Elysium, also called the Elysian Fields or the Isles of the Blest. Another is the punishing Hell-like realm of Tartarus, and a third is a Middleworld of sorts called the Fields of Asphodel, in which the spirits live as shades in an "in-between" state, having been neither villainous nor virtuous in their human lives.

Greco-Roman mythology includes detailed descriptions of the layers and levels of the Underworld, the sorting process of the soul, and the role the gods play in life after death. In that sense, it's similar to the Norse or Ásatrú view of souls moving through the various worlds of *Yggdrasil* upon death.

The ancient Egyptian version of the Underworld was known as the *Duat* (or Tuat). This is seen as a world consisting of various planes, including Amenti, where the soul would be questioned upon death before either entering the Hall of the Gods (a heavenly realm) or being eaten and permanently destroyed by the crocodile god Ammut. The outcome for souls was seen as being dependent on their approach to life and living, things they had and had not done when incarnated, as well as the person's reverence for the Great Ones. The symbol for the Duat was a five-pointed sunburst shape within a circle, quite similar to the pentagram. Egyptian pharaohs and other members of royalty would prepare their whole lives for this judgment and secure themselves a good afterlife. The recognition and mythologization of death were prominent in Egypt. Both life and death were seen as equally important occurrences.

Ancient Hittites recognized primordial deities as dwelling in the Underworld alongside spirits of the dead. The Semitic Akkadians called them by the name Anunnaki, and those deities are currently theorized by some esoteric researchers to be a race of alien beings incorporated into classical mythology, possibly actually belonging to the "twelfth planet" (called Nibiru, Wormwood, or Planet X) which is scientifically unrecognized as part of our solar system at present. The Hittites had a unique method of communicating with Underworldly spirits and deities. They would dig a deep pit in the earth that was used to leave offerings to the deities and spirits below. They would then stand in the pit and perform communicatory exercises, necromantic and otherwise, believing that contact was made much easier when being physically closer to "their terrain," beneath the earth's usual surface level. Pits were used as gateways for the spirits to move from the earth plane to the Underworld, and vice versa. This type of chthonic magick was commonplace in Hittite society. They would summon Underworldly deities not only for oracular work, but also to present them with offerings and convince them to help purify living quarters and bestow blessings.

Tibetan Buddhists long prepare for the time of their death, feeling that "in order to know how to live well, one must know how to die well." They, and many other traditional Buddhists, believe that the soul experiences a series of afterlife *bardos* or transitional states. It is even believed that humans exist in one of these temporary stages, called the "bardo of existence." Tibetan Buddhists believe that there is a post-death bardo period lasting forty-nine days, in which the soul of the deceased faces various choices and challenges. At the point of death, the soul disconnects from the physical body, viewing their own body and surrounding friends and relatives performing ritual around the newly dead. When a person is dying, they are believed to be extraordinarily sensitive to sound and energy. Because of this, prayers, mantras, and recitations of The Tibetan Book of the Dead are of utmost importance for the dying person's well-being in the afterlife.

After entering a state of pure mind and emotion, the soul of the dead enters a bardo wherein they are faced with two lights. One light is extremely bright, nearly blinding. Most spirits are said to be very frightened by this light, though the tradition states that it is the light of pure Buddhahood and is ruled by Lord Vairochana, the ethereal Buddha of Wisdom. Because this blinding light frightens most souls, they choose to take refuge in a smaller, dimmer light off to the side. That light represents rebirth and re-entrance into the cycle of samsara (suffering). The concept of these two lights is most likely taken from the Hindu belief of the light of the sun and moon appearing at the time of death. If a person is drawn to the sun, they are said to enter heavenly realms, not returning for a future incarnation. If a person takes the path of the moon, they enter the cycle of rebirth. Both Buddhism and Hinduism believe that one also encounters a number of peaceful and wrathful deities upon death, which may very well be manifestations of personal pleasures and fears. Both traditions also believe that when one is reborn, they are born as a particular being in a particular set of circumstances based on their precise energy pattern, having come from lessons learned and deeds accomplished in the previous lifetime. Death is seen entirely as a transition—just another stage of being, rather than an ending.

Wiccans and Celtic Pagans refer to the Upper afterlife plane as the Summerland. This is opposite the Shadowland, and both planes coexist on the astral. The Summerland is called the Land of Eternal Summer and is associated with the Celtic (Welsh) view of *Arran*, the uppermost level of the afterlife world of *Annwyn* (Annwfn). The mythology surrounding Annwyn comes about from the Welsh poem *Preiddeu Annwfn* and, because so much information was lost with the coming of Christianity, it is often equated with the general consensus of the Celtic afterworld belief system.

Arran, the Summerland, is a heavenly realm of pure joy, whose energy is pleasant and serene. The season is always summer and fun is always to be had. It is often associated with Avalon, the "Isle of Apples," and is linked to the legend of King Arthur.

The Celtic Middleworld, being a bit more optimistic than the Greco-Roman take, is *Caer Feddwid*. This is seen as the "kingdom of intoxication," where wine flows and enchanting music plays eternally. Also present is an elixir of life that the inhabitants drink to sustain existence in this realm.

The third and darkest layer of Annwyn is *Caer Wydyr*, the desolate, gloom-ridden Underworld of Celtic mythology. This realm can also be called the Shadowland. All souls here are lost, wallowing in ignorance, emptiness, and loneliness.

Wicca, rooted predominantly in Celtic mysticism, naturally recognizes the Summerland. Pagans of other cultural leanings may not identify the afterlife experience as the Summerland or Shadowland. Instead, they would base their ideas on their own individual belief system. Not all Witches and Pagans have a concrete agreement on what happens to the soul when one dies. All simply understand that the soul lives on, existing in the Otherworld for a period of time, usually prior to reincarnation.

All of the aforementioned belief systems are just a few examples of the numerous conceptions of the afterlife from various cultural perspectives. Virtually every cultural mythos includes a version of an Upperworld, Underworld, and sometimes Middleworld. It's surprising how much mythology overlaps between cultures throughout time, and how similarly the afterlife experience is viewed worldwide.

BLOOD MAGICK

Bloodwork is most certainly a part of shadow magick, but is not something to be taken lightly; it should be performed with caution and awareness.

Being introspective people, Dark Witches are not averse to the prospect of shedding their own blood for serious ritual work that can cause actual change in one's own state of being. Although it may freak out some magickal practitioners, Dark Witches and magicians find blood magick to be a natural, strong element of high-energy work. In fact, many of us emphasize bloodletting as one of the most effective methods for working personal magick. This makes sense, because the blood contains DNA and is naturally linked to the practitioner on a multitude of levels.

Even so, many magicians and Witches are not interested in practicing blood magick. Some use tears to amplify the intention of emotionally rooted magick, namely that which revolves around banishing sorrow. Others simply use saliva, hair, or nail clippings to provide an energetic link between the spell and the caster.

Blood holds ancient memory. In fact, it holds every memory of human existence within it. Drawing a bit of blood unlocks energetic keys buried within. The DNA we have now is but a new combination of the same genetic structure of ancient humans. Because of this, energy lies dormant in the blood (possibly in the "dead cells"), waiting to be accessed.

Blood is the ever-flowing substance encompassing the physical body as a whole, cycling and circulating again and again. It comes from the physical body and remains patterned to both one's physical body and the soul inhabiting it. Blood contains a person's ethereal essence through and through. Any magick performed on oneself or another person is naturally magnified with blood as a connecting substance.

DNA-linked magickal workings are part of what is called contagious magick in accordance to the Law of Contagion. That is, when an item contains a sample of one's genetic structure (including hair and nails) it has a direct link to the individual from whom it came. This theory may be extended to include the idea that any item a person touches or is somehow in contact with has a direct energetic link to the person as well. Even if the physical link is severed between a person and an object, an imprint still remains. These ideas have been used in person-to-person magick since the dawn of time.

Not much blood needs to be shed. Because a single strand of DNA holds the entirety of our genetic makeup, one drop of blood is more than enough to add a boost of power and bind a working to the practitioner's energy pattern. According to some occultists, extracting a small amount of blood is essential in any strong-willed releasing spell. It's a good idea to begin the ritual by saying *"May this cut (or prick) be the only pain experienced from this rite."*

In magick, blood may be shed in moderation for deeply personal magick like encouraging an end to internal suffering. Blood provides an ethereal link to the magickal practitioner and sympathetic workings being performed. Many female Witches use menstrual blood in magick to symbolize the Divine Feminine and connectedness to the lunar cycles.

Blood is one of the most powerful substances one can possibly use in magick. If a few drops of blood are added to a personal spellbag, potion, or oil, or anointed on a burning candle, written glyph, or sigil, then the magick of the working is immediately amplified and bound to your person.

Adding a bit of blood to a scrying bowl is very effective for divination concerning personal matters. When a drop of your own blood is added to a bowl of water used for scrying purposes, a multifold of doorways will open, and unseen issues of the soul will come into clarity if enough focus is directed. Diluted blood may also be applied to the edges of Tarot cards, runes, or another divinatory device that is used only by the practitioner.

Any blood work needs to be approached responsibly and with sterility. Cleanliness is a necessity, as any incision in the skin poses the risk of infection. As another forewarning, the precise place that bears the cut must be carefully mapped out so as to avoid hitting a vein or artery. This is very important when responsibly extracting blood for ritual use. Because extracting blood requires cutting or pricking, there is a slight level of physical pain involved. When you break the flesh, it's a symbolic act. The pain felt at the initial incision triggers a reaction in the brain. The energy of this can be focused into the ritualistic procedure at hand, and the actual blood drawn can be its conduit.

Risks in Bloodwork

Bloodwork is extremely powerful. If someone can get past the socially placed discomfort about bleeding, the practice can be carefully utilized to bring about extreme change. Emotions arise when the blood is shed. When the profound energy stored in the blood is accessed, it's like opening a floodgate. That's why a person must be ready to perform it. This specific form of magick causes the hidden to become seen and the repressed to come to the surface. If practiced prematurely, bloodwork can have results that are overly intense and even developmentally detrimental!

Iron is present in blood, and this is something to take note of when working with blood in magick. Mars rules the metal iron, and thus rules blood. The properties of the planet Mars are those of motivation, strength, power, aggression, and even war (i.e. bloodshed). This is a reason why blood magick should be undertaken with great focus and care. If used improperly or out of anger, it can send the energies awry and into a state of discombobulated chaos. If used with focused intention and precision, it will add a multilayered boost to spellcrafting, providing an amplified and more personal experience of weaving magick and raising energy. In other words, plan any blood magick carefully and be seriously smart about it; an intelligent approach to potentially risky rituals is a key to mastery.

Blood magick is very powerful but can also be dangerous. If someone approaches these practices with a high level of mental or emotional imbalance, the results can be devastating and unsafe, especially if the person is accustomed to cutting themselves out of depression. The energy of shedding blood in a depressed or manic state is completely different from the energy of shedding blood in a ritualistic setting. For those who don't approach these practices mindfully, the powerful energy released in cutting oneself has potential to overtake the practitioner. This can lead to overuse and a lack of precaution when approaching this type of ritual.

Be very mindful of the amount of blood you personally use and how often you cut or prick yourself in ritual. Analyze what purposes you have in mind when performing this intense form of shadow magick. The spell in which blood magick is used should not be frivolous, temporary, or superficial. Map out very carefully the area that you choose to cut yourself (not near a vein or artery) and decide if other people might possibly notice your cuts. However, I strongly believe that there should not be more than one healing cut present at any moment in time.

Please do not perform blood magick on a regular basis. The less frequently you shed blood in ritual, the more powerful the spell. This is due to the fact that a greater amount of personal energy gets built up in the body and energy field over time. If blood is shed more often than necessary, the practitioner will undoubtedly suffer a depletion of personal energy. Not to mention, psychiatric help may be the next step if a misunderstanding person assumes the wrong reason for self-inflicted wounds. I highly recommend no more than one cut or prick every moon cycle. Each cut or prick should be treated. Wash each one gently and apply some antibacterial ointment, bandaging appropriately to avoid infection. Ensure that the blood that's shed stays in an area where others won't unsuspectingly touch it.

I recommend against using a razor or another ultra-sharp tool when extracting your own blood. (Also, don't use your athamé for this because it should be reserved for energetic purposes, not used for physical ones.) If high energies are being raised, the practitioner may not have full conscious awareness of the physical plane, including the body. This can be very dangerous, even lethal. The safest tools to use for extracting blood are medical lancets, pieces of porcelain, or pieces of another earthen substance. The pieces should be used only once for sterility's sake, and may require a series of scratches on the skin to extract a little blood. This "scratching" allows the magician greater focus on the actual act of drawing the blood, and poses a much lesser risk of over-cutting.

I cannot more highly advise the use of medical lancets for the extraction of blood. Lancets are used by doctors for single-drop blood sampling and by diabetics for blood-sugar (glucose) level testing. One can purchase a lancing device along with a number of lancets, which are inserted into the device. Each lancet is disposed of after use, but the device can be reloaded. I prefer to use self-contained lancets, which are small plastic pieces containing a spring-loaded lancet. Like the lancets used with the lancing device, the needle is immediately retracted and only a single drop of blood is extracted. Both methods are sterile and virtually painless, and the pricks heal very quickly, leaving no wound. I think that lancets are the greatest thing ever for use in personal magick. Finally, if blood magick just isn't for you, consider getting a tattoo or piercing with magickal significance in mind.

MEMENTO MORI: NECROMANCY

Because of the intrigue surrounding the reality of death, people study and philosophize about it in order to come to terms not only with the passing of loved ones, but also the impending reality of their own deaths. Throughout time, people have sought to communicate with ancestral spirits for specific reasons. Communication with those who were once physically incarnated can be called necromancy.

Necromancy is not common practice in Wicca nor in most forms of modern Witchcraft. It takes training, dedication, and caution to accurately hone that ability. Some experienced Witches incorporate necromantic practices into their magick, but most have no need or desire to do so, unless it's for rituals on or around Halloween.

Necro- or neku- simply means "the dead," referring to a person or persons. It comes from the word *nekros*, meaning "corpse." The suffix –mancy comes from the Greek word *manteia*, meaning "to prophecy." In the most traditional sense, necromancy is divination by way of contacting the deceased.

The word *goetia* was originally synonymous with necromancy but over time came to refer to the art of summoning demons (the sorcerers were called *goētes*). Grimoires of the magick of King Solomon are still extant, including *The Goetia: The Lesser Key of Solomon*, which is concerned with communion with Otherworldly demonic entities rather than the spirits of once-living humans. This is not actually necromantic work, but a form of interdimensional evocation. It is important to distinguish between necromantic magick and other forms of spirit communication. The word necromancy is used *loosely* in modern times to refer to any magickal working in which the magician somehow makes use of the spirits of deceased human beings, or interacts directly with the energy of death itself. This general term is recognized even amongst some modern scholars on the topic, despite its linguistic roots emphasizing divination in particular. Modern practitioners tend to deem intentional communication with the dead as necromancy.

Ancient Necromancy

In classical times, the philosopher was also a magician. The Greek philosopher Pythagoras taught, among many other things, that dying people had a better ability to easily communicate with the dead than did young or middle-aged people, as their souls were departing from their bodies at the last stages of life. Pythagoras claimed to have received prophecies from the dead, particularly in his old age. He would also drink water from an underground well (attuned as a physical doorway to the Underworld) to communicate with chthonic spirits and gain prophecy. One of the prophecies received was the fall of Athens. Pythagoras's main goal in necromancy seems to have been simply that of prophecy, with no ulterior motives. His intentions were not self-serving or mundane, but held importance to himself and the greater community. His perceived encounters presumably acted as the bases for some of the philosopher's teachings in his magickal order. Greco-Roman society is the most appropriate culture to look at when studying ancient necromancy, considering the number of mentions of the practice in literary texts throughout time.

Mentions of necromancy began to appear in Mesopotamian texts around 900 BCE and extend to the transition into Coptic Christianity. Many of these mentions actually have to do with the dead appearing to a person in dream. There is no evidence of necromantic practice in Egypt, Anatolia, Levant, or other East Mediterranean cultures until the time of the Assyrian king Esarhaddon's reign (c. 600 BCE). Because Mediterranean cultures showed evidence of necromancy at a later time than the Mesopotamians, it is theorized that they borrowed the idea and practice from the Mesopotamians. This was most likely due to King Esarhaddon's expansion of the Assyrian empire, reaching and influencing areas like Egypt. Evidence for necromantic rituals in Greece also shows up at this time, suggesting that they also may have borrowed the practice from early Mesopotamian cultures.

The Greek Magical Papyri, which date between approximately the first and fourth centuries CE, include a number of necromantic spells that were certainly practiced by magicians in antiquity. Spells such as these were likely traded, bought, and sold by magick-practicing aristocratic men, taking into account that they were virtually the only people educated in reading and writing, as the majority of peasants remained illiterate.

PGM (*Papyri Graecae Magicae*) IV 2140-44 is probably the best example of an "executable" ancient necromantic spell. It is called "Pitys the Thessalian's spell for questioning corpses." It describes a method of communicating with the dead, which is to write "AZĒL BALEMACHŌ" on a flax leaf. The ink is to be made of red ochre, burnt myrrh, juice of fresh wormwood, evergreen, and flax. The magician is then to put the completed flax leaf in the mouth of the corpse to induce oracular communication with the departed spirit. It is a very short spell compared to most of the rest of the PGM material, and its simplicity is profound considering the goal. It doesn't describe what the magician can do after summoning the spirit, but only explains how to get a spirit in one's presence. The discovery of possible reasons behind it must be left up to cultural analysis. The ingredients and procedure of this ancient Greek spell aren't nearly as arcane and even humorous as many of the other translated PGM workings, which are very rarely practiced by modern Greco-Roman reconstructionists. Curiously, most modern Witches put little, if any, stock in these crazy ancient spells and many consider them magickally obsolete. If nothing else, they are at least fascinating historical writings!

In literature, necromancy has more often than not been portrayed in a slanderous light. It's usually equated with Witchery, and it's the Witchy women in classical literature who raise the dead and work spells with people's dead body parts. For example, in the second century CE, Roman author Lucian's sixth book of the Pharsalia, we encounter the Witch Erictho, living in Thessaly. After the battle of Pharsalus, she is portrayed scavenging the cremation grounds, gathering bones, ashes, and body parts of the newly dead, and even kills someone herself to obtain more materials. She is an old and vile-looking stereotypical hag, and in the story reanimates the corpse of a soldier by performing a spell so that he may foretell to her client the outcome of a battle before it happens. The soldier's ghost first appears next to his corpse and he actually refuses to fulfill the spell until Erictho threatens the spirit, causing him to finally reenter the body to answer her questions.

Homer's *Odyssey*, a mythological heroic tale having come into written form around 700–650 BCE, is the earliest detailed mention of classical necromancy. Because of its inclusion in a fictional piece, it's only right to assume that necromancy was practiced, or at least considered, at the time. In Book XII, Odysseus had just begun his journey to the house of Hades. The demigoddess Circe had just instructed him to voyage there to consult the shade (ghost) of Tiresias, a Theban prophet. Upon reaching the Underworld, he first encountered the spirit of his newly deceased friend, as well as his mother, whom he was mournfully shocked to encounter in the realm of the dead. After Odysseus gave offerings to Tiresias, the spirit revealed to him a prophecy about returning home to Ithaca, mentioning the trials and tribulations he would have to endure to preserve his own life and eventually return home.

In this case, the motivation behind necromantic ritualism is self-motivated but doesn't support destruction to anyone else for the sake of self-gain. It's surprising and reassuring that necromancy is not portrayed as a malicious endeavor in this case, though it is still dark and controversial. The Odyssey also crowns Circe as the first Witch in literature to incorporate necromantic practice into her "bag of tricks."

One of the most commonly known (and only arguably historical) documentations of divinatory necromancy is in the Bible. The Book Samuel was written in the Greek Archaic Period, specifically the eighth to seventh centuries BCE, and is set in approximately 1050 BCE. The relevant passage is in Samuel 1:28 and talks about Saul—and I don't mean Saul Goodman—having an encounter with the Witch of Endor. Samuel was dead, his body burned and spirit released. The passage mentions that Saul had banished all the mediums and spiritualists from the land but still wished to find a medium that had the power to summon his acquaintance back from the dead. His attendants told him of a Witch in Endor with whom he could inquire. Saul disguised himself and sought out the Witch. Upon summoning Samuel from the dead, Saul bowed before him, asking for advice as to why the Lord God no longer answers to him. Samuel, clearly upset by the disturbance, explains that Saul did not obey the Lord and is now being punished via God's silent treatment. He also predicts the future, which is the fall of Israel to the Philistines, as well as the death of Saul and his sons.

Additional classical literature showing now-ridiculous depictions of the "evil nature of women" speaks to us of the social context of the time. Similar depictions to the Pharsalia's Witch (aforementioned) are seen in the writings of Theocratus (the Witch Samytha), Horace (the Witch Canidia), and Apuleius (the hags in *Metamorphoses: The Golden*

Ass). Is this, in addition to portrayals by the Church, the source of the stereotypical view of the Witch we have now? It certainly is feasible; in that time, women were generally seen as men's property and as inherently tainted (even the goddesses), and thereby more susceptible to fall into a cycle of malicious behavior like Witchery and self-motivated necromancy. It's also worth considering that men of the time had an insatiable desire to be fulfilled by the woman through marriage and childbirth for the sake of companionship and procreation, as well as acceptance by the community, thereby fulfilling the social milieu. I believe one reason that literary depictions of feminine necromancy are portrayed in such a negative light is that men of the time wanted their desire for women to seem minuscule or nonexistent, so as to not show signs of "weakness" or dependency.

Necromancy is a relatively obscure topic when studying the classical world. Its mention is rarely specified in anything but fictional stories, and the accuracy of the information in those tales cannot serve as a gauge for the actual practices of the art in that time. However, the information suggests that yes, necromancy was incorporated into ritual and practiced alongside other forms of magick. Because of the obscurity of documentation, assumptions founded in comparative research tend to be the most accurate assessments of the place of the practice in Greco-Roman society. Mentions of ancient necromantic practice are both similar and dissimilar to modern practices.

Modern Necromancy

Modern necromancers seek contact with and understanding of death energy. A lesser form of necromancy is practiced on the holiday Samhain, when the Witch communicates with their ancestral spirits and leaves libations and offerings for their departed souls. Commemorative altars and shrines are constructed with the loved ones in mind, and offerings are left to satisfy their spirits. This sometimes includes one-on-one communication with the soul of the departed individual and is still considered a respectful form of necromantic communion.

Some Witches, as well as a number of other magickal practitioners, engage in necromancy much more regularly. Modern necromancers don't limit themselves to divination via departed spirits. To do so would be self-serving and disrespectful to the energy of death.

Instead, they will practice anything from transcendental meditation on death to pointing ghosts in the right direction to move onward. Modern necromancers work with death energy in its many forms, including the personification of Death itself.

Death energy is traditionally personified as an archangel named Azrael, who is, according to Hebrew and Islamic mythology, both the psychopomp and the record keeper of life and death. With the birth of every human, he/she/they write the person's name in their giant grimoire; when a person dies, they erase the name. They are said to have four thousand wings and as many eyes as there are people on earth. When a person dies, an eye blinks. Like all spirits and gods, Azrael's form has been mythologized and personified, and is highly symbolic. If worked with ritualistically, their form will most likely appear differently to everyone, based on personal interpretation of the energy of death. Many simply see them as a grim reaper figure, which is a modern form commonly associated with death of any kind. The grim reaper itself is said to have its origins in sixteenth century France, when an artist depicted what he felt was the personification of death.

Azrael's name means "he who helps God" in Hebrew. In the scripture, Azrael was said to have brought God (YHWH: Yahweh or Jehovah) a handful of dirt to help create Adam when the other angels refused to, heeding Earth's warning against it. Some theorists believe that the name Azrael comes from a person named Azra, who was devoted to spreading the Divine lessons of God following the Babylonian Exile. Additionally, the Angel of Death is given alternative names in different scriptural cultures, each of which have their own, often similar, attributions given to the angel's characteristics.

Regardless of origin, the energy of death has been personified through Azrael's name throughout time. When necromancers work with Azrael, they work with society's anthropomorphized image of death to uncover the truth of the dying process. A certain vibrational force has been attributed to the energy of death, and even if a practitioner doesn't believe in Azrael's original mythology verbatim, that energy is still accessible through their name; this is because social associations have built up significant amounts of energy around the entity in the same way that any other spirit or deity is astrally reinforced. Because death is so often socially feared, many necromancers have found that Azrael's image has become tainted and their spirit saddened. Necromancers seek to remedy this as much as is in their power, paying homage to the beauty and necessity of the death cycle. For people like us who have an inherent admiration of the dark and mysterious, working positively with the Angel of Death may prove a bit easier than it would for most.

In what may be termed high necromancy, the practitioner performs a communicative ritual in the presence of a cadaver. The corpse serves as a conduit for death energy. The physical body is a shell for the soul, and when the soul has been removed from its frame, death energy lingers about it until the body is fully decomposed (or cremated) and has returned to the elements. When a person or animal dies, the energy of death is immediately present, permeating the body and the room where they passed. Communicating with the Angel of Death is highly effective in this case. This is why high necromancers prefer to work directly in the presence of death energy, or in places reserved for death energy, such as cemeteries and graveyards (these two words are virtually interchangeable in modern parlance).

It isn't exactly easy or desirable to perform ritual with a corpse… Please don't rush out and try it. A graveyard, crypt, catacomb, or mausoleum is an ideal place to feel death energy, even if full contact isn't made directly in the presence of an "empty shell." Contrary to popular belief, a rule of high necromancy is to *not* cause harm to another being, especially for the purposes of magick. This includes no human or animal sacrifices. Something as absurd and cruel as performing ritual homicide not only induces cycles of horrible Karma, but renders the death energy impure. It is also a horrible insult to Azrael, who would have taken the soul in due time. Murder has no place in the Magickal Arts, even necromancy, and it would be foolish to think it does.

If someone performs high necromancy in the presence of a body, the person or animal worked with must be given absolute respect in the process, and it's ideal if they died from natural causes (having naturally endured the process of dying). It takes a very particular type of person to perform this type of magick. The rituals are very intense and exacted, and pose the possibility of either lifting someone to extreme (not always pleasant) states of consciousness or damaging their spirit if performed improperly or in the wrong state of mind. Because of the risks associated with high necromancy, I won't include any rituals dealing with that form of magick in these pages. However, I have included a meditation on the Angel of Death. This is a necromantic rite that poses little risk to the practitioner, yet is quite effective in that it is a face-to-face experience with death energy as performed in the confines of a sacred space.

In addition to murder and violence, another misunderstood element of necromancy is necrophilia, which is defined as an erotic attraction to corpses, usually including sexual intimacy with a dead body (in modern terms). To necromancers, this is considered a defilement of the beauty of death energy and is an extreme disrespect to the Angel of Death. High necromancers don't seek sexual gratification from empty shells. When a person passes from their body, the energy lingers until all of the tissue is completely decomposed. Even then, traces of a person's energy are stored in bones or ashes. To perform sexual acts with a corpse is not only disrespectful to the soul who once housed the body, but is…how you say…effed up?!

For those who wish to further research the implications of modern necromancy, I can't recommend the following titles highly enough (also listed in the Bibliography):

- *The Necromantic Ritual Book* by Leilah Wendell
- *The Witches' Book of the Dead* by Christian Day
- *Death & the Afterlife* by Clifford A. Pickover
- *Walking the Twilight Path: A Gothic Book of the Dead* by Michelle Belanger
- *Cemetery Gates: Death & Mourning through the Ages* by Corvis Nocturnum

Ritual Meditation:
Encountering the Angel of Death

Most of human culture fears death, and this makes Azrael's energy dense and mournful. He/she/they have not always appeared this way, harkening back to a time when death was ultimately accepted and embraced, not pushed aside or romanticized. Death energy is the energy of transition and the rawness of the loss of life. Death energy is the liminal stage between this incarnation and the next, and is something to be respected and worked with carefully.

The meditation below is aimed at making contact with Azrael. For some people, this can provide comfort and acceptance of the reality of death, particularly if someone you know is dying or has recently passed. This ritual is actually a form of minor necromancy and is a great introduction to the beauty of necromantic practice. Written out, it seems brief. Performed, and with enough time given between each step, it can last for much longer, even several hours. Everyone's experience is different and this is simply an outline for sparking temporary contact with the personification of death. Read through the ritual first and see if it's right for you. If now is not the time, save it for later down the road. If it is the time, approach the ritual with caution and honest soul-searching. Your intuition will tell you the answer.

This meditation should not be performed carelessly or nonchalantly. It should be performed in Perfect Love and Perfect Trust; if there is great fear in your heart, it will fail. This is not something to do at a slumber party, nor is it a way to make you a more powerful Witch. If performed properly, it will make you more aware, accepting, and reverent of death…and thereby more knowledgeable of life. It should only be performed if you are seriously contemplating the mysteries of the afterlife. This working should be well thought out, planned, and finally embarked on, ever remembering that the time will eventually come when the Angel of Death takes your hand once again.

During the working it is preferable to burn jasmine incense, which is said to be appeasing to Azrael. It is ideal to light a black candle or be surrounded by a number of them. You should also secure a nice piece of dark violet amethyst to cup in your hands or place near your heart during the meditation. In addition to the amethyst, you can also hold melenite, apache tear, dark tiger's eye, jet, or a combination of any of these. It is also beneficial to use an elestial stone, which is any stone with a number of terminations or jagged points along one side, also called "record keepers." If using an elestial stone, smoky quartz is a great option, as very few stones are capable of forming this design.

It's a good idea to surround yourself with sprinklings of graveyard dirt ("graveyard dust"). Simply go to a cemetery and respectfully gather a handful of dirt from any part of the land. Be certain not to accidentally desecrate any area; even a few pinches will do. Be respectful when gathering the dirt. Tell the spirits you wish them no disrespect, and that you are gathering the dirt to honor and connect with the energy of the Great Beyond. It's a good idea to leave a small offering as well, like an apple, tobacco, cornmeal, or any flower. This will appease the spirits and inform them of your intentions.

If a cemetery is not accessible to you for one reason or another, graveyard dirt may be substituted by a combination of as few or as many of these herbs as you'd like: mullein, valerian, patchouli, sage, and any nightshade. Grind these into a powder and sprinkle them around your ritual space before performing the rite. This will aid in communication with Azrael by securing the space with the subtle vibration of death.

The best time to gather or create the dirt is at midnight on a Dark Moon. If going to the cemetery, beware of traveling spirits. Some spirits may emerge when the veil is thin on the Dark Moon, and may not always have your best interests in mind, especially if they feel threatened.

It would also be beneficial to use animal teeth or bones by keeping them with you in the ritual, or even pieces of fossil. Though the animal's death has most likely not occurred recently as far as the bones are concerned, it still happened, and the imprints of both life and death are accessible through them. If you have a long bone to use, it may be consecrated as a wand and used in the same manner when casting the circle. Just don't make it your magick wand for every ritual; its energy is very specific. You can also use a small branch of an evergreen yew tree for the same purpose. This should be (preferably) freshly cut, and must be cut only with the tree's permission, with thanks given to its spirit or Dryad. All parts of the yew tree are quite poisonous, so be careful if you choose to do this.

As with all meditations, this may be prerecorded, memorized, or read softly in monotone by an accompanying friend. A strong circle should be cast beforehand, including the Lesser Banishing Ritual of the Pentagram (LBRP) if it is part of your regular practice. You may also perform calls to the Watchtowers/elements/quarters and create a strong rampart of protection. Though this meditation is not designed to put you at risk, a practitioner is more susceptible to unknown energies when working with this type of magick. Also, it's ideal to wear all black and powder your face a pale white, applying some eyeshadow around your eyes and slightly on your lips. Doing so will help invite Azrael's presence and pays respect to the necessity of death as a sacred aspect of life.

1. After constructing sacred space around you by casting a circle and calling the quarters as you normally would, sit comfortably to start the journey. Begin by clearing your mind. Take three deep breaths in through the nose and out through the mouth. Let the thoughts of the day drift away like moving clouds. This is not the time to focus on what happened today or what you need to do tomorrow…allow the common world to dissipate as you enter the sacred terrain of the mind. For several minutes, sense the oxygen entering your nostrils and exiting your lips. Bring absolute focus to your breath.

2. Take slow, deep breaths to calm and balance your energy, in turn lowering your vibrations. Meanwhile, clear your mind of any unnecessary thoughts. Your only thought should be that you, as a spiritual being, wish to make contact with the essence of death itself. Gradually make your breathing slower, longer, and deeper. Stop breathing for a few seconds at the peak of each inhale and exhale. This will change your normal breathing pattern, further aligning you to the sensation of departing the body. Feel free to additionally make sounds vocally as you will, so long as it feels natural, such as long sighs and quiet *uhhhh*s. Maintain a steady breathing pattern for an extended period of time before moving on, so that your energy may enter an altered state. Return to normal breathing when finished.

3. Now it's time to visualize. You are surrounded in darkness. Shadow permeates your being and is all around you, within and without. Blackness is all there is, and you are void of any light. Let the blackness fill you. Comfortably embrace it rather than fearing it, for darkness is the essence of all creation. Feel its soft ambience permeate your being, reminding you of your own mortality.

4. Begin to chant the name of the Angel of Death when you are ready. The chanting should be deep and guttural, extended and intense. This is the only vocal part of the meditation besides the opening and closing. Start with a whisper and repeat the

sacred name louder and louder until you have reached your vocal peak, if circumstances permit.

"AZ-RAY-EL...
AZZZ-RAYYY-ELLL...
AZZZZZZ-RAYYYYYY-ELLLLLL..."

Speak the name as many times as feels natural; there is no need to count. Follow by reciting in your mind any other invitations you feel appropriate. Ask Azrael to appear before you and inform them that you would like to better understand who they are. Make it known that you wish to increase your wisdom of life and death, and that you come with peace in your heart.

5. You will feel their presence around you. Keep your eyes shut. A shadow may form before you in your mind's eye, or you may simply be surrounded by the energy. Everyone's reaction will be different. Simply feel it for what it is, and know that you are safe. This is a glimpse of the hollow feeling of death: ultimate departure from the earth plane. You may feel tingling or coldness, joy or sorrow. Cry and scream if you feel the need. Shout and shiver, or remain perfectly still. React however feels right, dancing with the present energy. Remain respectful in death's presence. Be in the moment and accept any visions, thoughts, and emotions that flow through you. Just be.

6. Pay attention to what you feel, as well as the information you are given, even if it's only in energetic form. Take note of what energies you are encountering. Simply be in the presence of Azrael and allow yourself to learn from the energy at hand. Take time to experience this presence.

7. Now experiencing Azrael's energy, communicate with them in your mind. Tell them why you invited them here, thank them for being the escort when your time comes, and tell them that you wish to know some of the mysteries of the afterlife while still in this body. Communicate only mentally, from your mind

and heart, and continue to approach them with utmost respect. This is your time to mentally express what you are feeling and receive sacred messages in return. Do not question their need to take souls, and do not project upset or fearful vibrations. Simply bathe in the energy around you, ever minding death's presence at your side. Take as long as you need before moving on. Seek to understand death and the reality of change. Know Thyself.

8. You will feel when the time is right to part ways. When this has come, thank Azrael for their presence and pay them proper, heartfelt respect. Acknowledge their role and inform them that you will walk beside them in peace when it is time for you to leave this earth. Gratefully ask them to depart, making sure that their energy is dissipating. When you feel the energy begin to fade, close the ritual by saying aloud, *"Thank you and bless you, now and evermore…hail and farewell."*

9. Any images around you are fading back to normality. Your energy is becoming calm, centered, and stable. You are becoming aware of your body and the space around you. Sink into the present moment, knowing you just experienced a brush with death, and that you are stronger, less fearful, and more aware as a result. You have danced with magickal darkness and have come out a being of light. Only speak of this experience to those who understand, and remain silent to those that won't. The experience is yours and yours alone, because it was this that you have willed.

10. Allow yourself enough time to ground and come back to this present stitch in time. Close the circle as you normally would, and smile, knowing that life and death are one and the same. You have made connection with the unseen and your spiritual sight has expanded to one degree or another. It's a good idea to take a bath after the meditation, or hit the sack and sleep like the dead!

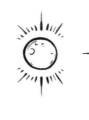

Conclusion

The sun falls beyond the horizon at the close of the day…the Wheel annually turns to the bitter seasons…we sleep and we dream…we create art from the unconscious and work magick from the subtle planes…the shadow is never separated from our very existence, and demands that we pay it attention, lest we remain in ignorance. Whether it's the overwhelmingly vast, blackened sky above us or the pitch blackness of the coffee we're drinking, darkness is all around us in one form or another, as well as in our minds.

Spiritually working with darkness, in whatever form it takes, is a technique of the shaman and the Witch, and is not something to be dismissed or disregarded. For those of us who walk a path that is more altruistic than self-serving, foreboding ideas of darkness can easily be replaced with ideas of wisdom and actual empowerment.

Far too often, people who have devoted themselves to magick and spirituality approach the shadow from an imbalanced perspective. For some, it seems comfortable and spiritually aligned to entirely avoid—to suppress and repress—those aspects of the self and observations of the human experience that could be considered "dark." On the flipside, some individuals who are drawn to the power and ability of the Magickal Arts delve into the more negative—and seemingly more potent—dimensions of magickal work, often for the purpose of gaining control, feeling darkly cool, or justifying anger. Still, either approach is imbalanced: the shadow can be a scary and frightening place as well as a powerful and empowering platform, indeed, but in the end, it's just as important as the lighter side and can, ideally, be equally revered.

Nature makes no distinction between light and dark, life and death, day and night. The polarities of existence uphold the natural paradigm, including our own. Part of honing one's spiritual ability and aligning to the tides of the natural world includes an acknowledgment of all sides of the spectrum; nothing can be left out of focus. The infinite nature of darkness and spiritual subtlety is an indispensable aid in our search for clarity and balance.

As these pages have shown, shadow magick manifests within many religions, cultures, and creeds worldwide, having always been a component of the human psyche. Shadow can be defined in countless ways, but the most significant is always one's own interpretation. The shadow is not to be feared, but rather embraced as a progressive contrast to the lighter aspects of spirituality. The shadow takes numerous forms, and part of its beauty is in its interpretation.

The modern practitioner is fortunate to be able to draw on many valuable components of a variety of beliefs and to work idiosyncratically with them. When we examine the hidden or destructive aspects of our psyches, as well as those of the world around us, we are given the tools for limitless spiritual progression. Appreciating and aligning with the beautiful darkness of Nature and the mystical planes of reality are keys to our holistic development. We are no longer required to fear and vilify the supposedly "dark" aspects of our religious and psychological constitutions. Instead, we may use these to elevate our consciousness and our spirit toward greater understanding and compassion, both for the self and for others. We are able to experience an integration with the cosmos in all of its glory, both light and dark. This is the essence of shadow magick.

Bless and Be Blessed,

~ O. R. D. N. ~

x

Bibliography

Andrews, Ted. *Animal Speak: The Spiritual & Magical Powers of Creatures Great & Small*. St. Paul, MN: Llewellyn, 1993.

Ankarloo, Bengt, and Gustav Henningsen, eds. *Early Modern European Witchcraft: Centres & Peripheries*. Oxford, UK: Oxford University Press, 1990.

Aron, Elaine N. *The Highly Sensitive Person: How to Thrive When the World Overwhelms You*. Secaucus, NJ: Birch Lane Press, 1996.

Attar, Farid-Ud-Din. *Conference of the Birds: A Seeker's Journey to God*. Translated by R. P. Masani. York Beach, ME: Weiser, 2001.

Auryn, Mat. "The Hex Appeal of Activism." *For Puck's Sake* (blog). July 9, 2017. http://www.patheos.com/blogs/matauryn/2017/07/09/the-hex-appeal-of-activism.

Baab, Lynne M. *Fasting: Spiritual Freedom Beyond Our Appetites*. Downers Grove, IL: IVP Books, 2006.

Bardon, Franz. *Initiation into Hermetics: The Path of the True Adept*. Salt Lake City: Merkur Publishing, 2001.

Belanger, Michelle. *Vampires in Their Own Words: An Anthology of Vampire Voices*. Woodbury, MN: Llewellyn, 2007.

———. *Walking the Twilight Path: A Gothic Book of the Dead*. Woodbury, MN: Llewellyn, 2008.

Bennett-Goleman, Tara. *Emotional Alchemy: How the Mind Can Heal the Heart*. New York: Harmony Books, 2001.

Beyerl, Paul. *The Master Book of Herbalism*. Custer, WA: Phoenix Publishing, 1984.

Blake, William. *The Marriage of Heaven & Hell*. Oxford, UK: Oxford University Press, 1975.

Blavatsky, Helena P., and Katharine Hillard (editor). *Abridgment of H.P. Blavatsky's Secret Doctrine*. Edited by Katherine Hillard. Whitefish, MT: Kessinger Publishing, 1996.

Bruce, Robert, and Brian Mercer. *Mastering Astral Projection: 90-Day Guide to Out-of-Body Experience*. St. Paul, MN: Llewellyn, 2004.

Chopra, Deepak. *The Seven Spiritual Laws of Success: A Practical Guide to the Fulfillment of Your Dreams*. Hertfordshire, UK: Motilal Books, 2003.

Cole, W. Owen, and Hemant Kanitkar. *Teach Yourself Hinduism*. Chicago: McGraw-Hill, 2003.

Coughlin, John J. *Out of the Shadows: An Exploration of Dark Paganism & Magick*. Bloomington, IN: Waning Moon Publications/1stBooks Library, 2001.

Crowley, Aleister. *Magick, Book Four: Parts I–IV*. York Beach, ME: Weiser, 2004.

Cunningham, Scott. *Cunningham's Encyclopedia of Magical Herbs*. St. Paul, MN: Llewellyn, 1985.

Daly, Mary. *Gyn/Ecology: The Metaethics of Radical Feminism*. London: Women's Press, 1979.

Dass, Ram. *Remember; Be Here Now*. San Cristobal, NM: Hanuman Foundation, 1978.

Davida, Michael Alexandra. *Dominus Satánas, the Other Son of God: Rethinking the Bad Boy of the Cosmos*. Boulder, CO: CLSM Publishing, 2002.

Day, Christian. *The Witches' Book of the Dead*. Newburyport, MA: Weiser, 2011.

del Campo, Gerald. *New Aeon Magick: Thelema Without Tears*. St. Paul, MN: Llewellyn, 1994.

d'Este, Sorita, and David Rankine. *Wicca Magickal Beginnings: A Study of the Possible Origins of the Rituals & Practices Found in this Modern Tradition of Pagan Witchcraft & Magick*. London: Avalonia Press, 2008.

Digitalis, Raven. *Esoteric Empathy: A Magickal & Metaphysical Guide to Emotional Sensitivity*. Woodbury, MN: Llewellyn, 2016.

———. *Goth Craft: The Magickal Side of Dark Culture*. Woodbury, MN: Llewellyn, 2007.

———. *Shadow Magick Compendium: Exploring Darker Aspects of Magickal Spirituality*. Woodbury, MN: Llewellyn, 2008.

Digitalis, Raven, and Konstantin Bax. *The Empath's Oracle.* Woodbury, MN: Llewellyn, 2022.

DuQuette, Lon Milo. *The Magick of Aleister Crowley: A Handbook of Rituals of Thelema.* Boston: Weiser, 2003.

Emboden, William A. *Bizarre Plants: Magical, Monstrous, Mythical.* New York: Macmillan, 1974.

Endredy, James. *Beyond 2012: A Shaman's Call to Personal Change & the Transformation of Global Consciousness.* Woodbury, MN: Llewellyn, 2008.

Faraone, Christopher A., and Dirk Obbink, eds. *Magika Hiera: Ancient Greek Magic & Religion.* New York: Oxford University Press, 1991.

Farrar, Janet, and Gavin Bone. *Progressive Witchcraft: Spirituality, Mysteries & Training in Modern Wicca.* Franklin Lakes, NJ: New Page Books, 2004.

Farrar, Stewart, and Janet Farrar. *Spells & How They Work.* London: Robert Hale Ltd., 1992.

———. *A Witches' Bible: The Complete Witches' Handbook.* Custer, WA: Phoenix Publishing, 1996.

Filan, Kenaz. *The Haitian Vodou Handbook: Protocols for Riding with the Lwa.* Rochester, VT: Destiny Books/Inner Traditions, 2007.

Flint, Valerie I. J. *The Rise of Magic in Early Medieval Europe.* Princeton, NJ: Princeton University Press, 1991.

Freuler, Kate. *Of Blood & Bones: Working with Shadow Magick & the Dark Moon.* Woodbury, MN: Llewellyn, 2020.

Goleman, Daniel. *Emotional Intelligence: Why it Can Matter More Than IQ.* New York: Bantam Books, 1995.

Graf, Fritz. *Magic in the Ancient World.* Translated by Franklin Philip. Cambridge, MA: Harvard University Press, 1997.

Graves, Robert. *The White Goddess: A Historical Grammar of Poetic Myth.* New York: Farrar, Straus & Giroux, 1999.

Greer, John Michael. *Atlantis: Ancient Legacy, Hidden Prophecy.* Woodbury, MN: Llewellyn, 2007.

———. *Secret Societies & Magical History.* San Jose, CA: Presentation at PantheaCon, 2007.

———. *The New Encyclopedia of the Occult.* St. Paul, MN: Llewellyn, 2003.

Gregory, Ruth W. *Anniversaries & Holidays.* Chicago: American Library Association, 1983.

Grimassi, Raven. *The Witch's Familiar: Spiritual Partnership for Successful Magic.* St. Paul, MN: Llewellyn, 2003.

Hagen, Steve. *Buddhism Plain & Simple.* New York: Random House/Broadway Books, 1998.

Harner, Michael, ed. *Hallucinogens & Shamanism.* New York, NY: Oxford University Press, 1973.

Harris, Stephen L., and Gloria Platzner. *Classical Mythology: Images & Insights.* Mountain View, CA: Mayfield Publishing, 1995.

Hicks, David, ed. *Ritual & Belief: Readings in the Anthropology of Religion.* 2nd ed. New York: McGraw Hill, 2001.

Hollis, James. *Why Good People Do Bad Things: Understanding Our Darker Selves.* New York: Gotham Books, 2008.

Johnston, Sarah Iles. *Restless Dead: Encounters Between the Living & the Dead in Ancient Greece.* Berkeley, CA: University of California Press, 1999.

Judith, Anodea. *Wheels of Life: A User's Guide to the Chakra System.* Woodbury, MN: Llewellyn, 2006.

Jung, Carl Gustav. *The Collected Works of C.G. Jung, vol. 9ii: Aion.* Princeton, NJ: Princeton University Press, 1959.

———. *Psychology & Religion.* London: Routledge, 1970.

———. *The Wisdom of Carl Jung.* Edited by Edward Hoffman. New York: Citadel Press, 2003.

Kaushik, Jai Narain. *Fasts of the Hindus Around the Year: Background Stories, Ways of Performance & Their Importance.* Delhi: Books For All, 1992.

Kemp, Daniel. *The Book of Night: Legends of Shadow & Silence.* Patchogue, NY: IRAYA Publications, 1990.

Kieckhefer, Richard: *Magic in the Middle Ages.* Cambridge, UK: Cambridge University Press, 1989.

Kinney, Jay, ed. *The Inner West: An Introduction to the Hidden Wisdom of the West.* New York: Tarcher/Penguin, 2004.

Kors, Alan Charles, and Edward Peters, eds. *Witchcraft in Europe, 400–1700: A Documentary History.* 2nd ed. Philadelphia: University of Pennsylvania Press, 2001.

Kraig, Donald Michael. *Modern Magick: Eleven Lessons in the High Magickal Arts.* St. Paul, MN: Llewellyn, 1997.

Larner, Christina. *Enemies of God: The Witch-Hunt in Scotland.* London: Chatto & Windus, 1981.

Lehmann, Arthur C., and James E. Myers. *Magic, Witchcraft & Religion: An Anthropological Study of the Supernatural.* Mountain View, CA: Mayfield Publishing, 1985.

Leland, Charles G. *Aradia, or the Gospel of the Witches.* Franklin Lakes, NJ: New Page Books, 2003.

Levack, Brian P. *The Witch-hunt in Early Modern Europe.* New York: Longman, 1987.

Lewis, Michael, and Jeannette M. Haviland-Jones, Jeannette M. *Handbook of Emotions: Second Edition.* 2nd ed. New York, NY: Guliford Press, 2004.

Low, Clifford H. *Black Magic & Dark Paganism.* San Jose, CA: Presentation at PantheaCon, 2008.

Lupa. *New Paths to Animal Totems: Three Alternative Approaches to Creating Your Own Totemism.* Woodbury, MN: Llewellyn, 2012.

Maslow, Abraham H. *Religions, Values & Peak-Experiences.* Columbus, OH: Ohio State University Press, 1964.

Matt, Daniel Chanan, trans. *Zohar: The Book of Enlightenment.* Mahwah, NJ: Paulist Press, 1983.

McLaren, Karla. *The Art of Empathy: A Complete Guide to Life's Most Essential Skill.* Boulder, CO: Sounds True, 2013.

McNevin, Estha. *Opus Aima Obscuræ.* Tradition materials and lesson notes. Missoula, MT, 2003–2019.

Mesich, Kyra. *The Sensitive Person's Survival Guide: An Alternative Health Answer to Emotional Sensitivity & Depression.* Lincoln, NE: iUniverse, 2000.

Metcalf, Peter. *A Borneo Journey into Death: Berawan Eschatology from Its Rituals.* Philadelphia: University of Pennsylvania Press, 1982.

Michelet, Jules. *Satanism & Witchcraft: A Study in Medieval Superstition.* Secaucus, NJ: Citadel Press, 1939.

Nanamoli, Bhikkhu. *The Life of the Buddha: According to the Pali Canon.* Kandy, Sri Lanka: Buddhist Publication Society, 1972.

Nocturnum, Corvis. *Cemetery Gates: Death & Mourning through the Ages.* Atglen, PA: Schiffer Publishing, 2011.

———. *Embracing the Darkness: Understanding Dark Subcultures.* Fort Wayne, IN: Dark Moon Press, 2005.

Ogden, Daniel. *Greek & Roman Necromancy.* Princeton, NJ: Princeton University Press, 2001.

Paramananda. *A Practical Guide to Buddhist Meditation*. Birmingham: Windhorse/Barnes & Noble, 1996.

Penczak, Christopher. *Invocation, Channeling, & the Oracular Mysteries*. San Jose, CA: Presentation at PantheaCon, 2007.

———. *The Inner Temple of Witchcraft: Magick, Meditation & Psychic Development*. St. Paul, MN: Llewellyn, 2002.

———. *The Temple of Shamanic Witchcraft: Shadows, Spirits, & the Healing Journey*. St. Paul, MN: Llewellyn, 2005.

Pickover, Clifford A. *Death & the Afterlife: A Chronological Journey from Cremation to Quantum Resurrection*. New York: Union Square & Co., 2015.

Plotkin, Mark J., *Tales of a Shaman's Apprentice: An Ethnobotanist Searches for New Medicines in the Amazon Rain Forest*. London: Penguin Books, 1994.

Poe, Edgar Allan. *Poems*. Edison, NJ: Castle Books, 2000.

Pollack, Rachel. *The Kabbalah Tree: A Journey of Balance & Growth*. St. Paul, MN: Llewellyn, 2004.

Purkiss, Diane. *The Witch in History: Early Modern & Twentieth-Century Representations*. Oxon, UK: Routledge, 1996.

Roderick, Timothy. *Dark Moon Mysteries: Wisdom, Power & Magic of the Shadow World*. Aptos, CA: New Brighton Books, 2003.

———. *The Once Unknown Familiar: Shamanic Paths to Unleash Your Animal Powers*. St. Paul, MN: Llewellyn, 1994.

Russell, Jeffrey Burton. *Witchcraft in the Middle Ages*. Ithaca, NY: Cornell University Press, 1972.

Sangharakshita. *Know Your Mind: The Psychological Dimension of Ethics in Buddhism*. Birmingham: Windhorse Publications, 1998.

Scholem, Gershom. *Major Trends in Jewish Mysticism*. New York, NY: Schocken Books, 1946.

Shakespeare, William. *Four Tragedies: Romeo & Juliet, Macbeth, Julius Caesar, Hamlet*. New York: Washington Square Press, 1963.

Silverknife, Zanoni. *Lessons in Georgian Wicca, 101–104*. Class handouts & lecture notes. Missoula, MT, 1999.

Stace, W. T. *Mysticism & Philosophy*. London: MacMillan Press, 1961.

Starhawk, M. Macha NightMare, and The Reclaiming Collective. *The Pagan Book of Living & Dying: Practical Rituals, Prayers, Blessings & Meditations on Crossing Over*. San Francisco: HarperOne, 1997.

Stavopoulos, Steven. *The Beginning of All Wisdom: Timeless Advice from the Ancient Greeks*. New York: Marlowe & Company, 2003.

Streeter, Michael. *Witchcraft: A Secret History*. Hauppauge, NY: Barron's, 2002.

Subramuniyaswami, Satguru Sivaya (Gurudeva). *Merging With Siva: Hinduism's Contemporary Metaphysics*. Kapa'a, HI: Himalayan Academy Publications, 2003.

Sylvan, Dianne. *The Circle Within: Creating A Wiccan Spiritual Tradition*. St. Paul, MN: Llewellyn, 2003.

Tenebris, Frater. *The Philosophy of Dark Paganism: Wisdom & Magick to Cultivate the Self*. Woodbury, MN: Llewellyn, 2022.

Thomas, Keith. *Religion & the Decline of Magic: Studies in Popular Beliefs in Sixteenth and Seventeenth-Century England*. New York: Charles Scribner's Sons, 1971.

Tipton, Harold F., and Micki Krause Nozaki. *Information Security Management Handbook*. 6th ed. Boca Raton, FL: CRC Press, 2012.

Too, Lillian. *Chinese Wisdom: Spiritual Magic for Everyday Living*. London: Cico Books, 2001.

Trobe, Kala. *Invoke the Gods: Exploring the Power of Male Archetypes*. St. Paul, MN: Llewellyn, 2001.

———. *Magic of Qabalah: Visions of the Tree of Life*. St. Paul, MN: Llewellyn, 2001.

———. *The Witch's Guide to Life*. St. Paul, MN: Llewellyn, 2003.

Tyson, Donald. *Soul Flight: Astral Projection & the Magical Universe*. Woodbury, MN: Llewellyn, 2007.

Valiente, Doreen. *An ABC of Witchcraft*. Custer, WA: Phoenix Publishing, 1988.

von Worms, Abraham, Georg Dehn, Steven Guth, and Lon Milo Duquette. *The Book of Abramelin: A New Translation*. Newburyport, MA: Weiser, 2006.

Wedeck, Harry E. *Dictionary of Magic*. Brooklyn, NY: Philosophical Library, Inc., 1956.

Wendell, Leilah. *The Necromantic Ritual Book.* New Orleans: Westgate Press, 1991.

Wimbush, Vincent L., and Richard Valantasis, eds. *Asceticism.* New York: Oxford University Press, 1998.

Zalewski, Pat. *Kabbalah of the Golden Dawn.* Edison, NJ: Castle Books, 2000.

Zell-Ravenheart, Oberon. *Grimoire for the Apprentice Wizard.* Franklin Lakes, NJ: New Page Books, 2004

MORE BY CROSSED CROW BOOKS

The Bones Fall in a Spiral by Mortellus
A Spirit Work Primer by Naag Loki Shivanaath
Circle, Coven, & Grove by Deborah Blake
Witchcraft on a Shoestring by Deborah Blake
The Way of Four by Deborah Lipp
Magic of the Elements by Deborah Lipp
Merlin: Master of Magick by Gordon Strong
Your Star Sign by Per Henrik Gullfoss
The Complete Book of Spiritual Astrology by Per Henrik Gullfoss
The Eye of Odin by Per Henrick Gullfoss
Icelandic Plant Magic by Albert Bjorn
The Black Book of Johnathan Knotbristle by Chris Allaun
A Witch's Book of Terribles by Wycke Malliway
In the Shadow of Thirteen Moons by Kimberly Sherman-Cook
Witchcraft Unchained by Craig Spencer
Wiccan Mysteries by Raven Grimassi
Wiccan Magick by Raven Grimassi
A Victorian Grimoire by Patricia Telesco
Celtic Tree Mysteries by Steve Blamires
Star Magic by Sandra Kynes
Witches' Sabbats and Esbats by Sandra Kynes
Flight of the Firebird by Kenneth Johnson
Witchcraft and the Shamanic Journey by Kenneth Johnson
Travels Through Middle Earth by Alaric Albertsson
Be Careful What You Wish For by Laetitia Latham-Jones
Death's Head by Blake Malliway
The Wildwood Way by Cliff Seruntine
Ecstatic Witchcraft by Fio Gede Parma
Aisling by Jeremy Schewe
Mastering the Art of Witchcraft by Frater Barrabbas
Transformative Initiation for Witches by Frater Barrabbas
Sacramental Theurgy for Witches by Frater Barrabbas
Sleep and Sorcery by Laurel Hostak-Jones

Learn more at
www.CrossedCrowBooks.com